War, Women, and Power

Rwanda and Bosnia both experienced mass violence in the early 1990s. Less than ten years later, Rwandans surprisingly elected the world's highest percentage of women to parliament. In Bosnia, women launched thousands of community organizations that became spaces for informal political participation. The political mobilization of women in both countries complicates the popular image of women as merely the victims and spoils of war. Through a close examination of these cases, Marie E. Berry unpacks the puzzling relationship between war and women's political mobilization. Drawing from more than 260 interviews with women in both countries, she argues that war can reconfigure gendered power relations by precipitating demographic, economic, and cultural shifts. In the aftermath, however, many of the gains women made were set back. This book offers an entirely new view of women and war and includes concrete suggestions for policy makers, development organizations, and activists supporting women's rights.

Marie E. Berry is an assistant professor at the Josef Korbel School of International Studies, University of Denver.

War, Women, and Power

From Violence to Mobilization in Rwanda and Bosnia-Herzegovina

MARIE E. BERRY

University of Denver

CAMBRIDGE
UNIVERSITY PRESS

CAMBRIDGE
UNIVERSITY PRESS

University Printing House, Cambridge CB2 8BS, United Kingdom

One Liberty Plaza, 20th Floor, New York, NY 10006, USA

477 Williamstown Road, Port Melbourne, VIC 3207, Australia

314–321, 3rd Floor, Plot 3, Splendor Forum, Jasola District Centre,
New Delhi – 110025, India

79 Anson Road, #06–04/06, Singapore 079906

Cambridge University Press is part of the University of Cambridge.

It furthers the University's mission by disseminating knowledge in the pursuit of
education, learning, and research at the highest international levels of excellence.

www.cambridge.org
Information on this title: www.cambridge.org/9781108416184
DOI: 10.1017/9781108236003

First published 2018

Printed in the United States of America by Sheridan Books, Inc.

A catalogue record for this publication is available from the British Library.

Library of Congress Cataloging-in-Publication Data
Names: Berry, Marie E., 1983– author.
Title: War, women, and power : from violence to mobilization in Rwanda
and Bosnia-Herzegovina / Marie E. Berry.
Description: New York: Cambridge University Press, 2018. |
Revision of the author's thesis (doctoral) – University of California,
Los Angeles, 2015. | Includes bibliographical references and index.
Identifiers: LCCN 2017053512 | ISBN 9781108416184 (hardback) |
ISBN 1108416187 (hardback) | ISBN 9781108401517 (paperback)
Subjects: LCSH: Women and war – Rwanda. | Women and war – Bosnia
and Herzegovina. | Rwanda – History – Civil War, 1994. | Rwanda – History –
Civil War, 1990–1993. | Yugoslav War, 1991–1995 – Bosnia and Herzegovina. |
Women – Political activity – Rwanda. | Women – Political activity – Bosnia and
Herzegovina. | Social change – Rwanda. | Social change – Bosnia and Herzegovina.
Classification: LCC JZ6405.W66 B47 2017 | DDC 303.66082–dc23
LC record available at https://lccn.loc.gov/2017053512

ISBN 978-1-108-41618-4 Hardback

– To all women survivors of war around the world

&

– To M., T., Y., and P., who survived genocide but cannot speak freely or live safely in their country today

"Violence is destructive; it constrains, it devastates, and it undoes … Yet the conflicts and activities in which violence is involved are not always purely destructive. In destroying, violence can also keep things in place; it can even set in motion change and the construction of the new."

– Christopher Cramer (2006: 279)

"Inside the word *emergency* is *emerge*; from an emergency new things come forth. The old certainties are crumbling fast, but danger and possibility are sisters."

– Rebecca Solnit (2016: 13)

Contents

Figures

Tables

Maps

Acknowledgments

While writing this book I heard a radio interview with a man in Syria whose apartment building had been bombed many times. He described the exhausting repetition of bombs breaking windows, shattering belongings, and sending his family to take refuge in the windowless stairwell of the building. While describing the constant fear he lived in, he commented that before the war he had not known any of his neighbors. Now, with regular shelling of the building, the neighbors had become close; they had started playing games, singing, and comforting each other while stuck in the stairwell during each attack.

This short interview made a lasting impression on me for two reasons. First, as I write this, mass violence unfolds in several countries around the world. This is deeply, morally tragic. After studying and working in Rwanda and Bosnia over the past decade, what sticks with me most is the abhorrent nature of war and that it is never over when it is "over." Instead it persists, in different forms, for years and decades to come. The fact that such brutal forms of conflict still exist in the twenty-first century after years of proclaiming "Never Again" should be of the deepest moral concern to all human beings.

The interview also stuck with me for a different reason. It is in these periods of destruction, these periods of pain and fear, that devastation can be forged into something new: new forms of social organization, new activities, new gender roles. The idea that war is not only a period of destruction but is also a period of transformation motivates this project.

It has been a tremendous privilege to work on this project over the past decade, which stems from my dissertation in sociology at UCLA. It is to the individual women in Rwanda and Bosnia who agreed to sit with me for an interview that I am the most grateful. Their extraordinary stories of resilience and strength are at the root of this study and humble me every day. It was an honor and a privilege to be invited into their homes, share food, meet their children, and try to understand their struggles.

I am also deeply grateful to my dissertation committee for its support and guidance throughout the duration of this project: Abigail Saguy, Andreas Wimmer, Gail Kligman, Michael Mann, and Bill Roy. Each contributed something different to my growth as a scholar and helped make UCLA a truly supportive and intellectually rigorous place for me to pursue my graduate work. I am grateful to many other faculty members at UCLA, including Zsuzsa Berend, Rogers Brubaker, CK Lee, Geoff Robinson, Megan Sweeney, Stefan Timmermans, Ed Walker, and Maurice Zeitlin, for their support and mentorship throughout my years in graduate school.

There are too many others to thank at UCLA who supported me and this project as it evolved. I am most grateful to Pamela Prickett, Elena Shih, Molly Jacobs, Matt Baltz, and Laura Orrico for their friendship, feedback, and encouragement on this project. And I am thankful for the friendship and intellectual support of many others at UCLA over the years, including Kyle Arnone, Gustav Brown, Becca DiBennardo, Yuval Feinstein, Noah Grand, Kjerstin Gruys, Susila Gurusami, Wes Heirs, Nicole Iturriaga, Lisa Kietzer, Laura Loeb, Zeynep Ozgen, Caitlin Patler, David Schieber, Michael Stambolis, Forrest Stuart, Danielle Wondra, and others I am certainly forgetting.

Many others have contributed valuable insights, critiques, and encouragement. I am especially grateful to Susan Watkins for convening regular dinner meetings at her house with Tara McKay, Tom Hannan, Amy Zhou, and Saskia Nauenberg. Sid Tarrow, Doug McAdam, and the members of the SSRC's 2010 DPDF Contentious Politics "Gang" were essential in the development of this research and in helping me find my own confidence and voice. And, Julie Waxman who profoundly supported me throughout my years in graduate school.

My fieldwork in Rwanda was fraught with frustrations but was also a period of tremendous learning. I am very grateful to several Rwandan friends and research assistants who were my partners in this research. I would love to mention each of you by name, but out of respect for you and in acknowledgment of the political environment in Rwanda that is intolerant of criticism, I choose to omit. In addition to them, I am grateful for the support of many in the field, including Iina Älli, Perttu Saralampi, Jesse Hawkes, Sarah Watkins, Kate Doyle, David Loewenguth, Keri

Schmit, Shelly Rosen, Nicky Fox, Erin Jessee, Tim Williams, Laura Heaton, Shirley Randall, Rebecca Davis, Marcella Pasotti, Samantha Pritchard, Elizabeth Powley, Maggie Zraly, Yolande Bouka, Susan Thomson, and many others I am certainly forgetting. The FFRP in Parliament and the Center for the Study of Gender at the Kigali Institute of Education also provided research support and affiliation. Of course, only I am responsible for the ideas discussed in this book.

In Bosnia I am grateful to Julianne Funk, Julia Dowling, Adis Hukanović, Mona Talebreza, Vahidin Omanović, Miki Jacević, Jakov Čaušević, Lejla Aličić-Ćoralić, Muamer Ćoralić, Đina Kopić, Ken Palmer, Amna Hadžikadunić, Maja Barisić, Azra Karabašić, Emir Elezovic, Ena Hubić, Doris Zubać, Lana Ackar, and many others who provided me contacts, friendship, advice, and coffee dates. Nicolas Moll, in particular, provided tremendously helpful feedback on my Bosnia historical chapter. A special thanks goes to an amazing group of research assistants: Halil Dedić, Mirza Slatina, Elida Vikić, Doris Zubac, Emina Gasal, and especially Emir Slatina.

My fieldwork in both countries had the unexpected and delightful surprise of introducing me to some extraordinary, resilient women who have become my closest friends. I am deeply grateful for the richness Hollie Nyseth Brehm, Milli Lake, Laura Mann, and Jessica Smith have brought into my life and to this project.

At the University of Denver, I've been lucky to find a deeply supportive intellectual community as I completed this book. I am grateful to Erica Chenoweth, Deborah Avant, Rebecca Galemba, Alan Gilbert, Cullen Hendrix, Kyleanne Hunter, Oliver Kaplan, and Tim Sisk for their feedback and support on various parts of this project. I am especially grateful to Emily Van Houweling for her friendship and encouragement. Research assistants Annie Kraus, Alex Smith Davis, Sarah Chasin, Fawn Bolak, Kate Morgan, and Leah Breevort also provided essential support. Trishna Rana, in particular, has been my confidant and collaborator throughout the final stages of fieldwork and writing. I am also grateful to Colleen Jankovic for critical editing assistance, and Joseph Ryan for help with all of the visuals. At Cambridge University Press I am grateful to Sara Doskow, Katherine Tengco-Barbaro, and the anonymous reviewers who provided tremendously helpful feedback. I am also thankful to Marnie Galloway, who designed the front cover art.

The work itself benefited from the generous financial support of many centers at UCLA, including the Department of Sociology, Graduate Division, International Institute, Center for the Study of Women,

xvi   *Acknowledgments*

Center for European and Eurasian Studies, and the Charles E. and Sue K. Young Foundation. I am also grateful for financial support from the Social Science Research Council and the IREX Individual Advanced Research Opportunities (IARO) Program, with funds from the State Department Title XIII Program. After arriving at the Josef Korbel School of International Studies in 2015, I have been lucky to receive support for this project from the University of Denver Faculty Research Fund and the Carnegie Corporation of New York.

Finally, this project would not have been possible without the support of my family. My father introduced me to military history and the atrocities in Rwanda at a young age. My mother embodies the resilience of women. I am grateful to them, and most especially to Sam Kidder, for responding to my long absences and morbid party chatter with patience, encouragement, and love.

Cast of Characters: Rwanda

Bagosora, Theoneste: Hutu Power extremist within Habyarimana's government; member of the Akazu. De facto head of Rwandan government during the genocide. Major architect of the violence.

Bizimungu, Pasteur: Hutu member of the RPF, was appointed president of Rwanda during the immediate post-genocide period. Considered the head of the "Government of National Unity."

Habyarimana, Juvenal: President of Rwanda from 1973 to 1994. Head of the MRND political party. Hutu. From Gisenyi. Shifted power base of Rwanda to the north of the country.

Kagame, Paul: Current president of Rwanda. Commanding general of the RPF.

Kanjogera: Queen Mother during Musinga's reign.

Kayibanda, Gregoire: President of Rwanda from 1962 to 1973. Head of the PARMEHUTU political party. From the south of Rwanda. Hutu.

Mitterand, Francoise: President of France during the genocide, close ally of President Habyarimana.

Musinga: Tutsi King (*mwami*) of Rwanda from 1896 to 1931.

Ndadaye, Melchoir: Hutu president of Burundi, assassinated on October 21, 1993.

Rwigyema, Fred: Early leader of the RPF in Uganda, killed during the first days of the RPF invasion of Rwanda in 1990. Former army chief of staff and deputy minister of defense in Uganda after fighting in Museveni's National Resistance Movement.

Sindikubwabo, Theodore: Interim president of Rwanda during the genocide.

Uwilingiyimana, Agathe: Hutu prime minister of Rwanda from 1993 to 1994. Assassinated on the first day of the genocide.

Abbreviations

ADLF   (Alliance des Forces Démocratiques pour la Libération
            du Congo-Zaïre): National Army of the Democratic
            Republic of Congo that brought Congo President Laurent
            Kabila to power in the First Congo War (1996–1997).
CDR   (Counsil National du Développment): Extremist
            political party that spun off from MRND and supported
            Habyarimana, before deeming him too moderate. This
            party became one of the key organizers of the genocide.
FAR   (Forces Armées Rwandaise): The Rwandan government's
            military during the Habyarimana regime and the
            genocide-era government. FAR troops were responsible
            for committing much of the genocide, and also engaging
            in the civil war against RPF forces.
MDR   (Mouvement Démocratique Républicain): The primary
            opposition party to Habyarimana's MRND; later a
            coalition partner in the "Government of National Unity."
MRND   (Mouvement Républicain National pour la Démocratie,
            or Mouvement Révolutionnaire National pour le
            Dévelopment): Habyarimana's political party that
            controlled the state from his assent to power in 1973. Its
            leaders were heavily involved in planning and executing
            the genocide.
PL   (Parti Libéral): Opposition party to Habyarimana's
            MRND. Counted many Tutsi among its members. Later a
            coalition partner in the "Government of National Unity."
PSD   (Parti Social Démocrate): Social democratic party that
            was one of the largest opposition parties and later a
            coalition partner in the "Government of National Unity."

RPA   The military arm of the RPF.
RPF   (Rwandan Patriotic Front): The political arm of the
              guerrilla movement led by Paul Kagame that originated
              in Uganda.
UNAMIR   (UN Assistance Mission in Rwanda): Initially consisted of
              2,500 peacekeepers, but this number was reduced to 270
              during the first days of the genocide.
UNHCR   Office of the UN High Commissioner for Refugees, or the
              UN Refugee Agency.

Cast of Characters: Bosnia

Boutros-Ghali, Boutros: UN Secretary-General from 1992 to 1996.

Broz, Josip (Tito): Founder of Communist Yugoslavia, leader of the Partisan resistance movement during World War II, ruled Yugoslavia from 1945 until his death in 1980.

Izetbegović, Alija: Founding leader of the Muslim Party of Democratic Action (SDA) who became president of the Presidency of Bosnia-Herzegovina from 1990 to 1996, when he joined the rotating tripartite presidency until 2000. Died in 2003.

Karadžić, Radovan: President of Republika Srpska. Indicted for war crimes by the International Criminal Tribunal for the Former Yugoslavia (ICTY). Sometimes referred to as the Butcher of Bosnia. Trained as a psychiatrist. In hiding for years after the war. Finally arrested in 2008 and is currently on trial at the ICTY.

Milošević, Slobodan: President of Serbia. Indicted for war crimes by the ICTY. Died during trial at ICTY in 2006.

Mladić, Ratko: General in command of the Bosnian-Serb Army beginning in 1992. Indicted for war crimes by the ICTY in 1995, but lived as a fugitive for years after the war. Finally arrested in 2011 and is currently on trial at the ICTY.

Morillon, Philippe: Commander of UN forces in Bosnia from 1992 to 1993.

Orić, Naser: Led resistance from Srebrenica in 1992. Former bodyguard for Milošević.

Plavšić, Biljana: Member of the prewar Bosnian Presidency. Serb nationalist.

Ražnatović, Želkjo-Arkan: Commander of notoriously brutal paramilitary group known as Arkan's Tigers. Accused of war crimes. Killed in 2000. Indicted for crimes against humanity by the ICTY.

Silajdžić, Haris: Prime minister of Bosnia from 1993 to 1996, became the Bosniak representative to the rotating presidency from 2006 to 2010.

Tudjman, Franjo: Founder of Croatian Democratic Union (HDZ) and first president of Croatia after independence. Died in 1999.

Abbreviations

AFZ   Antifascist Front of Women within Tito's Partisans and
             later within the Communist Party in Yugoslavia.
HDZ   (Hrvatska demokratska zajednica Bosne i Hercegovine,
             or Croatian Democratic Union): Croat political party in
             Bosnia.
ICMP   International Commission on Missing Persons.
JNA   Yugoslav National Army, commanded by Milošević
             during the Bosnian war.
OHR   Office of the High Representative, the institution in
             Bosnia charged with implementing the Dayton Accords.
OSCE   Organization for Security and Cooperation in Europe.
SDA   (Stranka demokratske akcije, or Party of Democratic
             Action): Conservative Bosniak political party founded by
             Alija Izetbegović.
SDP   (Socijaldemokratska Partija Bosne i Hercegovine, or
             Social Democratic Party): Social-Democratic political
             party that is multiethnic (although primarily supported
             by Bosniaks).
SDS   (Srpska Demokratska Stranka, or Serb Democratic
             Party): Serb political party founded by Radovan
             Karadžić.

Summary

In 1994, Rwanda experienced one of the most horrific periods of mass violence in history. Less than ten years later, Rwandans surprised people around the world by electing the world's highest percentage of women to parliament. The ascent of women in Rwandan politics complicates the popular image of women as merely the victims and spoils of war. Perhaps even more surprising, while Rwanda may be an extreme case, it is not an exception: war is correlated with increases in women's political representation in dozens of other countries across the globe. In countries such as Bosnia, women's formal political representation did not increase after war; however, women launched thousands of community organizations that became spaces for informal political participation. This book offers the first in-depth attempt to explain the processes through which war can facilitate women's mobilization at the grassroots. Comparing the Rwandan and Bosnian cases, it argues that war can serve as a period of rapid social change that reconfigures gendered power relations by precipitating interrelated demographic, economic, and cultural shifts. These shifts culminate in women's increased engagement in both informal and formal political capacities. The stories and experiences of more than 260 women animate this book, highlighting the multifaceted and varied ways that violence restructured women's lives. As the concluding section shows, however, many of these gains were short-lived, as the political settlement, international actors, and patriarchal norms intervened to constrain and set back women's progress.

I

War, Women, and Power

As a child in the south of Rwanda, Ignatinne had dreamed of becoming a doctor. Despite the trauma of her father's violent death in 1973 during a wave of ethnic violence targeting Tutsi, Ignatinne excelled in secondary school. Because of her ethnicity, however, she was denied entrance to university. When the genocide broke out in April 1994, Ignatinne's husband and many of her family members were killed. After the bloodshed, she found herself alone. As she put it to me in an interview, to move forward "wasn't a choice, it was an obligation. Either you do it, or you die. Either you provide for yourself, your children, or others, or you die" (Interview #7, July 2009).

Instead of dwelling on the loss of her husband, Ignatinne resolved to help the thousands of children who had suffered during the violence. She managed to go back to school, take a job with UNICEF working with children who were incarcerated or living on the streets, and join other initiatives and organizations advocating for children's rights. Soon, desiring to make an even greater impact, Ignatinne felt like she needed to ascend to a higher level. In 2008, she ran for political office. Her first campaign was successful – today, Ignatinne sits in Rwanda's parliament, which boasts the highest percentage of women legislators of any country in the world.

While dominant narratives emphasize the destructive effects of war, this book is concerned with how women like Ignatinne experience war, bear witness to its effects, and exert agency in ways often obscured by analyses of violence that emphasize women's suffering, shame, and victimhood. To do so, I compare the impact of wars in Rwanda and Bosnia-Herzegovina on women in their aftermath. I argue that while war is destructive, it is also a period of rapid social change that reconfigures gendered power relations by precipitating interrelated demographic, economic, and cultural shifts. Despite the many differences between the cases, I show how war in both countries catalyzed women's mobilization and forged spaces for their political engagement at the household, community, and national levels. War, contrary to expectations, can lead to increases in women's political agency. Ultimately, I also show the erosion of women's gains after war and unpack the various social processes that can fracture women's organizing and undermine women's progress.

WOMEN AND WAR

Much scholarship and media coverage have emphasized the destructive effects of war on women (Elshtain 1987; Goldstein 2001). War causes displacement, institutional breakdown, psychological damage, physical suffering, economic collapse, and myriad other harms. In recent violence in Sudan, Iraq, and the Democratic Republic of Congo, journalists fixated on women's experiences in two primary roles: as victims of sexual violence and as refugees. In contrast, men were shown in combat fatigues, bearing weapons, rendering them "active" subjects meant to protect "passive" subjects such as women and children.[1]

Yet Ignatinne's story reminds us that images of "weeping women, wringing hands" (Del Zotto 2002: 1) obscure the immense range of women's roles and experiences during violence. Further, such depictions do not reflect a robust literature on the active roles women play both during and after episodes of violence (see Aretxaga 1997; Lorentzen and Turpin 1998; Baumel 1999; Enloe 2000; Bop 2001; Sharoni 2001; Sjoberg and Gentry 2007; or Thomas and Bond 2015 for an overview). For instance, while relatively few serve as combatants, women's presence in fighting roles continues to grow. In the second half of the twentieth century, women's involvement in Algeria's war of independence from France (1954–1962) revealed the potential for revolution to catalyze processes of women's liberation. Women also played active combat roles in subsequent conflicts in Nicaragua, Vietnam, Iran, Zimbabwe, Eritrea, El Salvador, Argentina, Mozambique, Sri Lanka, Nepal, Lebanon – and, most recently, among Kurdish forces in Syria. In the first decades of the twenty-first century, there has been a markedly increased focus on women's capability to serve as violent actors, especially in light of women serving in militant extremist organizations like the Islamic State of Iraq and the Levant and Boko Haram. Moreover, many Western states – including the United States – have fully integrated women into combat roles within their militaries (see Segal 1995; Hunter 2017).

In these varied conflicts, women's mobilization in combatant roles has challenged traditional gender hierarchies, sometimes opening space for women to participate in new political roles. For instance, in El Salvador, women's mobilization as guerrillas led to the FMLN integrating women into leadership positions within the political branch of the movement (Viterna 2013). In Mozambique, women's participation in FRELIMO as fighters and organizers helped lead to (albeit incomplete) progress toward women's greater economic and political equality with men in the aftermath (Urdang 1989). Most recently in Nepal, women fought as Maoists and continued fighting against the constraints of both caste and gender for inclusion in the postwar political system (Lohani-Chase 2014).[2]

Women's increased political participation during and after war does not only stem from their participation as combatants; it can also emerge through public protest and civil resistance. In East Timor, an indigenous women's association fought to liberate women from the patriarchal structures of Timorese society and simultaneously challenged the Indonesian military's occupation of the island nation (Franks 1996).[3] In Liberia, a diverse coalition of women organized public sit-ins and protests to demand an end to the civil war, and, mirroring the Greek play *Lysistrata*, led a much-publicized campaign to withhold sex from their husbands until they agreed to put down their weapons (Fuest 2008; Moran 2012). In Israel and Palestine during the First Intifada, feminist organizations like Women in Black organized silent protests to condemn the violence in their homeland and resist the militarization of the conflict (Sharoni 1995; Helman and Rapoport 1997). Since, organizations like Four Mothers and, most recently, Women Wage Peace, have extended this legacy and situated women at the forefront of conversations about building durable peace in the region.

Women's peace movements, particularly many "mothers' movements," also draw on essentialized notions about women's "more peaceful" nature to make their claims. Feminist scholars like Gayatri Chakravorty Spivak (1993) have noted that subaltern or oppressed groups sometimes consciously use "strategic essentialisms" to simplify differences that might raise problems in existing structures of power. Groups that highlight women's peaceful and caring nature essentialize women; yet such "essentialisms" can afford women an opportunity to make political claims on the basis of their gender (Helms 2013; Tripp 2016). Some feminist scholars, however, caution that emphasizing women's differences from men may ultimately exclude women from political spaces and prevent them from gaining sustainable power (Lorber 1994; Epstein 1997). While mothers' movements typically do not attempt to upend patriarchal hierarchies or even criticize women's role in society, they establish motherhood as a basis of legitimacy and thereby implicitly challenge conventional gender norms. Motivated by grief over the loss or conscription of their children, mothers' movements tend to thus invert traditional notions about women's passive status as "bearers of the nation" by agitating for justice for crimes committed during the war (Femenía 1987; Noonan 1995; De Alwis 1998; Ray and Korteweg 1999). Members of some mothers' groups have eventually run for political office, and some groups – like Las Madres de la Plaza de Mayo in Argentina, whose activism helped bring down a brutal regime – have gained official political status (Hunt and Posa 2001). In these and other contexts, we see how women can serve as voices of resistance to war, often challenging the male-dominated, patriarchal military machine (see Tickner 1992; Aretxaga 1997).

While the aforementioned scholarship reveals that women are not simply passive victims during war, recent quantitative studies find something even more surprising: countries that have experienced war since the 1980s have higher rates of women in their legislatures than countries that have not experienced war (Hughes 2009; Hughes and Tripp 2015). Melanie Hughes (2009) incorporated war into standard statistical models explaining women's political representation (see Paxton 1997; Matland 1998; Kenworthy and Malami 1999; Reynolds 1999), finding that certain types of armed conflict in low-income states were associated with an increased percentage of women in parliament. Her subsequent study of this phenomenon with Aili Mari Tripp narrowed the analysis to Africa. They found that states that have experienced civil wars since 1980 had 4–6 percent higher rates of women's legislative representation, suspecting openings in the "political opportunity structure" (Tarrow 2011; McAdam, Tarrow, and Tilly 2001) after war – including peace talks, constitutional referendums, and new electoral commissions – as the cause. In other words, war created opportunities to build new institutions.[4] The historical timing of the conflict is important, as women's initiatives after more recent conflicts have built on women's increasing rights to press for even greater equality (Hughes and Tripp 2015).

Tripp's book, *Women and Power in Post-Conflict Africa* (2015), extended this line of research even further. Drawing on data from Liberia, Angola, and Uganda, Tripp's groundbreaking research found that women have made remarkable political gains in countries that have experienced devastating violence in Sub-Saharan Africa, and that the severity of war is positively correlated with the level of political mobilization. At the core of Tripp's argument is that war can require a wholesale renegotiation of domestic power, opening opportunities for the domestication of international frameworks. Critically, Tripp argues that local women's movements are essential for women activists to take advantage of the political openings created by the disruption of war.

Inspired by the scholarship on women and war in general and on war's mobilizing potential in particular, this book offers an important extension of this recent research by illustrating the processes through which large-scale armed conflict can open unexpected spaces for women's increased engagement in public and political roles. Oversimplified depictions of women's suffering, shame, and victimhood do not reflect the full range of identities and experiences women undertake and encounter during war. With these varied experiences in mind, this book compares the impact of war on women in Rwanda and Bosnia-Herzegovina, making a processual argument about the specific ways war can precipitate women's increased political engagement. Unlike studies that focus only on women's engagement in formal politics, here I draw from the feminist truism that "the personal is political" to explore spaces of women's political agency that fall both inside and outside the institutional political realm. I show how women's strength and boldness amid the horrors of war led to shifts in gendered power relations at all levels of society. Ultimately, however, I show how many of these gains were short-lived, as the political settlement, international actors, and patriarchal norms intervened to fracture women's organizing and constrain women's progress. This book thus calls attention to crucial issues for social scientists, students, activists, and policymakers concerned with war, women, and power in different contexts across the world.

TRANSFORMATIVE POWER OF WAR

To understand the impact of war on women, we must first understand war's transformative potential. Historical sociology and political science literatures demonstrate how states experience long periods of institutional stability that are punctuated by periods of flux and structural change. War is the paradigmatic example of a period of flux. Referenced in different literatures as "critical junctures," "crises," or "unsettled times," these periods of significant change reflect an interruption of the status quo and the possibility for new social processes or institutional arrangements (Swidler 1986; Collier and Collier 1991; Mahoney 2000; Pierson 2004; Capoccia and Kelemen 2007; Mann 2013).

War can transform the people who live through it in myriad ways; it can abruptly destroy lives, families, and material possessions, leading to death, despair, suffering, and financial destitution. War can also bond people together as comrades in arms, victims, or neighbors. For example, World War I veterans saw their experience as a personal transformation that distinguished them from the rest of the population (Leed 1981). In Spain, the Spanish Civil War conditioned political identities and voting patterns in the population decades later (Balcells 2012). Political scientists and economists have looked specifically at the unexpected positive consequences of civil wars (Bellows and Miguel 2009; Blattman 2009; Annan et al. 2011; De Luca and Marijke 2015). Drawing on trauma studies in psychology, Blattman (2009) and Bellows and Miguel (2009) found that individuals and households that directly experienced high levels of violence during wars in Uganda and Sierra Leone were more likely to vote and actively participate in community politics in the aftermath than those who witnessed lower levels of violence. Violence, in other words, can – however terrifyingly and unwittingly – transform individual lives.

Just as war transforms individuals' sense of community and political engagement, it can also have aggregate political consequences. Max Weber understood war as a powerful force leading to state formation and capitalist development in Europe. The development of bureaucratic rationality within militaries was particularly important and eventually allowed for the development of modern state institutions (Weber [1922] 1978). Subsequent scholars have further developed this idea. Charles Tilly (1986) famously identified interstate war as an essential factor driving the formation of modern Europe, noting that "wars make states" because war forces states to develop their administrative, coercive, and extractive capacities and forge strong national identities among the population (Moore 1966; Mann 1986, 1993; C. Tilly 1986). Military structures then transform into civil bureaucracies, and states strengthen as they attempt to harness their populations' productive capacity. Michael Mann argued that "war is ubiquitous to organized social life" (1986: 48) and posited that certain economic and military power relationships culminated in the emergence of the state itself.

In the twentieth century, wars likely killed more than 130 million people (Leitenberg 2006). Since World War II, an estimated 260 civil wars have occurred around the world,[5] and civilians have comprised as many as 90 percent of the casualties (Carnegie Commission 1997; Kaldor

2013). While political scientists and sociologists have used cross-national datasets to quantitatively analyze the outbreak, scale, and duration of war (see Small and Singer 1982; Fearon and Laitin 2003; Collier and Hoeffler 2004; Sambanis 2004; Wimmer, Cederman, and Min 2009), historical sociologists have looked at war's consequences for other macro-level processes. These processes include the emergence of revolutions (Moore 1966; C. Tilly 1978; Skocpol 1979; Goldstone 1991; Mann 1993), the welfare state and civic organization formation (Skocpol 1992; Skocpol et al. 2002), citizenship rights and civic participation (Markoff 1996; Kestnbaum 2002), and the entrenchment of autocracies (Celestino and Gleditsch 2013). These studies illustrate the many ways war can shape institutions and social structures for years to come (see Wimmer 2014 for a review).

However, few studies have used gender to animate war's transformative effects. Research on women and war is typically confined to disciplinary subfields, including feminist international relations or security studies, and principally examines women during war, paying less attention to war's gendered impact on institutions and social structures in the aftermath. Given the ubiquity of war in the first decades of the twenty-first century, this absence seems shortsighted: better understanding the legacy of war on women's power is of fundamental moral and political importance, and of value to both social science theory and policy.

Indeed, war may be one of the few comprehensive disjunctures that opens social and institutional space for women's gains. Women's status across the world has been on a slow, if steady, upward trajectory over the past few centuries. Since Mary Wollstonecraft's *Vindication of the Rights of Women* in 1792, women's movements have gradually become more prominent worldwide. In the nineteenth century, women in Europe, the United States, and beyond campaigned for suffrage, education, and legal rights. In 1893, New Zealand became the first country to give women the right to vote, and countries across the world began to extend political rights to women. Progress has not been swift. In the United States, for example, women gained the right to vote in 1920, entered the labor force in great numbers only during World War II, and then were pushed out of these new positions after the war. Moreover, these rights and opportunities were granted primarily to white women; women of color, indigenous women, and immigrant women have long worked the most physically demanding, precarious jobs with long hours, and continue to face substantial obstacles to controlling their legal and political rights. The Civil

Rights Act of 1964 provided women formal protection against sex discrimination, but not until the following decade did the courts clarify the
substantive terms of this protection.[6] Today, women in the United States
lag behind men in many key areas, including in political representation,
income, wage employment, and managerial positions. Women with marginalized identities lag even further behind their white counterparts in
these areas.

Despite these limitations, the history of American women's rights alerts
us to the transformative role war can play in the quest for gender equality.
The suffrage granted to American women immediately after World War
I was due, in part, to suffragist movements engaging in nonviolent direct
action by joining with broader peace movements during the war effort
(Clemens 1999; Taylor and Rupp 2002). The women's movement gained
momentum during the war, and international feminist organizations,
such as the Women's International League for Peace and Freedom, forged
networks between activists around the world. World War II ushered in a
political sea change in American women's roles, as women's employment
in the wage economy increased by 50 percent during the war (Anderson
1981; Hartmann 1982; Milkman 1987). As the United States mobilized
for war during both periods, women were depicted as essential to the war
effort; they became not only mothers and wives, but also workers, citizens, and soldiers (Hartmann 1982: 20). Women's domestic tasks were
thus infused with a broader nationalist purpose.[7]

Thus, while war indisputably has certain negative impacts on women,
we see how interstate wars also shaped American women's employment
patterns and political rights. Moreover, recent scholarship suggests a
link between war and women's legislative representation in low-income
countries around the globe. Case studies have revealed how women
organized during wars in places like Sri Lanka, Algeria, and Nepal and
challenged traditional expectations about women's roles in the domestic
sphere as they got involved in everyday struggles to demand peace, reject
militarism, and advocate for political change. We also know from the
case-specific literature that wars can shape women's lives by motivating
collective action or inspiring new social bonds.

However, we know little about how war causes structural shifts that can
precipitate ordinary women's mobilization in less formal political capacities, or about the processes that facilitate women's mobilization after war
has ended. Such ordinary political action is not captured in quantitative
cross-case analyses on women's parliamentary representation after war,
nor in historical accounts that look principally at macro-level outcomes.

That is where this book comes in, utilizing Rwanda and Bosnia as case studies for understanding the demographic, economic, and cultural processes through which mass violence impacts women's political mobilization, and employing a theoretical approach that conceptualizes political participation from two perspectives: "everyday" politics and the formal political realm.

UNDERSTANDING FORMAL AND EVERYDAY POLITICS

Studies of political participation have tended to distinguish between formal participation in elections, political parties, and government offices on one hand, and informal participation in neighborhoods, communities, and identity-based activities on the other, reflecting a long-running debate about the opposition between public and private spheres. The public, formal political realm is centralized, highly institutionalized, bureaucratic, permanent, resource-intensive, and largely concerned with *de jure* change. It is based on particular forms of cultural and social capital – such as formal education and credentials – which, throughout history, have predominantly been afforded to men from dominant groups. Such formal political spaces require little explanation: women's legislative representation is one of the most visible indicators of women's status, as underrepresentation is one of the most pronounced forms of inequality in the world today.

Yet debates endure over *substantive* versus *descriptive* representation when it comes to women's formal participation (see Lovenduski and Norris 1993; Phillips 1995; Walby 2005; Wangnerud 2009). In 2017, Rwanda had the world's highest percentage of women in parliament at 64 percent. Comparatively, in the United States, women hold approximately 20 percent of the seats in both houses of Congress, and in countries like Lebanon, Haiti, Thailand, and Tonga, women comprise less than 5 percent of the legislature (Inter-Parliamentary Union 2017). While women's legislative representation serves as an indicator of women's formal political power, and understanding the political, social, cultural, and economic conditions conducive to the advancement of women in politics has been the subject of extensive study, such statistics are a poor indicator of women's power more broadly. This is only in part because the advancement of women in formal political positions is often done for the benefit of the patriarchal status quo and ruling male political elites. More alarmingly, recent scholarship has drawn much-needed attention to the fact that gender-sensitive legal reforms or women's empowerment efforts can be used instrumentally to mask more nefarious political motives behind a guise of progress (see Goluboff 2007; Berry 2015b; Lake, Muthaka, and Walker 2016; Berry and Lake 2017). For instance, in Rwanda, women's political power has been used to distract international donors away from human rights abuses conducted by the authoritarian-leaning regime. Such limitations of women's formal political representation call for our increased recognition of spaces of women's political agency that fall outside of the formal politics.

Further, the boundaries between the formal political sphere and the private one are not always clear.[8] Limiting the analysis of political participation to the formal sphere overlooks vast arenas of women's informal political action. Informal political spaces, by virtue of their deinstitutionalized nature, require more explanation. They are more decentralized, less bureaucratic, emotional, emergent, resource-light, and more concerned with immediate, *de facto* gains. Such realms privilege forms of social and cultural capital beyond formal education or credentials.

To further explore informal political realms that bridge the public/private divide, I borrow from the micro-politics and resistance paradigms pioneered in works by James C. Scott (1985, 1990), Lila Abu-Lughod (1990), Asef Bayat (1997, 2007, 2010), and others. These approaches are useful for understanding political activities that occur outside of formal political realms and help reveal the complexity of power relations in a given society. Moreover, in political or cultural contexts where organized resistance is infeasible, such an approach investigates alternative spaces and forms of struggle. Foucault's (1980: 96) notion of decentered power underscores much of this perspective, holding that power exists in the center as well as in more regional and local institutions at the "extremities" of society and works through the "citizen-subjects" themselves. For Foucault, power circulates; it therefore is not confined solely to state institutions. Similarly, Gramsci's (1971) concept of civil society views power as rooted in institutions outside of the formal political realm.

In order to make sense of how everyday activities can be political, I draw in particular on Bayat's (2010) work that discusses a "politics of practice": the idea that the ordinary activities of the subaltern can be political, even if they look different than most Western understandings of contentious politics. Instead, people selling items in public, working outside of the home, building houses, pursuing education, playing sports, and the like can be political as they quietly impinge on appendages of the state and accepted behavior, reflecting a "social nonmovement" within constrained political environments. Such actions are not necessarily consequential on their own, but as large numbers of ordinary people struggle to survive and improve their lives, their actions can accumulate and lead to new forms of organizing outside the political realm. In turn, these forms of everyday politics can foster movements for social and political change that challenge the authority of the state.

Crucially, Bayat notes that the state is never absent from these contestations of power. The everyday political activities of the subaltern can both strengthen and undermine the stability and legitimacy of the state, and they are in turn constrained and shaped by the reach of state power. For instance, Bayat notes that in the context of women's actions in Iran, women's daily activities bore little resemblance to what we generally think of as acts of defiance or collective action – they were not public protests, labor strikes, or mass demonstrations. Instead, women juggled in public parks, raced cars, and let their hijabs slip to reveal a few inches of hair beneath their headscarves. These activities were intimately tied to daily life, because the state tightly controlled citizens' ability to engage in public actions (Bayat 2010: 17).[9] As tens of thousands of women participated in these daily activities that resisted the status quo in Iran, their activities began to accumulate, ultimately establishing new roles and rights for women.

This "everyday politics" approach is particularly useful after the upheaval of war, as people take on new social roles intimately tied to survival and the ordinary activities of daily life. As we will see in Rwanda and Bosnia, women were more likely than men to assume new roles that impinged upon the established social order (e.g., doing "men's work"); this led women to make small claims that became "stepping stones" for further claims, and eventually generated new opportunities for women to demand rights (Bayat 2010: 17). These everyday encroachments catalyzed the formation of community organizations, which soon became a space for political organizing outside of traditionally male-dominated political realms. These organizations ultimately codified women's leadership at the local level and provided a platform for some women to launch political careers. As Figure 1.1 captures, these processes of mobilization overlapped: only by first having massive numbers of women engaged in new social roles did community organizations form, which then allowed some women to participate in formal politics (Rwanda) and protest movements (Bosnia).

This theoretical approach builds on past feminist research that shows how women's collective action often occurs outside of the formal political

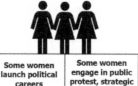

| Some women launch political careers (*Rwanda*) | Some women engage in public protest, strategic humanitarianism (*Bosnia*) |

Many women form and participate in organizations to support daily needs

Masses of ordinary women engage in new social roles tied to daily life

FIGURE 1.1 Overlapping Process of Women's Political Mobilization

realm (L. Tilly 1981; Marx Ferree 1992; Clemens 1993; Ray and Korteweg 1999; Taylor 1999). Particularly when looking at the Global South, feminist scholars have challenged assumptions that women only have power if they enter the "male" political domain (Elshtain 1981; Sharoni 1995, 2001; Yuval-Davis 1997; Gal and Kligman 2000). Given that institutions within the personal sphere – marriage, family, and home – are highly political, these spheres also reflect spaces for women's political engagement (Stanley and Wise 1983; Miles 1996; Enloe 2000). Thus, statistics on the percentage of women in government or parliament are not a fully satisfactory measure of women's political power, as national parliaments are hardly the only venue for political action (Gal and Kligman 2000: 13; Heath, Schwindt-Bayer, and Taylor-Robinson 2005).

Instead, civil society is a critical space for analysis. When cut out of politics, women – and notably African women (Tamale 1999; Bop 2001) – often retreat to the civil sector. As is frequently the case in the developing or post-socialist world, nongovernmental organizations (NGOs) can represent a dynamic space in between the public "male" government realm and the private "feminine" one. Such an in-between space – or "third sector" – must be considered when looking at women's political power. For example, Elisabeth Clemens (1993) showed how American women invented a new model of non-electoral political action by founding women's organizations in the late nineteenth century. Gal and Kligman (2000) described how civil society in East Central Europe after the end of the Cold War – especially the collection of informal aid

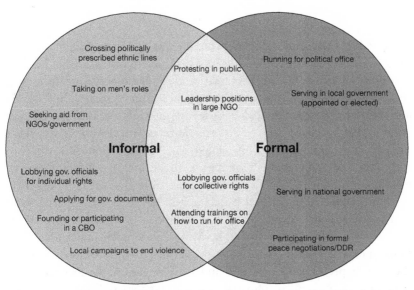

FIGURE 1.2 Examples of Women's Informal and Formal Political Participation

networks and community organizations – was dominated by women, and increasingly became the primary arena of women's political action. Aili Mari Tripp also showed how women in Uganda engaged in politics through the pursuit of tangible results on the ground; in addition to demonstrations and electoral politics, women mobilized to solve the problems at hand (2000: 16–17; see Ray and Korteweg 1999 for a review of similar research). Looking beyond formal politics is thus essential for understanding women's political engagement after war. I show some examples of these varied types of political action in Figure 1.2.

To be sure, it is important not to over-romanticize these forms of everyday politics and resistance (see Scott 1985: 29–30; Abu-Lughod 1990: 42; Bayat 2010: 55). While such forms of political action are not trivial, we should not read every action "as signs of the ineffectiveness of systems of power and of the resilience and creativity of the human spirit in its refusal to be dominated" (Abu-Lughod 1990: 42). Furthermore, mass violence can lead large numbers of people to experience shifts in their ordinary daily activities, not all of which reflect new forms of political organization. As such, this book looks at women's political agency alongside the structural transformations precipitated by war, and as something that unfolds temporally: in stages and in many different social locations.

ARGUMENT

Informed by the sociological literature on war and the feminist literature on spaces of political contention, my central argument in this book is that war can loosen the hold of traditional gendered power relations as it restructures the institutional and structural layout of society. In Rwanda and Bosnia, war precipitated a series of interrelated and overlapping structural shifts that occurred at variable rates and temporalities. These include: (1) a demographic shift, due to the disproportionate death, conscription, and imprisonment of men and the massive displacement of people from their homes; (2) an economic shift, due to the destruction of infrastructure, agricultural capacity, and the arrival of international humanitarian aid; and (3) a cultural shift, due to the reconceptualization of women as legitimate public actors, as women juxtaposed their "more peaceful" nature with men's propensity for war. Combined, these three shifts produce the outcome under investigation: the increased participation of women in informal political capacities. Under additional conditions – including the installation of a new, gender-sensitive political regime, which occurred in Rwanda but not in Bosnia – women's informal political mobilization may culminate in women's increased participation in formal political capacities.

In this book, I focus on both informal and formal politics, allowing me to analyze the multifaceted and varied ways that violence restructured women's lives and allowed for some women's increased participation in public, political spaces.[10] Women's claims to rights and justice were often made urgent and amplified by war, and women's everyday activities during and after violence – such as providing for their families, going outside of the home to find food or cooking fuel, and resisting the idea that they were involved in the violence – reflected a "politics of practice" whereby women took on new political roles in their households and communities. These new roles led women to form community organizations, which created spaces for women to build new social networks and engage in collective projects. While broadly perceived as extending women's domestic care work, these organizations simultaneously became a new form of political organization, institutionalized women's leadership at the community level, and served as a springboard for some women to participate in more formal political capacities. In Bosnia, these organizations also facilitated women's protest movements.

Comparing Rwanda and Bosnia allows me to illustrate similarities and differences in how war facilitated women's grassroots mobilization; further, it allows me to trace the processes through which women's

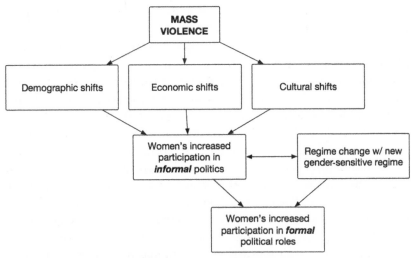

FIGURE 1.3 Impact of Mass Violence on Women's Informal and Formal Political Participation

grassroots mobilization eventually led to women's legal gains, greater freedoms, and more formal political participation. Ultimately, I show how in both cases, many of these gains were set back as a variety of social processes intervened. These include the domestic political settlement, which created *hierarchies of victimhood* that facilitated new social divisions and undermined the possibility of a cross-cutting women's movement; the arrival of international humanitarian actors, which prioritized technocratic knowledge over local expertise and distributed funding on the basis of rapidly changing donor priorities; and the revitalization of patriarchy, in which women's gains were met with a violent *patriarchal backlash* as men sought to preserve hegemonic control. In both countries, violence extended beyond the theater of war and entrenched itself into women's daily lives. Combined, these processes have set back many gains women made after the wars in Rwanda and Bosnia and raise questions about the extent to which postwar mobilization and formal, institutional rights can be harnessed for genuine, intersectional gender emancipation.

RESEARCH DESIGN: A HISTORICAL-INSTITUTIONALIST APPROACH

My approach in this book falls within the framework of historical institutionalism, as I attempt to explain variation in real-world problems or events over time (Skocpol 1979; Tilly 1984; Pierson and Skocpol 2002; Mahoney and Rueschemeyer 2003; Pierson 2004; Waylen 2009). Historical institutionalists explain large-scale structural changes, identifying the "critical junctures" that instigate change and the causal processes and mechanisms that emerge from such periods. They also pay attention to the temporality of social change, looking at how events transform structures and produce social processes that are both path dependent and contingent. Such an approach understands events – like war – as moments of institutional transformation and creativity, which set in motion processes that are then constrained by the cultural and social structures that predate the event (Sewell 1992, 1996; Mahoney 2000; McAdam and Sewell 2001; Pierson 2003). Here, historical institutionalists ask about other possible outcomes at every stage of the event trajectory, engaging counterfactuals and expecting contingency. When studying the impact of war, such an approach is essential, since hindsight often leads to overly deterministic explanations of war's occurrence and impact.

In this book, I focus particular attention on the gendered elements of institutional and structural transformation during war. As such, I analyze how actors in a given institutional context are shaped by gendered power dynamics (Skocpol 1992; Thelen 1999; Waylen 2009), thereby taking up Georgina Waylen's (2009) call for more "feminist historical institutionalism."

Case Studies

A case study approach also informs my analysis (Ragin and Becker 1992; Ragin 1999; Mahoney and Rueschemeyer 2003; George and Bennett 2005; Gerring 2007). Through case studies of Rwanda and Bosnia, I delve into the specific historical context to identify the institutional changes that occurred during violence and the resulting repercussions for gendered power relations. Interviews with individual Bosnian and Rwandan women serve as the primary data for these cases studies, allowing me to analyze institutional transformation through the life stories of those directly affected by it. This approach provides richness and nuance to a literature dominated by more top-down accounts of institutional transformation after violence.

I designed the case studies through the paired case comparison method of historical analysis. When I initially began this project, I selected the two cases based on a "most similar conditions" research design with a divergent outcome. Rwanda and Bosnia shared experiences of mass violence in the early 1990s that featured the mass killing of noncombatants, ethnic antagonisms, widespread sexualized violence, and massive population displacement. In the aftermath, the status of women looked very different. Rwanda appeared to be an extremely positive case: women reached the world's highest percentage of seats in parliament, as well as top positions in the judiciary, police, and government ministries. At first glance, Bosnia was a negative case: women saw few gains at the national political level, and, in the first postwar elections, women were elected to less than 3 percent of the seats in the national legislature. As I delved further into the cases and considered political engagement more broadly, however, it became clear that Bosnia was not a strictly negative case. Indeed, the violence in both countries pushed women into new social and political roles and facilitated women's mobilization in many areas. While looking only at the national political level immediately after the violence suggests a divergent outcome, women in Bosnia participated in informal political spaces in many of the same ways as women in Rwanda, suggesting a more universal pattern in how war impacts women's political engagement in the aftermath. Thus, the comparative logic in this book is designed to illuminate the patterns in how war impacted women's informal political mobilization in both cases.

There are, of course, many differences between the cases. While Rwanda was transitioning from a single-party authoritarian system of government to a multiparty democracy before the violence, little real change had occurred and its authoritarian leader was firmly entrenched when the war broke out. Bosnia, on the other hand, was undergoing a massive transition from the socialist era as it broke off from the collapsing Yugoslav federation. This left Bosnia reeling from both political and economic turmoil; the country had barely declared its independence when the war broke out. The end of each conflict also presents a notable difference; in Rwanda, the violence was ended by the invading Rwandan Patriotic Front (RPF), a mostly Tutsi rebel army based out of Uganda, whereas in Bosnia, the violence was ended by NATO's military engagement and the subsequent Dayton Accords, an internationally brokered peace agreement. Furthermore, the differential death toll between the two cases is important: there were approximately 100,000 wartime deaths in Bosnia, compared to a best estimate of 800,000 deaths in Rwanda (Straus 2006; Research and Documentation Center 2013; Verporten 2014). This amounts to approximately 2.4 percent versus 11.2 percent of the total populations of each country.

These differences are important. Still, at the core of the comparison is a shared experience of mass violence in the early 1990s, which allows me to sketch out the conditions under which violence can be transformative for gendered power relations. In addition, it allows me to analyze patterns produced by violence itself, identifying the impact of demographic, economic, and cultural shifts on women's power in the aftermath.

Conducting Research in Rwanda and Bosnia Today

The war in Bosnia broke out less than a decade after Sarajevo hosted the 1984 Winter Olympics, and Bosnia's location in Europe rendered the war highly visible to Western audiences. As the first war was covered by the twenty-four-hour televised news cycle, nightly broadcasts from besieged Sarajevo featured images of children dodging sniper fire and of prisoners starving in concentration camps (Keenan 2002). Western horror ultimately led to NATO's involvement in the conflict, which culminated in the Dayton Accords. Yet, following a rapid invasion of foreign diplomats and "colonization"[11] by international nongovernmental organizations (INGOs) and humanitarian aid agencies, the involvement of internationals faded around 2002.[12] In the years since, Bosnia has had comparably less international media attention than Rwanda.

By contrast, Rwanda has become increasingly familiar to Western audiences since the violence. Books like Philip Gourevitch's *We Wish to Inform You That Tomorrow We Will Be Killed with Our Families* (1998) and Samantha Power's *A Problem from Hell* (2002), and movies like *Hotel Rwanda* (George 2004) sparked a global conversation about genocide and the human capacity for evil. In addition, the country's purported development success over the past two decades has made it a darling of the international aid community. Today business students and entrepreneurs travel to Rwanda not only to visit the country's genocide memorials, but rather to witness its innovative development programs firsthand.

Yet, in recent years Rwanda has been the subject of a heated debate. On one hand, many journalists and some scholars have heralded the country as a model of reconciliation and development (see Gourevitch 1998; Kinzer 2008; Crisafully and Redmond 2012). On the other hand, the state's increasing authoritarianism has generated many critics, who accuse President Paul Kagame and his government of extrajudicial killings during the war and intense repression of political rivals and ordinary citizens who fall afoul of the regime (see Reyntjens 2004, 2011, 2014; Longman 2006, 2011; Prunier 2009; Thomson 2013). While I attempt to stay agnostic in some of these debates, my findings nevertheless echo many of the concerns raised by the most critical of scholars: I too find that many of the narratives about Rwanda's success obscure the daily reality for ordinary citizens. I also find that the high percentage of women in parliament is likely part of a broader political strategy aimed to distract attention from the overwhelming number of Tutsi in government and to win accolades from the international community, rather than a genuine effort to advance women's power and freedom. This should cause us to pause and reconsider using national legislative statistics to capture women's empowerment; it should also inspire us to look critically beyond formal political spaces in order to more accurately understand gendered power relations.

DATA AND METHODOLOGY

The core data for this book come from semi-structured biographical interviews I conducted with 152 women in Rwanda and 109 women in Bosnia during a combined year of in-country fieldwork between 2009 and 2016. Alongside the interviews are corroborating sources from government documents, organizational reports, secondary literature, and archival collections of survivor testimonies. I analyzed more than 200 organizational reports and briefing papers, including from international organizations (e.g., Human Rights Watch, Amnesty International, the World Bank, the International Conflict Group, and the International Labor Organization) and local community organizations. Many of these reports contain excerpts from interviews, which provided another useful source of women's experiences during and after the violence.

Further, the analysis herein draws from my many experiences in the field. These experiences included countless informal conversations with friends, government employees, international development workers, expatriates, and many other locals (both women and men). In addition, in each country I engaged in participant observation with women's organizations, parliamentary sessions, NGO conferences, and human rights organizations. These observations greatly informed the research. My fieldwork also benefited from my status as a board member of a nonprofit organization, Global Youth Connect (GYC), which has run human rights education programs in both countries over the past decade. My work with GYC during two previous summers spent in Rwanda (2007 and 2008) also informed the research, and granted me networks and connections I was able to use to gain access to certain populations.

I selected interviewees using a stratified purposive sampling design, targeting women respondents from three social groups: (1) high-level government officials and NGO executives ("elite" women);[13] (2) founders, employees, and members of smaller NGOs and community-based organizations (CBOs); and (3) poor urban and rural women ("ordinary" women). Eventually I largely abandoned the formal distinctions between categories 2 and 3, as many women of various class and ethnic backgrounds claimed membership in some sort of formal NGO or CBO. It thus became unnecessary to formally differentiate between the two categories; however, I still aimed to interview women who were leaders in NGOs/CBOs in addition to women who were the beneficiaries of these organizations.[14] I individually approached interviewees from category 1 via email, phone, and various contacts. I approached interviews from categories 2 and 3 through a variety of strategies, primarily local interlocutors and community associations.

Between 2009 and 2013 I conducted three research trips to Rwanda (2009, 2012, 2013) for a total of six months in the country. I conducted forty semi-structured interviews with women in Rwanda's government, including twenty-five members of Rwanda's parliament. While it is illegal to discuss ethnicity in Rwanda today, based on each elite woman's biography, I estimate that 35 percent (fourteen) were widows or survivors of genocide (likely Tutsi), 38 percent (fifteen) were returning refugees (likely Tutsi), and 28 percent (eleven) made no mention of their victimization during the genocide (ethnicity unknown, likely Hutu).[15] I conducted an additional 112 individual or small-group interviews with "ordinary" Rwandan women in women's associations, school groups, and rural cooperatives. After the initial period of fieldwork, I revised my one-on-one interview strategy and conducted interviews with thirty women from low economic backgrounds in small groups (between three and five women in each). This facilitated a more open and comfortable environment for my participants, and served to cultivate more substantive and detailed answers to my questions. I conducted the majority of my interviews in the capital city of Kigali, but conducted additional interviews and fieldwork in two additional sites: Musanze, in Northern Province, and Bugesera, in Eastern Province. This allowed me to make subtle comparisons between the regions, which experienced different levels and types of violence during the war.

I took five research trips to Bosnia (2010, 2013, 2015, and 2016) for a total of six months in the country. During these trips, I interviewed twenty high-ranking women in the state and Federation-level governments.

TABLE 1.1 *Completed Interviews in Rwanda and Bosnia-Herzegovina*

Category of Respondent	Rwanda	Bosnia
Political elites, NGO executives	40	20
Ordinary women, women involved in foundation of CBOs	112	89
Total completed interviews	152	109

Within this group of elite respondents, 50 percent (ten) of the women were Bosniak, 25 percent (five) were Serb, 10 percent (two) were Croat, and 15 percent (three) were of mixed ethnicity. I also interviewed eighty-nine Bosnian women not affiliated with the government, most of whom were members of various NGOs and CBOs. Like in Rwanda, while I conducted the majority of the interviews one on one, to facilitate a more open environment, I conducted twenty-two interviews in small groups of between two and five women, typically with additional follow-up interviews one on one.[16] I conducted approximately one-half of the interviews in Sarajevo, and approximately one-quarter each in the Krajina and Drina Valley regions of the country. In particular, I concentrated on the towns of Kozarac (in the Krajina region), and Potocari and Tuzla[17] in the Drina Valley. Like in Rwanda, different field sites within the country allowed me to more thoroughly analyze how different processes and logics of violence affected women differently in the aftermath of war.

I conducted some of the interviews in each country in English, but conducted the majority in the local languages of both countries (Kinyarwanda or Bosnian-Serbian-Croatian) with the help of local translators. I recorded the interviews with an audio recorder and with the permission of the interviewees; when permission was not granted, I took extensive notes by hand.[18] I transcribed the vast majority of the interviews and analyzed the interview transcripts in Dedoose, a qualitative coding software.[19] I selected the quotations included throughout this book to represent themes consistent in multiple interviews. These quotations have been lightly edited for clarity, while keeping the original meaning intact.

In order to preserve the anonymity of my interview subjects who are not public figures or who did not grant me permission to use their names, I assign pseudonyms from a list of common Rwandan and Bosnian female names, or simply refer to their interview numbers.[20] I use the real names of organizations and places in order to give credit for their work and to provide a roadmap for future researchers. In general, I protected the identities of my Rwandan interviewees more vigorously than my Bosnian ones, given the tense political climate in Rwanda today. This involved altering and randomizing basic identifying details (e.g., age, profession) about many respondents.

ON THE "POLITICS OF NAMING" AND THE GENOCIDE DEBATE

At the outset of this book it is prudent to clarify one thing. Many scholars, human rights activists, and journalists refer to the violence in Rwanda and Bosnia as "genocide." This term is more commonly used in reference to Rwanda, but it is also used to refer to Bosnia, especially as the International Criminal Tribunal of the Former Yugoslavia (ICTY) and the International Court of Justice (ICJ) formally declared the massacre at Srebrenica to be an instance of genocide (see Cigar 1995; Bećirević 2014; Nyseth Brehm 2014). In an attempt to resist the "politics of naming" (Mamdani 2010), here I refer to specific elements of the violence as genocide, and yet I generally refer to both cases as "mass violence" or "war." There are a few theoretical, moral, and political reasons for this, which are worth explaining at the outset.

The 1948 UN Genocide Convention[21] defined genocide as "the intent to destroy, in whole or in part, a racial, ethnical, religious, or cultural group." The Convention was signed in the immediate aftermath of the Nazi Holocaust against Jews, the archetypal genocide in which the Nazi-controlled German state was undoubtedly the perpetrator and exhibited clear "intent to destroy" the Jewish population.[22] The Convention describes genocide as "an odious scourge" that must be condemned by the "civilized world," establishing genocide as violence that is evil, immoral, and barbaric. In the years since the Holocaust, the term has been used to refer to a certain subset of violent conflicts – most genocide scholars put Armenia, Cambodia, Rwanda, and Bosnia on the list. Scholars debate whether other cases – such as East Timor, Guatemala, or Darfur, Sudan – should be included, often evaluating whether there was clear evidence of "intent to destroy." In recent years, a debate has also emerged over whether the destruction of indigenous populations in the Americas, Australia, and elsewhere should also be considered cases of genocide. Participants in these debates are generally human rights activists, genocide scholars, and, increasingly, policymakers from the West. Their role is a powerful one, because naming violence as genocide ostensibly commands an international responsibility to intervene. While military intervention is generally considered a last resort to foreign crises, the Responsibility 2 Protect (R2P) doctrine established it as an acceptable choice to confront genocide – although interventions have nevertheless been exceedingly rare.

Yet, herein lies the problem. To begin, I reject the idea that genocide alone is evil or immoral, while war is considered the normal – and acceptable – purview of states (see also Žarkov 2008; Mamdani 2010; Gibbs 2015). War itself typically involves the aggression of one state against the people of another (Walzer 2015). A genocide is an aggressive war more extended. Further, whether war is aggression by one state or self-defense against it, targeting civilians is a distinct horror. Targeting civilians is, of course, counter to the Geneva Conventions, international humanitarian law, and every other "rule" of war. Yet one only has to look at the high rate of civilian deaths in all wars in the twentieth century to note that the targeting of civilians (or at the minimum, the acceptance of civilians as "collateral damage") is a defining feature of wars. Civilian casualties have climbed from an estimated 5 percent in nineteenth-century wars to between 50 percent and 90 percent in recent wars of the 1990s (Roberts 2010). One could argue that this makes all modern wars immoral and barbaric. Indeed, civilian deaths in many current wars – including Iraq, Syria, and the DR Congo – far outnumber combatant deaths.[23] This even sets aside the fact that many combatants in modern wars are young men who may have had little choice over becoming combatants in the first place.

Moreover, the term "genocide" tends to simplify complex, overlapping conflicts into a neat framework, wherein one social group is the perpetrator and another is the victim. This Manichean understanding of good versus evil is rooted in reference to the Nazi Holocaust – the most one-sided destruction of a people in recorded history. This schema of categorization precludes the possibility that members of the "perpetrator" group could be victims, or that members of the "victim" group could be perpetrators. And yet, when we look closely at episodes of genocide – such as Rwanda and Bosnia – we see that such categories are rarely clear-cut (see Fujii 2009; Luft 2015). For instance, as I discuss in the chapters that follow, the Tutsi-led Rwandan Patriotic Front (RPF) massacred tens of thousands of Rwandans as it invaded and took control of the country. Further, the Bosnian Armed Forces and affiliated armed groups also murdered civilians during the course of the conflict. Even further, some members of each ethnic group committed atrocities against their co-ethnics; for example, Hutu extremists killed tens of thousands of Hutu who were political opponents of the regime, were married to Tutsi, or who refused to participate in the violence. Hutu men also raped Hutu women. A paramilitary group that defended Sarajevo eventually turned on it, raping and stealing from the population it was ostensibly protecting.

Morally speaking, Manichean categories disguise these Rwandan and Bosnian crimes. Politically speaking, there are many within the so-called genocidal group who oppose the violence and are victims of it. Genocidal racism, in other words, harms many beyond the target group. In any case, when we exclusively refer to these conflicts as genocides, we unintentionally neglect these diverse and multilayered logics of violence. Understanding those killed in genocidal violence as somehow more definitive victims than those killed in more conventional military engagements can create hierarchies of victimhood that intensify social divisions, thwart reconciliation and justice, and perpetuate cycles of violence.

Further, the term "genocide" can let certain people off the hook. By elevating genocide as the "crime of crimes," human rights activists and genocide scholars implicitly view violence that is perpetrated by states or insurgents against civilians for reasons *other* than to destroy an "ethnic, national, racial, or religious group" as less offensive than genocide. It is this classification that establishes Nazi Germany as the leading villain during World War II, and lets Japan comparably off the hook for its rape and murder of millions of Chinese and Korean civilians. More recently, it allowed Western activists to rally against genocide in Darfur – during which between 200,000 and 400,000 civilians were killed – while more than 400,000 Iraqi civilians were dying as a result of the U.S.-led invasion.[24] It is the term's embeddedness within structures of power that allows U.S. policymakers and those with power to hide behind labels like "legitimate war." These same policymakers label conflicts like Darfur as genocide, but hesitate to label others like East Timor and Guatemala as such, perhaps because U.S. foreign policy emboldened genocidal processes in these places. When Secretary of State John Kerry deemed the Islamic State guilty of committing genocide in 2016, his declaration appeased domestic constituencies and helped justify U.S. military strategy in the region.[25] Power and interests thus determine how crimes are labeled and whose deaths are mourned.

The term can also facilitate lazy scholarship. In Rwanda and Bosnia, exclusively using the term "genocide" oversimplifies both conflicts and leads to determinist explanations of both cases by allowing *what we know now* to shape the evidence included in our analyses. Both cases of violence had multiple fronts and different groups perpetrating violence at different times. Both conflicts began as civil wars, in which armed forces engaged in "legitimate" armed combat against state-backed armed groups. All sides committed atrocities against civilians, although certainly not at the same level. Members of each ethnic group committed atrocities against their co-ethnics. When the wholesale massacre of Tutsi civilians began in Rwanda, it certainly constituted genocide. The shift in the type of violence from civil war to genocide, however, can only be understood by looking at how the violence unfolded temporally and spatially, and by accounting for contingency in every step of the process. Many of these atrocities were not the result of a planned system of annihilation, but rather a series of contingent escalations resulting from contestations over state power and fear of military defeat. Furthermore, a civil war and other forms of political violence unfolded concurrently with the genocide. Referring to the entire episode simply as the "Rwandan genocide" thus misses these additional logics of violence.[26]

Selectively using the term "genocide" in reference to these cases creates a privileged hierarchy of victims, while simultaneously giving impunity to other forms of violence. Further, it deepens the "Orientalist" or neo-colonialist gaze of the West, which sees the savagery with which some countries experience genocide as a different phenomenon from our annihilation of indigenous populations, bombing campaigns against civilian targets, or invasions of Vietnam, Iraq, or Afghanistan. Even the UN mandate that signatories to the convention undertake to "prevent and punish" the crime of genocide situates the West in the "savior" category, ignoring the role of the West in furthering processes of militarism, capitalism, and neocolonialism that shape the emergence of genocide itself.

Given the problems the term "genocide" raises in these contexts, I only use it in reference to specific events (i.e., in reference to the specific instances and dynamics of violence that constituted genocide during the broader civil wars, particularly in Rwanda). In so doing, I do not intend to minimize the severity of violence or human suffering in either case; rather, this approach stems from my conviction that no violent death should matter more or less than any other violent death.[27] It is my hope that this approach allows for a more careful and dynamic analysis of the multifaceted processes of violence that unfolded in each place. Moreover, doing so allows me to situate these cases within the broader social science literature on war and thereby to draw on established theoretical frameworks to understand the impact of violence on women in the aftermath.

STRUCTURE OF THE BOOK

This book consists of three sections. The first two sections, on Rwanda and Bosnia respectively, contain three chapters each. I first sketch out a historical overview of the status of women in each country (Chapter 2 for Rwanda, Chapter 5 for Bosnia). These historical chapters outline the context in which the war occurred and illustrate the role of past violence in shifting women's roles. I next analyze the major structural shifts caused by the violence in each place (Chapter 3 for Rwanda, Chapter 6 for Bosnia). These chapters examine the demographic, economic, and cultural shifts caused by war in an effort to specify the particular ways that war can be transformative for gendered power relations. Here I extend current research that looks at the puzzling positive relationship between violence and political engagement by identifying the structural shifts and social processes through which this relationship arises. In the third and final chapter of each section, I unpack the outcome of these structural shifts by assessing how they impacted women's political engagement in both informal and formal political capacities (Chapter 4 for Rwanda, Chapter 7 for Bosnia). Despite the differences between the violence in Rwanda and Bosnia, delving deep into the various processes that emerged reveals many patterns between the cases.

The third section, Chapter 8, asks two essential questions: has women's political mobilization continued in the years since the violence? If not, what social processes have intervened to undermine or limit women's gains? Despite increases in women's political engagement during the immediate postwar period, as time progressed, much of this progress was ultimately lost or set back. This occurred for similar and different reasons in each case that were intertwined with power dynamics and instability in the postwar period. Three general themes emerged from my interviews. First, the political settlement in both cases fractured women's organizing across ethnic and class divides and created new barriers to women's participation in political spaces. In order to consolidate power in the aftermath of violence, political elites in both Rwanda and Bosnia mobilized ethnically defined social groups and elevated certain constituencies as those most victimized by the violence. In the process, these efforts created *hierarchies of victimhood* that facilitated new social divisions and undermined the possibility of a cross-cutting women's movement. Second, foreigners who arrived after the violence often exacerbated these hierarchies, as they knew little about the local context and were alienated from ongoing work at the grassroots. The funding priorities of INGOs changed rapidly, which inhibited the growth and formalization of informal, grassroots organizations without the capacity to adjust to changing demands. Moreover, internationals often valued technocratic skills over local knowledge, which ultimately undermined efforts to organize around particular community needs. Third, and finally, both countries experienced a revitalization of patriarchy in the aftermath, as violence extended beyond the theater of war and entrenched itself in women's daily lives. While the gender order was in flux during the war and women made many social and legal gains in the aftermath, this progress was undermined by an uptick in gender-based violence. This may have been a reaction to women's gains and increased autonomy during the war, which threatened men's power and thus triggered a *patriarchal backlash*. In both cases, foreign and domestic efforts to mitigate women's subordinate status in the aftermath of war at times unintentionally reinforced it.

In the concluding chapter, I suggest ways that future studies might extend this framework to other cases of mass violence. I also highlight the implications of my arguments for different fields of social science research, as well as for policymakers and NGOs interested in implementing more effective peacebuilding and women's empowerment programs in conflict-affected states. Speaking to those broadly concerned with gender, peace, security, political violence, genocide, and social movements, I conclude by reflecting on the continued cycles of violence that persist in our world today, and the importance of understanding war as a period of destruction that is simultaneously a period of rapid social transformation. Better understanding war's impacts on women reveals spaces of agency and resilience amid devastation, signaling areas where efforts to champion peace and intersectional emancipation may find success in the future.

2

Historical Roots of Mass Violence in Rwanda

Rwanda is a small, landlocked, densely populated country in the Great Lakes region of Central Africa. In the early 1990s, it was the site of a brutal war and genocide. Today, it boasts the world's highest percentage of women in parliament and impressive economic growth, and has garnered accolades for ease of doing business and low corruption.[1] When I first traveled to Rwanda in 2007, these dualities were striking. Rwanda is a stunningly beautiful place: sunbaked red earth roads cut across rolling, verdant hills. At the same time, these hills are dotted with purple banners commemorating massacres and marking memorials where human bodies, skulls, and tattered, bloodied clothing are on display. As I traveled back to the country five times over the next six years, I came to understand Rwanda as a country full of paradoxes, which, as Filip Reyntjens rightly put it, makes the country "difficult for outsiders to comprehend and to apprehend" (2011: 1). It is at once a place of tremendous hope and overwhelming suffering, economic prosperity and entrenched poverty, women's progress and women's oppression.

My own understanding of the country evolved dramatically since my first visit, when I came to the country as a delegate on a cross-cultural human rights program. During my first weeks there, I sat down with a handful of young genocide survivors – mostly men – and listened to stories about their experiences during the violence. One had watched militias kill his mother with his baby brother on her back, and then hid for weeks before a Hutu family took him to the neighboring Democratic Republic of Congo. A second described how, at sixteen years old, he had been forced by militias to beat an elderly woman who later died; if he

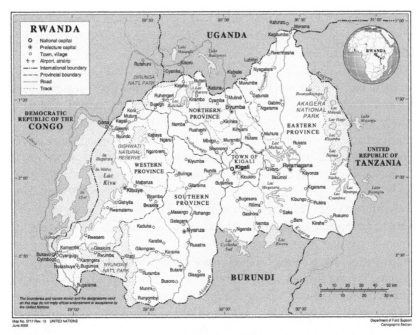

MAP 1 Rwanda

had refused, they would have killed him.[2] During my next trip in 2008, I met a man in his late-twenties who recounted how he escaped from a mob of *génocidaires* by hiding with friends at his boarding school, which was some distance away from where his parents and most of his siblings were killed. Another friend confessed that, at eight years old, he watched as militias raped his mother and then cut her body into pieces. These four men's stories profoundly shaped my desire to understand how human beings live and even thrive after such unimaginable atrocity.

During my subsequent visits to Rwanda, I began to turn toward the experiences of women during and after the violence. While conducting research for this project, I also continued to spend time with each of the young men I had met on my initial trip. As the years passed and trust grew, they began to tell me stories – quickly and in private – about things that worried them. At the same time, I began to hear concerning rumors: the family of a domestic worker I knew was blown up by a grenade after being invited to a community political meeting; the research assistant of another foreign researcher had turned up dead under mysterious circumstances; an impressive journalist I had met on my first visit had fallen ill, and everyone believed he had been poisoned. These rumors – true or false – began to complicate my impressions of the country's progress since the violence.

Between 2010 and 2013, all four of the young survivors I befriended on these earlier trips went into exile. I later learned that each had been targeted by agents of the state – physically beaten, threatened, and their family members poisoned – before fleeing to the United States, Canada, South Africa, or, in one case, to a small island nation near Madagascar. The purpose of this research project is not to explain why each of these young men was forced to leave his country, though several studies provide context for their experiences (see Reyntjens 2004, 2011; Straus and Waldorf 2011; and Human Rights Watch Reports from 2010 to 2015). Rather, I mention these men's experiences here because understanding any research that emerges from Rwanda today requires understanding the context in which such research is produced. Rwanda is not a free country: citizens and foreigners alike are surveilled and monitored. Academics who are critical of the current regime risk harassment from government agents on social media,[3] denial of entry or research permits, or limited or heavily curated access to people and documents while in the country. By limiting access to ordinary Rwandans and pressuring researchers to avoid openly criticizing the government, this hostile research environment stymies critical engagement. Indeed, foreign researchers have been practically kicked out (e.g., Christian Davenport), declared *persona non grata* (e.g., Gerard Prunier and Filip Reyntjens), involuntarily sent to so-called reeducation camps (e.g., Susan Thomson), and denied entry after years of living in and studying the country (e.g., the late Alison Des Forges). Human rights organizations and journalists do not fare any better.[4]

As a result, many foreign researchers today depend on the willingness of local elites to navigate the complicated government bureaucracy and conduct research in collaboration with various government institutions. This results in a skewed perspective because, since the war, local elites are predominately upper- or upper-middle-class Tutsi, most of whom grew up outside of Rwanda. These elites possess the linguistic skills necessary to work with foreign researchers, as well as the political connections to operate smoothly on the ground. Yet, relying on them limits the range of experiences and networks to which researchers are exposed. Many researchers also inadvertently end up with local fixers, who have an agenda to sculpt the image of Rwanda presented to foreigners and convince them of the Rwandan success story. Indeed, many Rwandans today eagerly praise President Kagame to foreigners and tell stories of how Rwandans have reconciled and forgiven each other since the genocide.

Attempting to dig deeper under the surface and past the façade often presented to foreigners, my own research follows recent studies by Fujii (2009), Burnet (2012), Thomson (2013), Purdeková (2015), Jessee (2017), and others who refuse to accept declarations of Rwanda's progress at face value, including the notion that Rwandan women are all "empowered." This approach required deliberately connecting with ordinary Rwandans and even with political dissidents, a strategy I believe considerably strengthened the project. However, I also practiced extreme caution when asking ordinary Rwandans about subjects that could be perceived as politically contentious, and was always aware that my actions as a researcher could complicate the lives of those I interviewed. Topics like ethnicity, for example, were almost completely off-limits. I was careful not to probe interviewees to criticize the government, and instead often asked open-ended questions – which still often resulted in short, neatly crafted answers towing the government's line. As a result, I lean heavily on secondary literature, NGO reports, and government documents to situate my original data (presented in Chapters 3 and 4) within a broader political and historical context.

ETHNICITY IN THE PRECOLONIAL PERIOD

At the outset it is important to clarify the historical background of Rwanda's three ethnic groups, as there has been much debate. While described by nonspecialists during (and after) the genocide as "tribes," the categories of Hutu (approximately 85 percent of the population), Tutsi (approximately 14 percent of the population), and Twa (approximately 1 percent of the population) have come to be understood as dynamic identities that have held different meanings during different time periods. Very little is known about how these ethnic categories were used before 1860 (Pottier 2002: 12). We do know that, in the precolonial era, the most salient social and economic distinction was between sedentary farming and pastoral animal husbandry. Pastoralists, who were predominantly Tutsi, held higher economic and social status than sedentary farmers, who were primarily Hutu. Pastoralists primarily raised cows, which were highly valued. Tutsi controlled the monarchy, whereas Hutu, in general, held a lower economic and social status. Despite these social distinctions, members of these groups traditionally spoke the same language (Kinyarwanda), lived in the same areas, practiced the same religion, and were both patrilineal and patrilocal (Newbury 1988; Prunier 1995; Mamdani 2001). Historically one's ethnicity was not necessarily fixed or stable: wealthy Hutu who obtained cattle could sometimes be considered Tutsi, and poor Tutsi farmers sometimes identified as Hutu (Newbury 1988; Fujii 2009). Most critically, Hutu and Tutsi belonged to the same clans, which served as the principal form of political organization in the precolonial era (Lemarchand 1970).

GENDER IN THE COLONIAL PERIOD: 1895–1962

Gendered power relations and the gendered division of labor in the home changed little between the late precolonial and colonial periods. Arriving in Rwanda in the mid-1880s, German colonialists (who formally established the colony as part of the German Empire in 1895) found a monarchal political system ruled by a Tutsi king (*mwami*), King Rwabugiri. The king was considered a divine being and the patriarch of the Rwandan nation (Prunier 1995: 9). His mother – known as the queen mother (*umugabekazi*) – also held substantial political and symbolic power (Watkins 2014). The Europeans immediately saw the Tutsi as a different race than the Hutu and Twa, noting that Tutsi were, generally speaking, taller, more slender, and of a slightly lighter complexion than their compatriots. Since Tutsi occupied all positions of prominence within the royal court and comprised the elite, the Germans also assumed them to be of a higher intelligence than the Hutu masses. The monarchy ruled the country through a decentralized government of chiefs, sub-chiefs, councilors, and administrative auxiliaries, who were almost exclusively men from the Tutsi ethnic group (Lemarchand 1970: 82).

King Rwabugiri's death in 1895 ushered in a period of political turbulence. While one of Rwabugiri's sons initially assumed the throne, Kanjogera, the queen mother, intervened, killing the king and proclaiming her own biological son Musinga as *mwami* (Prunier 1995; Watkins 2014). Musinga ruled until 1931, but Kanjogera and her brothers were the most powerful people in the kingdom. They eliminated those who opposed the transfer of power and even killed some of Rwabugiri's other sons whom they feared might someday threaten Musinga's rule (Lemarchand 1970; Des Forges 2011). Kanjogera's well-known ruthlessness ultimately shaped the way Rwandans imagined women in positions of power; she is remembered today either as a tyrant or as a powerful role model for women (Jessee and Watkins 2014).

Gender in the Household

Throughout the colonial period, the gendered division of labor in Rwanda was similar to that in other patriarchal agrarian societies in Sub-Saharan Africa.[5] Women and men had complementary, culturally defined roles within the household and community. Whereas men were generally in charge of animal husbandry and heavy labor, women took on the arduous farming tasks of digging, planting, and harvesting, as well as caring for children (Jefremovas 1991, 2002; Burnet 2012). Girls were expected to fetch water, complete household chores, and cook, while boys were often sent to watch over livestock. Motherhood was the primary duty of married women, and women averaged more than eight children each (Republic of Rwanda 2014).[6]

Polygamous marriages were common in elite Tutsi families. Wives typically raised their children in their own households on their husbands' land. At twelve or thirteen years of age, boys would move to their fathers' houses to join their other adult children. The growing popularity of Christianity in the early twentieth century limited the practice of polygamy to some degree, but even those in Christian marriages often discreetly took polygamous partners (Codere 1973: 143). Compared to Hutu women, many Tutsi women did not engage in physically demanding labor and enjoyed relative economic security. Domestic servants – either poorer Tutsi or Hutu – were common in Tutsi households. Due to Tutsis' elevated status in the social hierarchy, many regularly interacted with Europeans or men raised and educated in Europe or cosmopolitan urban centers.

Hutu families were generally less wealthy, and therefore less likely to practice polygamy, as most Hutu men lacked the means to support multiple households (Codere 1973: 145). Hutu women's primary profession involved their families' heavy agricultural labor: digging to cultivate the major crops in the Rwandan diet – maize, plantains, sweet potatoes, vegetables, and sorghum. A Hutu woman's burdens were lessened if she married a man who worked with her in the fields, particularly if they continued to live as part of a corporate unit with his parents, who could help with childcare and agricultural labor. But this household arrangement was uncommon; most Hutu women were expected to perform unrelenting physical labor from early childhood on (Codere 1973: 246). During the colonial period, most Hutu girls did not attend school. Some poor Hutu girls (and boys) were sent to live as domestic servants in wealthier households, which was particularly common among orphans.

Marriage was an important rite of passage for both Hutu and Tutsi women, as it marked the beginning of adulthood and the transition of a girl from her parents' home to that of her husband and husband's family. Before marriage, women derived their social identities from their fathers and brothers; after marriage, a woman joined her husband's patrilineage, relying on his family for access to land and property (Jefremovas 2002: 99; Burnet 2012: 42–44). Divorce was possible, although rare, and was almost always initiated by men. After the death of a spouse, a marriage was dissolved. Women had no property or inheritance rights; as such, they were often compelled to marry the brother of their late husband to remain in their home. Male widowers could remarry as they wished (Burnet 2012: 43). For women, premarital promiscuity or pregnancy was extremely stigmatized. Male family members would sometimes kill a girl who became pregnant before she was married (Codere 1973: 144).[7] Unmarried women were dubbed *femmes libres* (free women), a term that suggested their promiscuity and social marginalization, and many were the concubines of married men, who financially supported them without formally marrying them (Codere 1973: 144; Jefremovas 2002: 99).

Belgian Era: 1920–1962

Germany's colonial presence in Rwanda was minimal: by 1914, there were only five German administrators and ninety-six Europeans in the whole country (Newbury 1980: 102; Prunier 1995: 25). After World War I, Germany's claim to Rwanda was transferred to Belgium as part of the postwar settlement. During Belgian rule, the colonial administration expanded, using the Tutsi monarchy and chiefs as its proxies. Patron–client relationships between Tutsi landowners and Hutu peasants consolidated Tutsi power over state resources and sustained Tutsi wealth. During this period, typical economic relationships transitioned from kinship-based lineage groups to vertical patron–client relations, which curtailed women's access to land and power (Jefremovas 1991: 380).

During the Belgian colonial era, the vast majority of Hutu peasants worked in agrarian production and self-subsistence farming on plots of land owned by their Tutsi "patrons." Through the institution of *ubuhake* (translated variously as "contract of pastoral servitude" or "cattle contract"), these peasants became "clients" of Tutsi "patrons," who gave them rights to land and cattle in exchange for agricultural products grown on the land (Lemarchand 1970: 36; Newbury 1980: 17). Along with other coercive and exploitative labor institutions like *uburetwa*[8] and *umuheto*,[9] the *ubuhake* system fostered deep resentment across the countryside both within the peasantry and between the Hutu peasants and Tutsi chiefs (Newbury 1980: 102–107). Rather than cultivating social interaction, such labor systems inhibited the development of solidarity among the peasants, creating social cleavages that had dramatic consequences later in the century (Lemarchand 1970: 17; Verwimp 2013).

While male peasants sold their labor to Tutsi "patrons" or to the state, women tended their husbands' land and cared for children (Vidal 1974: 58–64). Women's labor was essential to household production; however, they had little to no control over any surplus they produced (Jefremovas 1991: 381–382). Men could earn money and then choose to spend it as they wished, which was often at bars. As Villa Jefremovas explained, this gendered division of labor in the home remained largely unchanged from the precolonial through the postcolonial period:

> Men have no obligation to use the cash they earn from cash crops or wages to contribute to the subsistence of the household ... Women in Rwanda have limited control over the cash they produce, whether it is gained by selling the crops they produce or through wage labour. Women can and do earn cash, but can only control small amounts of the income they generate. Any control they have over land and income depends on the personal relationship individual women have established with individual men. (1991: 382)

In 1933, amid the rising popularity of Social Darwinism and the eugenics movements in Europe, the Belgian colonial administration conducted a census of the Rwandan population. While the categories of Hutu and Tutsi were traditionally rooted in the country's social class system, at this point the colonial administrators formally codified the ethnic categories as different races. After observing and conducting measurements of individual Rwandans' physical features, Belgian social scientists declared that Tutsi were a nonindigenous "Hamitic" race descended from "Caucasoid" people from Egypt. As such, they were deemed to be close relatives of white Europeans, with an intellectual ability far superior to their Hutu counterparts. Hutu were declared indigenous, inferior Bantu "negroids" (Mamdani 2001: 99–102). Following this census, the colonial administration issued mandatory identification cards marking an individual's ethnicity. This newly codified racial hierarchy justified Tutsi political dominance and Hutu oppression, transforming what were previously more fluid social identities into fixed and binary ethnic categories that were extremely difficult to change.

This exclusionist political regime and exploitative labor system led to protests and riots in the mid-1950s. Belgian administrators felt pressured to grant the Hutu some political representation and slowly introduced reforms to that effect. A Hutu counter-elite thus emerged and began to develop a subaltern ideology devoted to breaking the Tutsi monopoly in government and transferring power back to the "indigenous" masses (Mamdani 2001: 117). Perhaps inspired by the wave of pan-African independence movements, Belgian colonialists began to support this new counter-elite, which was comprised of Hutu educated at missionary schools or the seminary when higher education was largely restricted to Tutsi (Lemarchand 1970: 141). The constant inability of this group of Hutu intellectuals to find decent employment because of their ethnicity had generated a burning sense of grievance. In 1957, nine members of this counter-elite produced the Bahutu Manifesto, which "challenged every conceivable feature of the feudal system" by demanding the equal education of Hutu children, the recognition of individual landed property, the promotion of Hutu to political office, and more (Lemarchand 1970: 149). These sweeping demands were a stinging indictment of the Tutsi regime.

THE CHANGING STATUS OF WOMEN DURING REVOLUTION AND THE POSTCOLONIAL PERIOD

Women's roles within their households and in public spaces began to shift in the postcolonial era. In 1959, King Rudahigwa died unexpectedly. Seizing the opportunity, bands of militants affiliated with newly forming Hutu political parties began assaulting Tutsi chiefs. Lemarchand explains how "violence spread like wildfire through the entire country" (1970: 111). During twenty-two months of fighting, militias killed an estimated 150,000 Rwandans of all ethnicities. Another 130,000 Tutsi fled the country, including many members of the monarchy (Lemarchand 1970). Belgium officially granted Rwanda independence in 1962.

Soon after independence, popular elections installed an exclusionist Hutu regime led by President Grégoire Kayibanda, a Hutu from the south of Rwanda. The new constitution granted women the right to vote and to run for political office (Burnet 2012: 50). However, the revolution and the subsequent transition to independence failed to produce many lasting social or economic reforms (Lemarchand 1970).[10] Indeed, by removing the former Tutsi elite and thus transforming the political power structure in Rwanda, the revolution sowed the seeds of the genocide thirty-five years later. In the initial months of the "Hutu Republic," violence drove Tutsi off their land and into exile so that Hutu revolutionaries could take their property. The revolution gave rise to a Hutu elite that assumed control of the state and created deep rifts between Hutu and Tutsi elites, as well as between Hutu factions in the north and south of the country.

Waves of killings during the decades after the revolution sent tens of thousands of Tutsi and political dissidents into exile in neighboring countries, including Uganda, Tanzania, the DR Congo, and Burundi. Tutsi rebel groups, dubbed "*inyenzi*" or cockroaches (perhaps because they often came at night), waged periodic attacks around the country in an attempt to destabilize the new Republic. Before long, Kayibanda's ruling party (PARMEHUTU) began to face internal conflicts between family clans and power networks from different regions of the country (Newbury 1998: 13). In 1973, during massive violence in neighboring Burundi, a coup d'état ushered Juvenal Habyarimana and his Mouvement Républicain National pour la Démocratie (MRND) political party to power. Habyarimana's reign continued the domination of Hutu politicians, but shifted the power center to the north of the country (Pottier 1993; Prunier 1995; Lemarchand 2009).

President Habyarimana was from Gisenyi, a city in Northern Province across the border from Goma, DR Congo. Habyarimana's wife, Agathe Kanziga, was from a powerful family that had ruled an independent principality that was incorporated into Rwanda in the late nineteenth century. Her family networks comprised the Akazu, a political faction that became the staunchest champion of Habyarimana's regime. During his tenure, Habyarimana and the MRND imprisoned or killed many politicians from the south of the country. Violence against Tutsi was generally limited, although institutional discrimination was rampant and restricted the number of Tutsi who could go to school or be employed by the government (Vidal 1969). Civil society was virtually nonexistent, as the regime exerted tight control over public spaces, although some small farming cooperatives formed in the 1970s (Uvin 1998).

From the perspective of the international community, Rwanda under Habyarimana was a successful model of strong state-led development. The country heavily depended on foreign aid, and received lots of it because of its reputation as a relatively uncorrupt, well-organized society (Uvin 1998). The Habyarimana regime enjoyed strong support from France and Belgium, relying on them for military and development aid, and also received aid from the United States, Switzerland, Australia, Canada, the Netherlands, and elsewhere (USAID 2000: 12). With this aid, which would later shape the dynamics of violence during the civil war and genocide, Habyarimana made notable improvements to Rwanda's infrastructure, education, and health care systems, and also implemented reforestation programs aimed at increasing agricultural production (Newbury 1995: 14; Uvin 1998). The development community celebrated these accomplishments and appreciated the political stability of the country – even if it fell far short of democratic ideals.

Women in the Postcolonial Period

A 1973 speech by the minister of justice summed up women's postindependence position in Rwandan society. He stated that a woman's "role as a producer ... reinforces her motherhood. Her dignity in work pays homage to her husband and reflects back on her" (quoted in Jefremovas 1991: 392–393). The minister's speech encapsulated the government's explicitly pronatalist position; despite being one of the most densely populated countries in the world, as of the 1970s Rwanda had instituted no formal family-planning policies (Verwimp 2013: 26). Throughout the postcolonial era, Rwandan women continued to have an average of eight children (Republic of Rwanda 2014).

Despite the Habyarimana regime's tight control over civil society, a small women's movement emerged in the 1980s (Burnet 2012: 52). In 1985, several Rwandan women attended the UN's Third World Conference on Women in Nairobi, where they learned new strategies for involving women in development. During this period, the percentage of women in formal political positions increased, as the percentage of seats women held in parliament increased from 12.9 percent in 1983 to 15.7 percent in 1988 (Burnet 2008: 370). The parliament, however, was largely ceremonial, since Habyarimana and his single-party regime controlled the state and the women who served in government were predominantly the wives or family members of Habyarimana's closest advisors. Nevertheless, a handful of women's organizations formed during this period with both Hutu and Tutsi members, including Haguruka, a women's legal advocacy group; Duterimbere, a micro-credit banking cooperative; and Réseau des Femmes, an organization dedicated to furthering the development of rural women. Based in Kigali, these organizations were generally comprised of elite women with close ties to the regime. Unlike in Bosnia (and many other places in the 1980s), these emergent women's movements were not tied to international feminist networks. Instead, they stemmed from the "Women in Development" framework promoted by the UN Development Program and the World Bank.

Despite some progress, women's legal rights still lagged far behind men's. Rwandan women gained the right to vote after independence, but still required their husbands' consent to open a bank account, engage in any profit-making activity, register a business, buy land, or undertake any legal action in court. Men controlled women's property and income and could withdraw money from their wives' accounts without permission. Unmarried women formally had full legal status, but in practice were considered wards of their fathers or brothers (Jefremovas 1991: 382–383; Longman 2005).

Moreover, independent women were subjected to repression from the state or its agents. Authorities launched a series of "moral cleanup" missions around Kigali in the 1980s (Verwimp 2013: 36). Police rounded up young, single, urban women who dressed stylishly or consorted with European expatriates, beating them and even reportedly stripping them naked in public. Authorities detained some of these women in moral "reeducation centers," where they were subjected to various forms of harm. The majority of women subjected to this mistreatment were Tutsi (C. Taylor 1999; see Verwimp 2013: 36 for a discussion). Educated women were not immune to rigid social control either; at the National University of Rwanda in Butare, school administrators and local officials detained women suspected of promiscuity, improper relationships, or drug use (Umutesi 2004: 14–15). These forms of paternalistic policing remain common in Rwanda today (see Berry 2015b; Human Rights Watch 2015).

ORIGINS OF THE RWANDAN PATRIOTIC FRONT

Women played important roles in the early days of the RPF. After the violence surrounding the Hutu revolution, a large number of Tutsi exiles ended up in Uganda, where they lived in large, semipermanent camps between the Rwandan border and Kampala. When combined with other Banyarwanda[11] already living in Uganda, they comprised the country's sixth largest ethnic group (Otunnu 1999; Mamdani 2001: 161). In the beginning, some passed as Ugandan, which meant they could attend school and find employment. Yet, despite this integration, between 1959 and 1973, political rhetoric emphasized the need to expel Tutsi refugees from Uganda, and various Ugandan governments made attempts to resettle or repatriate the refugee population (Jones 2012: 58-59). Discrimination against Rwandans in Uganda increased in the early 1980s, causing many refugees to seek opportunities to return to Rwanda (Prunier 1995; Mamdani 2001).

Increased repression against Rwandan exiles in Uganda motivated some Rwandan refugees to join Yoweri Museveni's National Resistance Army (NRA), a guerrilla army that aimed to overthrow Ugandan President Obote. Two Rwandan exiles rose to prominent leadership positions within the NRA: Paul Kagame and Fred Rwigyema. At least another 500 or so Rwandans fought in the lower ranks (Otunnu 1999; Prunier 2009).[12] Exiled Rwandans viewed Museveni's NRA as an important base from which they might eventually gain permanent status in Uganda or return to Rwanda (Waugh 2004). In 1986, after a grueling five-year bush war, the NRA successfully overthrew Obote's regime. This experience gave Rwandan exiles confidence in the possibility of overthrowing entrenched national governments, and it taught the leadership that "violence was not exceptional; it was a normal state of affairs" (Prunier 2009: 13). Later, Rwigyema became the Ugandan army chief of staff and eventually deputy minister of defense, while Kagame became acting head of the NRA's military intelligence.

Throughout this period, Kagame and Rwigyema were part of a Rwandan diasporic network that sought to organize an armed political movement for repatriating all Tutsi exiles and eventually securing a Tutsi presence in Rwanda's government and military. This movement was initially known as the Rwandese Alliance for National Unity (RANU); from 1987 on it was the Rwandan Patriotic Front (or RPF, and for the military wing, Rwandan Patriotic Army, or RPA).[13] Several of the leaders of this movement were admirers of Mao Tse Tung and Che Guevara, and were motivated by pan-Africanist struggles for independence and dignity around the continent (Waugh 2004: 37). The movement cultivated strong internal discipline, and its leaders began to seriously think about using military force to return to Rwanda. To do so, the RPF developed expansive financial networks among the diaspora, particularly in English-speaking countries, which benefited from the growing prominence of Rwandan refugees in Museveni's administration and the growing business success of many Rwandans in exile. Equipped with such military support and financial resources, the RPF grew into a sophisticated and disciplined politico-military organization (see further discussions in Prunier 1995; Otunnu 1999; Lemarchand 2009; Jones 2012, 2014).

Modeling itself on Museveni's NRM – which had also mobilized women – the RPF deployed women in a range of roles during its early days. According to several women I interviewed, women took on important roles in the refugee camps, sometimes after the violent deaths of their spouses. Men came to appreciate women's capabilities and support their involvement in the movement. As the RPF grew, women served as recruiters for the cause and also took charge of soliciting donations from the diaspora. Wherever Rwandan exiles lived, young and eager RPF members worked to build consensus and recruit members. Some women, including Aloisea Inyumba, rose within the ranks to hold senior positions on the political side of the movement. Others, like Rose Kabuye, rose in the military ranks. During my interviews with both women, each described the RPF's encouragement of women, saying, "We were never discriminated [against], and when we came to power, they never pushed us aside. They pushed us in the front; we were with them throughout" (Rose Kabuye, Interview #30, February 2013). The RPF gave all Tutsi exiles – women and men alike – the hope that one day they might experience respect within their own country's borders.

CIVIL WAR BEGINS

While the RPF grew in Uganda in the mid-1980s, the economy within Rwanda was experiencing a dramatic decline. The price of coffee, Rwanda's primary export, dropped 50 percent in 1989 (Newbury 1995: 14). The Structural Adjustment Programme mandated by the International Monetary Fund devalued the Rwandan franc by 67 percent, leading to the rapid inflation of basic commodities like food and fuel (Newbury 1995: 14; Mamdani 2001: 147). Tin prices also collapsed on the world market, shutting down Rwanda's tin mines and sending shock waves through the domestic economy (Prunier 1995: 84). With an estimated 90 percent of the population dependent on self-subsistence agriculture for their livelihoods, a famine – partially triggered by the economic crisis – haunted the south and southwest areas of the country and killed an estimated 300 peasants (Pottier 1993; Newbury 1995: 14). This crisis was exacerbated by the high tax burden placed on the rural population, which was expected to pay water fees, school fees, health care taxes, and more, on top of providing several days of labor each month to the state (Newbury 1995: 14; Prunier 1995: 87–88). At the same time as these economic shifts, unknown terrorists threw grenades into crowds in Kigali and at busy bus stations. A pervasive sense of uncertainty spread throughout the population.

Overpopulation was the most pressing issue for both the peasantry and the regime. In some parts of the country, there were more than 1,000 people per square mile (Newbury 1995: 14), which led to land grabs and unrest in the already overpopulated countryside (Prunier 1995: 88).

During the 1980s, the population had grown at an annual rate of 3.1 percent – one of the highest growth rates in the world (Verwimp 2013: 55). The average size of cultivated land per family dropped from 1.2 hectares in 1984 to just 0.9 hectares in 1990 (Republic of Rwanda 1984, 1989, 1991). As word spread that Tutsi exiles wanted to return to Rwanda and reclaim the land they had fled from in previous decades, Hutu peasants were alarmed – there was simply not enough space. Many, including extremists within Habyarimana's regime, began to imagine the country free of pastoralist Tutsi who threatened to suffocate struggling Hutu agriculturalists. Such an imagining of an ethnically pure country of small landholder peasants could not accommodate the RPF, which was knocking at the country's northern border.

In the context of this economic and political instability in Rwanda, the RPF decided it was an opportune time to initiate its military strike. On October 1, 1990, RPF forces attacked a border post at Kagitumba in the north of Rwanda (Prunier 1995: 93–97). They soon encountered the Forces Armées Rwandaises (FAR), the reasonably well-organized and trained Rwandan military of about 5,000 men. The FAR had technical military support from France, which helped it to push back the RPF offensive. Fred Rwigyema was killed under suspicious circumstances during the first few days of fighting, delivering a substantial blow to the movement.[14] Forced to reconsider its offensive, the RPF retreated to the mountainous region in the Virunga Mountains bordering Rwanda and Uganda.

Rwigyema's death elevated Kagame[15] to a central leadership position within the RPF. For several months, RPF members lived in the freezing cold mountains, where several froze to death. Because of the ongoing efforts of the RPF's network, however, funds and new recruits poured in. Many came from the Tutsi exile community in Burundi, and others still from DR Congo, Tanzania, and elsewhere in Europe and North America – although the leadership remained overwhelmingly "Ugandan" in origin. Most of those who joined the RPF were well educated; almost all had attended primary school, and nearly 20 percent had reached university (Prunier 1995: 117). The rebel army swelled in numbers: by 1992, nearly 12,000 fighters had entered the ranks.

To counter the growing threat from the RPF, the FAR rapidly expanded, growing to 30,000 troops by the end of 1991. France supplied the weapons for the expanded army and even aided in military operations (Prunier 1995: 113). Habyarimana commanded the elite Presidential Guard; primarily recruited from his home region, this group was loyal to the president and Akazu faction that comprised his core power base (Des Forges 1999: 45). Habyarimana also cracked down on domestic opposition, arresting between 8,000 and 10,000 people in Kigali alone immediately after the RPF attack (Verwimp 2013: 130). Local authorities organized civilian defense units by conscripting one man from every ten households. These armed groups set up road blocks and monitored activity in order to protect their neighborhoods from the rebel threat (Des Forges 1999; Straus 2006: 26; Verwimp 2013: 147). In 1992 and 1993, MRND leadership and military officers formed youth militias, dubbed *interahamwe* (variously translated as "those who stand together" or "those with a common goal"; Des Forges 1999: 50). The Presidential Guard selected certain promising men in these youth militias for additional military training, which allowed them to gain skills to resist the rebel onslaught (Des Forges 1999: 50; Straus 2006: 26–27). Later, these groups would be among those most involved in genocidal violence.

While the RPF regrouped, pogroms against Tutsi civilians within Rwanda increased, including one in the Matara region (Gisenyi Province), where Hutu militias massacred 348 Tutsi in mid-October 1990 (Prunier 1995: 110; Des Forges 1999: 46; Verwimp 2013: 129). Extremist members of the MRND organized Hutu to kill between 300 and 1,000 members of a Tutsi subgroup in February 1992 (Verwimp 2013: 130–132). The organizers of these massacres had hoped these killings would spread throughout the region; when they failed to do so, extremists faked an attack by the RPF on a military camp in an attempt to incite the local population to launch a counterattack the next day (Des Forges 1999: 47).

In January 1991, the RPF shifted its invasion tactics to a hit-and-run guerrilla strategy. RPF members attacked Ruhengeri – one of the key power bases of the Habyarimana regime – where they stormed a prison and captured weapons that would aid them in the fight. During the following months of the civil war, both RPF and FAR forces perpetrated small massacres of civilians. Some were committed against the Tutsi in "self-defense," as ordinary Rwandans feared the RPF and thereby understood all Tutsi as potential RPF accomplices (or *ibyitso*). Fake propaganda pieces suggesting Tutsi were coming to kill their Hutu neighbors helped rally peasants to participate in killing squads organized by local militias (Prunier 1995: 137; Straus 2006: 29).

By March 1993, approximately 860,000 people had fled in advance of the RPF army, which now controlled large parts of the north and almost all of Byumba prefecture (Prunier 1995: 136). Hutu civilians were increasingly terrified of the RPF, as rumors circulated that the rebels were killing civilians in order to take their land.[16] The RPF established its military headquarters in Mulindi, just sixty kilometers north of Kigali. Fearing insecurity if civilians were allowed to repopulate the area, the RPF prevented civilians from returning to their homes, condemning the displaced to the appalling conditions of the informal camps around Byumba (see Umutesi 2004; Dallaire 2003: 66–67). The RPF committed atrocities during this period, killing dozens (maybe hundreds) of civilians and even children (Amnesty International 1994; Umutesi 2004). Reports of these killings, while minor in comparison to the killings perpetrated by the FAR and affiliated extremist forces, reduced support for the RPF among the opposition parties in Kigali (Prunier 1995: 176).

"DEMOCRATIZATION"

During this ongoing crisis, international donors and domestic groups – including women's groups – pressured Habyarimana to initiate liberal reforms. Habyarimana's ministers and cabinet members were almost all from northern Rwanda (mostly from Gisenyi prefecture). This regional imbalance caused intense resentment among Hutu elites in the south of the country – particularly from former President Kayibanda's base. Fearing a loosening of his power, Habyarimana made plans to introduce a multiparty system of government (Newbury 1995: 14), including legalizing political parties beyond his own ruling MRND and opening political space in the country for pro-democracy supporters.

In 1991, Habyarimana announced plans to hold a constitutional referendum and even promised to erase ethnicity from future ID cards or official documentation (Prunier 1995: 122). In addition to MRND, several other political parties announced their formation, including the Parti Social Démocrate (PSD), the Parti Libéral (PL), and the Parti Démocrate-Chertien (PDC). Furthermore, the Mouvement Démocratique Républicain (MDR), banned after the coup d'état in 1973, was resurrected from Kayibanda's former political base in the south of the country. Each political party was essentially a patronage network with supporters from different segments of Rwandan society (e.g., the PL included many Tutsi). Many within these parties wanted to promote democracy and do away with ethnic politics. Habyarimana also encouraged the development of a group of "opposition parties," which had little power in practice (Prunier 1995: 128; Des Forges 1999: 28–38). This liberalization encouraged the growth of the newly formed women's organizations, as they now felt they could pressure Habyarimana to make women's issues a priority. In 1992, a small coalition of women's organizations – including Haguruka and Réseau des Femmes – successfully lobbied to create the Ministry for Women and Family Promotion.

Habyarimana, however, never seriously intended to relinquish any power, and retained tight control over the FAR and the police. Elite military forces silently assassinated many of his strongest political opponents, often using mysterious car accidents as camouflage (Newbury 1995: 13; Prunier 1995). In March 1992, a coalition of racist Hutu on the "lunatic fringes of radical Hutu extremism" (Prunier 1995: 129) also formed a party, called the Coalition pour la Défense de la République (CDR). Many of these extremists were fringe members of MRND and supporters of the Hutu Power movement, which in 1990 had published the Hutu Ten Commandments. These commandments deemed any Hutu who married, befriended, employed, or even associated with a Tutsi a traitor to his ethnic group, declaring that Tutsi women were deceitful temptresses who were not to be trusted (Kangura 1990). The CDR called for the total elimination of Tutsi from the government and army; thus by definition, it was opposed to any power-sharing negotiations stemming from the civil war, which would necessarily involve the RPF. This group of extremists situated the current threat posed by the RPF in a broader historical narrative, where Hutu, the indigenous people of Rwanda, had been exploited and abused by Tutsi invaders from the north and their colonial collaborators (Mamdani 2001). In radio programs, pamphlets, speeches, and rallies, CDR extremists emphasized that Hutu were victims of a historical injustice: the exploitative yoke of the Tutsi monarchy had made them suffer, and with increasing land scarcity in the country, there was simply no room for the invaders to return.

While Habyarimana tacitly supported many of the CDR's goals, he also was under domestic and international political pressure to begin negotiations with the RPF. The prospect of power-sharing, however, sent many hardliner MRND members into the streets, and in several regions the army mutinied. As a result, the opposition parties (MDR, PSD, and PL) initiated negotiations with the RPF. After these talks, the RPF – represented by its Hutu political chief, Pasteur Bizimungu – announced that the armed portion of its struggle was finished and that only the political struggle would continue. Plans were set to discuss the details of this agreement in Arusha, Tanzania, in July 1993 (Prunier 1995: 150). The Arusha Accords, as they became known, were designed to establish a power-sharing agreement that would end the civil war.[17]

The pending negotiations with the RPF caused extremists within the CDR and the president's own party to worry about ceding power. Evidence of death squads, coordinated by members of the Akazu, emerged at the end of 1992 (Prunier 1995: 168; Des Forges 1999: 59). Network Zero, a group of people close to Habyarimana, purportedly rejected his willingness to consider a power-sharing settlement. Some believe Network Zero began to formalize plans to kill Tutsi and other political opponents and stored weapons in secret arms caches around Kigali (Dallaire 2003: 143; Melvern 2006).[18] There is evidence that many extremists sought to radically halt the democratization process by murdering those who threatened the regime. Extremists, including Lèon Mugesera (a vice president of the MRND in Gisenyi with a PhD from Fort Laval University in Canada) began calling for the murder of Tutsi. Mugesera famously stated that Tutsi should be sent back to Ethiopia via the Nyabarongo River.

But it is important to note that Mugesera's rhetoric was not paradigmatic of political speech at the time; many Hutu elites openly criticized this extremism, and even called for the arrest of people using such racist language. Jean Rumiya, a former member of the MRND central committee, accused Mugesera of calling for murder "in order to launch an operation of ethnic and political purification ... I had hoped that the time when ritual murders were committed for political purposes is over" (Prunier 1995: 172). The minister of justice even issued a warrant to arrest Mugesera for inciting unrest, prompting Mugesera to flee the country (Prunier 1995; 172; Mann 2005: 444). This diversity of opinions on the RPF "problem" should temper allegations that the genocide was the culmination of a long-orchestrated plan by the Habyarimana regime as a whole.[19]

Four major political contingents operated in Rwanda during the early 1990s, each of which had vastly different political agendas and was suspicious of the other groups' motives (Straus 2006: 42). Hutu moderates were represented by opposition political parties like the MDR, PSD, and PL; extremist Hutu hardliners, including Habyarimana's MRND political party and the more extreme CDR, were orchestrated by the Akazu and its military and media allies; the RPF was led by Paul Kagame; and, last, the international community included roughly 2,500 UN peacekeepers and a diplomatic corps assembled by neighboring governments and Western powers. Perhaps most critically, Hutu hardliners were convinced that the RPF was just posturing during power-sharing discussions; many were certain that the rebels would not be satisfied until they took the country by military force and secured Tutsi control over the entire government and military (Straus 2006).

The Arusha Accords, signed in August 1993, established various protocols designed to bring about the end of the civil war, yet ultimately caused further deterioration of the situation. The agreement included a ceasefire and a power-sharing agreement that would grant RPF troops 40 percent of the military and 50 percent of the Officer Corps (Des Forges 1999: 33). A Broad Based Transitional Government (BBTG) would be formed to incorporate the RPF into the political system. Representatives from all major political parties were granted positions in the BBTG. Agathe Uwilingiyimana, a Hutu from the south of Rwanda, became the first woman prime minister of the country.[20] The agreement also granted the RPF five ministerial positions and allowed for the repatriation of Tutsi refugees.

The accords were extremely unpopular among many Rwandans for several reasons. For one, they completely excluded radical Hutu parties from power and deprived the MRND of its control over the cabinet. Moreover, the accords promised to demobilize 20,000 Hutu soldiers, stoking fears of mass unemployment (Mann 2005: 441). Further, the accords allowed for the return of hundreds of thousands of Tutsi from exile, generating fears of instability and land grabs. As a result, the political situation in Rwanda deteriorated further during the negotiations. The CDR refused to participate in any power-sharing agreements with the RPF, and tensions escalated. For protection, the accords granted the RPF permission to station 600 troops in Kigali, generating worry about a military escalation to the political crisis.

On October 21, 1993, in this tense political climate, members of Burundi's Tutsi-controlled army assassinated Melchior Ndadaye, the first Hutu president of Rwanda's southern neighbor. Earlier that year, Burundians had elected Ndadaye president in the country's first smooth transfer of power since independence. President Ndadaye had attempted to appease Tutsi and was widely seen as a political moderate. Violence erupted in Burundi after his assassination, and forces from both ethnic groups killed at least 50,000 people – Hutu and Tutsi – in the following months.[21] Another 700,000 Burundian refugees fled across the border into southern Rwanda (Eriksson 1996: 22). Ndadaye's murder sent shock waves throughout the Rwandan political system, bolstering Hutu Power sects in all opposition parties and fomenting anti-Tutsi rhetoric. The assassination particularly mobilized the extremists in the

CDR, who feared the RPF might similarly assassinate Habyarimana and attempt a coup d'état in Rwanda.

At this point, tensions in Rwanda were at an all-time high, and there was a general escalation in violence of all types.[22] Multiple delays in implementing the Arusha Accords prompted UN Secretary-General Boutros Boutros-Ghali to threaten to withdraw the UN assistance mission in Rwanda. Regional and donor governments also threatened sanctions. Eager to resolve the various conflicts and avoid a full-fledged civil war, officials from Tanzania, Kenya, Burundi, and Uganda met with Habyarimana in Tanzania on April 6, 1994. They scolded him for his failure to control the political situation in his country and for the many delays in implementing the BBTG (Prunier 1995: 221). Habyarimana left the meeting with the newly elected Burundian President Cyprien Ntaryamira to fly back to Kigali in Habyarimana's presidential jet. As the plane attempted to land in Kigali around 8:30 P.M., it was struck by two surface-to-air missiles, causing it to crash and killing all on board. Who shot the missiles continues to be a subject of much heated debate.[23]

GENOCIDE BEGINS, CIVIL WAR CONTINUES

Within hours of the plane crash, Habyarimana's inner circle blamed the RPF for the death of the president and declared that the RPF was attempting a coup d'état. Extremists within the regime mobilized the Presidential Guard, police, FAR, and *interahamwe* militias, and began to carry out supervised killings of political opponents. An interim government was set up, entirely comprised of members of the Akazu and other extremists. Théoneste Bagosora, a Hutu Power extremist at the center of the Akazu, emerged as the central power-holder in the government, and declared the politically meek Theodore Sindikubwabo interim president. Bagosora first aimed to eliminate all domestic opposition to his consolidation of power and commanded the Presidential Guard to spread out across Kigali (Guichaoau 2010: 255; Verwimp 2013: 151). The Presidential Guard began by callously killing opposition politicians, starting with Prime Minister Agathe Uwilingiyimana, who was constitutionally the next in line for the presidency. They continued rounding up the leaders of the other opposition political parties and their families, brutally murdering them under the guise of restoring order (Dallaire 2003; Straus 2006: 47).

Within thirty-six hours of the president's assassination, Bagosora established a "crisis committee" of extremists within the government that began to consolidate control. Its actions during the first twenty-four hours after Habyarimana's assassination were designed to scare the UN – particularly its Belgian forces – into withdrawing. The crisis committee made a political calculation that if several UN peacekeepers were killed early on in the violence, the international involvement in Rwanda would proceed like it had in Somalia and Bosnia: forces would swiftly withdraw. To this end, the militias murdered ten Belgian peacekeepers assigned to protect the prime minister. As intended, the UN Assistance Mission in Rwanda (UNAMIR) reduced the number of peacekeepers on the ground from 2,500 to just 270 Blue-Helmets. On April 7, widespread slaughter of civilians began across the country.

The killings mobilized the RPF, which still had 600 troops stationed in Kigali. RPF troops attacked Presidential Guard stations and command centers and attempted to establish a safe zone around their encampment. They also endeavored to defend the houses of RPF supporters living in Kigali. Clashes between RPF troops and government forces caused Hutu and Tutsi residents to flee the city (Umutesi 2004: 50). In her memoir as a Hutu survivor of the violence, Beatrice Umutesi captured how everyone in Kigali was petrified with fear, regardless of whether they were Tutsi or Hutu. She recalled:

Each group suspected the presence of armed elements in the other group. The Hutu thought that there were members of the RPF among the Tutsi, who in turn believed that there were militia among the Hutu who came from Kigali. The Tutsi provoked panic in the whole camp by running away when a vehicle carrying militia or soldiers passed by on a road. The Hutu caused everyone to run when they claimed they had seen young men armed with clubs and grenades in the areas occupied by Tutsi. At each alarm, people began to run in every direction, without really knowing what was going on. (2004: 51)

On the northern front, RPF forces also launched a full attack beginning on April 8. They advanced quickly. By late April, the RPF controlled the majority of north central and eastern Rwanda (Straus 2006: 50). When they came into contact with MRND political leaders or other extremists, the RPF was militarily aggressive. During its invasion, the RPF killed an estimated 25,000 to 60,000 civilians (both Hutu and Tutsi) – although this number is the subject of heated debate.[24] Many more FAR soldiers were killed in battle. Because of hate propaganda and rumors of RPF attacks, all Tutsi in the country were soon seen as the fifth column of the RPF, and thus legitimate targets in the eyes of the *génocidaires* (Straus 2006).

The international community debated intervening in the violence. Lieutenant General Roméo Dallaire, the chief of the UN Mission in

Rwanda, pleaded with U.S. and UN officials for additional forces, which he believed could curb the violence. His requests were in vain, as world powers exercised restraint in the aftermath of U.S. troop losses in Somalia. France was the exception: in June 1994, it sent 2,500 troops to Rwanda to establish a safe haven for fleeing Hutu civilians as part of Operation Turquoise (Prunier 1995; Dallaire 2003; Power 2003;). The mission was motivated by Habyarimana's long relationship with French President Mitterrand, and French leadership suspected that Habyarimana had been the victim of a Tutsi-led coup d'état. Thus, instead of stopping the genocidal militias, French troops were sent to protect Hutu civilians from the RPF invasion.

NATIONAL TRENDS IN VIOLENCE

The violence in Rwanda, as in Bosnia, unfolded with different speeds and intensities in different parts of the country. Here I outline some over-arching characteristics of the violence, as they are important for under-standing how women's experiences of violence affected their subsequent community engagement. For instance, the pervasiveness of sexual violence shaped the types of groups that women eventually formed around their experiences. The perpetrators of genocidal violence can be roughly grouped in four categories: (1) racist, anti-Tutsi extremists, most notably the Akazu and the CDR leadership; (2) those who wanted to maintain the gains of the 1959 Social Revolution and ensure continued Hutu access to land; (3) Hutu who were not ideologically committed to genocide but nonetheless went along with orders to kill or otherwise participate in the process; and (4) opportunists who turned against Tutsi to gain wealth, settle scores, or assume power (Verwimp 2013: 162). Specifying these categories of perpetrators is helpful for understanding the different dynamics of violence that unfolded over the next few months.

Racist Hutu extremists (category 1) used radio and other propaganda channels to rally ordinary Rwandans to join in the fight against Tutsi. Radio broadcasts encouraged citizens to avenge the president's death, and eventually explicitly called for blood (Prunier 1995: 224). A broadcast by the Ministry of Defense declared that the RPF was comprised of those "who [want] to reinstate the formal feudal monarchy," and encouraged Rwandans to destroy the enemy and any who might assist them (Straus 2006: 50). Radio programs sometimes used dehumanizing language that referred to Tutsi as "cockroaches" (*inyenzi*)[25] or "snakes." Most critically, hardliners emphasized that Tutsi were the enemy (*umwanzi*) or were accomplices (*ibiyitso*) of the RPF, who must be killed before they could launch their own attack (Straus 2006: 158).

Mobs of militias (often mobilized from categories 3 or 4) carried out attacks against Tutsi civilians around the country, usually under the control of an organized and trained military unit. Many of these genocide perpetrators were "marauding bands of violent, opportunistic, and often drunken thugs" (Mueller 2000: 62). Many were motivated less by pure ethnic hatred than by fear, a strong sense of ethnic justice, and the potential for material gain. Looting was pervasive, and killing squads or local militias profited from the violence by stealing livestock, possessions, or even building materials from the homes of those who were killed. Many of these ordinary citizens turned from looters into killers because they feared the RPF onslaught. There was a "kill or be killed" mentality, and many perpetrators feared sanctions from Hutu leaders if they failed to comply (Des Forges 1999; Mann 2005; Straus 2006: 155). Many Hutu saw no way to resist without being considered traitors (Verwimp 2013: 182).

Perpetrators used different killing strategies and techniques. Militias went door to door to known Tutsi houses, killing anyone known to be Tutsi or even those who looked Tutsi. Perpetrators targeted the elite and highly educated, regardless of their ethnicity (Des Forges 1999). Militias also set up roadblocks that prevented people from escaping their neighborhoods by car or on foot (Dallaire 2003: 253). Those who tried to pass the roadblocks were asked for their ID cards; if they were Tutsi or if their names were found on a wanted list, they were killed on the spot. Desperate to survive, many Tutsi fled to Rwanda's swamps and hid for weeks, often partially submerged in water and mud (Interviews; Gisozi Testimony Archive; Des Forges 1999). Others hid in the homes of sympathetic Hutu, and there are reports that some hid in Kigali's few mosques, protected by the imams, who were viewed as nonethnic (Kubai 2007). Tutsi also took shelter in churches, schools, and other large institutions, hoping for safety in numbers, only to discover that these institutions made them easy targets for mass murder. Prefects in some sectors even directed Tutsi to large stadiums, assuring their safety if they complied. This made it easier to use grenades, guns, and rudimentary weapons like machetes and knives to carry out the killing once many were gathered in a single place (Des Forges 1999).[26]

As noted, Hutu were also targeted. Des Forges (1999) and Straus (2006) estimated that the FAR and other Hutu militias killed approximately 10,000 Hutu during the violence. Initially, most of these victims were members of the political opposition or were known for their passive support of the RPF. Others simply looked Tutsi, or were in the wrong place at the wrong time. Some were married to Tutsi. Still others had valuables – including land and cattle – that militias coveted (André and Platteau 1998; Umutesi 2004: 60–61). In certain parts of the country (particularly in Kigali and Northern Province), Hutu from the south were also killed, as they were suspected of supporting opposition parties (Prunier 1995: 249). Beyond being targeted, many Hutu were beaten and coerced to kill; some youth, in particular, were told they would be killed or their mothers raped if they declined to participate. Rwandans with mixed ethnic backgrounds (e.g., a Hutu father and Tutsi mother) were at particular risk of violent coercion to ensure their participation.[27]

Sexualized Violence

In addition to killing, sexualized violence[28] was widespread. Like in Bosnia, rape was not an extension of interpersonal violence or one of the spoils of war; rather, perpetrators employed rape as a deliberate strategy of violence with ethnic, class, and gender dimensions. In many cases, rape was used to destroy the ethnic "other" by eliminating its source: women's biological capacity to reproduce. In patrilineal societies like Rwanda, women are considered the property of their male relatives; their value derives from bearing children that carry on men's lineage. Thus, perpetrators used rape to emasculate and humiliate Tutsi men by abusing their property. Rape became a political act designed to carry out an officially orchestrated policy (Buss 2009).

Yet sexual violence also often occurred outside of the problematic dyad of Hutu/perpetrator and Tutsi/victim: extremist militias raped many Hutu women and girls as the rule of law broke down, and RPF soldiers coerced women into sexual relationships in areas under their control (Burnet 2012: 98). Sexual violence took multiple forms, including sexual slavery, forced "marriage," gang rape, sexual torture, and sexual exchange (Norwojee 1996; African Rights 2005a). These forms of abuse did not follow the genocide script promoted by the postwar RPF regime, in which only Tutsi were victims of the genocide. Instead, these varied types of sexualized violence during war show that an array of factors shaped individual experiences (Buss 2009). Indeed, accounts from Hutu women suggest extremely high levels of sexualized violence perpetrated against them by their co-ethnics during the war (see Umutesi 2004; Thomson 2013).

Many sources cite the estimate that 250,000 women were raped during approximately three months after April 6, 1994, a figure that comes from a 1996 UN Special Rapporteur of the Commission on Human Rights.[29] Some suggest that the number may be as great as 350,000 (Bijleveld et al. 2009). However, these figures are likely inflated – later estimates are in the tens of thousands (Des Forges 1999; Sharlach 1999; African Rights 2004; Amnesty International 2004). Sexualized violence was sometimes part of the process of killing. *Génocidaires* raped women of all ages with objects like machetes and knives, killing most of them in the process (African Rights 2004). Human Rights Watch described these assaults in agonizing detail in its report *Shattered Lives* (Nowrojee 1996), noting how rape was often just one component of wholesale humiliation. One estimate is that only 20,000 to 50,000 women survived rape (Turshen 2001; Zraly and Nyirazinyoye 2010). While sexual violence against men was less common, it certainly occurred (Thomson 2013).

Mass rape in Rwanda left similar legacies to mass rape that occurred during war in Bosnia. Sexualized assaults left a physical legacy that included permanent damage to reproductive organs, bodily disfigurement, pregnancies, fistula, and HIV/AIDS and other sexually transmitted diseases (Nowrojee 1996; Amnesty International 2004; Zraly, Rubin-Smith, and Betancourt 2011). Sexualized violence also caused high rates of psychological trauma among survivors, including post-traumatic stress syndrome, anxiety, suicidal thoughts or behaviors, and persistent depression (Amnesty International 2004; Zraly et. al. 2011). To complicate these physical and psychological legacies, rape survivors faced stigma from their communities, and the legacy of rape affected kinship networks (Fox 2011). Perpetrators sometimes threatened to kill rape survivors because of their status as a living witness to genocide crimes (Zraly et al. 2010: 259). Because of this marginalization, women who survived sexual violence were particularly likely to live in extreme poverty and face constant hunger and housing instability in the aftermath (Cohen, d'Adesky, and Anastos 2005; Zraly et al. 2010).

The mass rapes in Rwanda and in Bosnia also left political legacies. Prior to the violence in both countries, rape had broadly been understood as an unfortunate by-product of war. In the wake of both cases – particularly in the wake of crimes in Bosnia – there was a movement to redefine rape as a systematic weapon of war that could be more broadly prosecuted. Women's groups and feminist organizations worked to legally define rape as a war crime and to establish a precedent for command responsibility (Hansen 2000; Mertus 2004; Engle

2005). In *The Prosecutor v. Jean Paul Akayesu* (ICTR-96-4-T, 1998), prosecuted at the International Criminal Tribunal for Rwanda (ICTR), rape was found as an integral part of the process of genocide and a crime against humanity. This ruling, and subsequent cases like *The Prosecutor v. Anto Furundžija* at the International Criminal Tribunal for the Former Yugoslavia (ICTY) (IT-95-17/1, 1998), legally recognized rape and other forms of sexual and gender-based violence as some of the most serious offenses of war. Later, the Rome Statute of the International Criminal Court defined rape as a war crime and a crime against humanity (Article 8),[30] and UN Security Council Resolutions 1325 and 1820 established that crimes of sexual violence must be excluded from amnesty provisions. While such legal cases were victories for the women's movement, they also codified distinctions between victims and perpetrators, as according to the ICTR only Tutsi women could be victims of genocidal rape (Buss 2009).

REGIONAL VARIATION

The violence in Rwanda ranged in intensity and timing around the country. Many scholars have conducted studies of specific regions in an attempt to understand how the genocidal dynamics emerged and played out in a particular area (see Verpoorten 2005; Verwimp 2005; Straus 2006; Fujii 2009; Guichaoua 2010; Mulinda 2010). Indeed, the number of people killed in a given commune ranged from 71 to upward of 54,700. The average number of deaths in a commune was just over 7,000 (Nyseth Brehm 2017). Violence began at different times across the country and often took on local logics. The areas of the country with the strongest support for Habyarimana's MRND – Gisenyi and Ruhengeri in the north, and Kigali – were the first to see violence, as party members were well organized and particularly motivated by revenge (Straus 2006: 60). In other parts of the country, the violence did not break out for several weeks. In Butare, for example, the local prefect opposed the killing and continually refused orders from national authorities to eliminate Tutsi. In order for killings to move forward, the interim government removed the prefect from his post and replaced him with an extremist (Prunier 1995: 244; Des Forges 1999).

As discussed in Chapter 1, the focus of the analysis in this book is on current residents of Kigali, with additional areas of focus in Musanze (formerly Ruhengeri) and Bugesera (formerly Kigali Ngali).[31] These areas were selected to capture different dynamics and levels of violence.

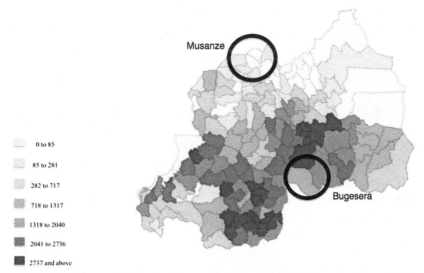

Legend:
- 0 to 85
- 85 to 281
- 282 to 717
- 718 to 1317
- 1318 to 2040
- 2041 to 2736
- 2737 and above

Musanze

Bugesera

FIGURE 2.1 Rates of Killing by Commune in Rwanda with Focus Regions Circled
Map courtesy of Nyseth Brehm (2014)

As such, I provide brief descriptions of the backgrounds of all three regions here.

Kigali

Prior to the outbreak of violence, Kigali was Rwanda's primary urban center. In 1991, it had a population of about 235,000, with Hutu comprising 81.4 percent of the population and Tutsi comprising 17.9 percent (Republic of Rwanda 2003). Kigali was the site of the initial violent fervor. As described earlier, within hours of the president's assassination, violence began. Extremists began to unearth stockpiles of weapons buried around the city (Des Forges 1999; Dallaire 2003). Over the next few weeks, Kigali witnessed the most concentrated violence in the country. The Presidential Guard and the FAR elements began going house to house, looking for political opponents or RPF sympathizers. Donatella Lorch, a journalist reporting for the *New York Times*, recalled the tumultuous state of the city a few days after the plane crash:

Food had run out, drinking water was scarce and the streets of this capital city, empty of residents, [were] a terrifying obstacle course today of drunken soldiers and marauding gangs of looters dressed in a patchwork of uniforms, armed with machetes, spears, bows and arrows and automatic weapons. Children carried hand grenades, and open-back trucks, loaded with angry men waving weapons at passing cars, sped through the city. As night fell, screams could be heard coming from a church compound where more than 2,000 Rwandans had taken refuge. A short time later, after the sound of machine-gun fire, the screaming stopped.[32]

During the first day of killing, the Presidential Guard and other extremist forces killed many members of government and several prominent journalists and priests (Prunier 1995: 230; Des Forges 1999). There was also fighting between factions of the FAR and the Presidential Guard, as some wanted to stop the slaughter, while other hardliners wanted to expand it (Prunier 1995: 229). Further, there was fighting between the 600 RPF members stationed in Kigali and government forces, creating confusion and chaos among civilians regardless of their ethnicity.

After the initial phase of targeted political killings, widespread killing of Tutsi civilians rapidly ensued. The killings in Kigali were particularly centralized, with the Presidential Guard carrying out much of the initial terror. In order to leave the city, people had to show an ID card at multiple roadblocks. Thousands of Tutsi civilians therefore became stuck, and many took shelter in Sainte-Famille and Saint-Paul Churches, in addition to Amahoro Stadium. Tutsi in these locations fared better than most, defended by a priest and UNAMIR troops, who used all available resources to prevent the *interahamwe* from entering (Prunier 1995: 254; African Rights 2004: 110–119). Others were able to survive in the Hotel Milles Collines, made famous by the movie *Hotel Rwanda*. While some UN peacekeepers remained in the city and provided a modicum of protection in these places, they ultimately had little ability to defend citizens as they lacked the authority to use lethal force. As a result, tens of thousands of the city's residents fled. By July 24, 1994, the *New York Times* reported that in Kigali, "the dead and the missing outnumber the living."[33]

The RPF secured control of Kigali in early July and then proceeded to rebuild the city's infrastructure and develop new buildings to accommodate an influx of people – including "old caseload" refugees, predominantly Tutsi Rwandans who had grown up in exile – who came in search of security amid ongoing regional violence. Commercial activities began in Kigali quickly after the violence, facilitated in large part by the influx of humanitarian aid organizations. These humanitarian organizations built new roads and repaired the communication infrastructure. Within the next decade, Kigali became a "showroom" for the progress of the country under Kagame and the RPF (Goodfellow and Smith 2013; Mann and Berry 2016). By 2002, the city had swelled to more than

600,000 residents, and by 2012 it had more than one million (Republic of Rwanda 2012).

Musanze (Ruhengeri)

Musanze, formerly known as Ruhengeri, is a district located in Northern Province bordering DR Congo. Musanze is also the name of the district's capital city. The district is Rwanda's most mountainous: to get there from Kigali, one drives for two hours along winding mountain roads, avoiding the steep cliffs that drop off just beyond the pavement. The region has rough terrain with elevated volcanic peaks and barrier lakes. Virunga National Park, home of Rwanda's famous mountain gorillas, is nearby.

Ruhengeri was the scene of many of the early battles between the RPF and the FAR from 1990 to 1993. During the genocide, however, it was relatively spared from massacres, as only 0.5 percent of the district's population was Tutsi (Republic of Rwanda 2003; Straus 2006: 55; Verwimp 2013: 56).[34] Due to the region's proximity to DR Congo, it experienced massive insecurity during the refugee exodus and influx after the genocide. It also witnessed violence again between 1996 and 1998, as militias from DR Congo waged periodic attacks across the border and Congo National Army (ADLF) and Rwandan forces attempted to clear the nearby refugee camps. This counterinsurgency continued for several years between the RPF and its proxy militias in DR Congo, the ADLF, and remnants of the *interahamwe* militias that fled Rwanda after the genocide. Ruhengeri saw battles as late as 1999. Because of high rates of violence over several years and widespread displacement in the area, Ruhengeri's economy suffered enormously.

As a whole, Ruhengeri Province had the highest population of all provinces in Rwanda before the genocide at 750,000. Its population increased to 894,000 by 2002 because of the influx of refugees (Republic of Rwanda 2003), and it remains one of the most densely populated provinces, with 540 people per square kilometer (the national average is 322 people per square kilometer). While before the war and genocide the sex ratio in Ruhengeri was 91.4 men for every 100 women, by 2002 the ratio had dropped to 87.7 men per 100 women. By 2012, the sex ratio had dropped even further, to 84.7 men per 100 women, with women heading 32.4 percent of all households in the province (Republic of Rwanda 2011: 45–46).

Bugesera (Kigali Ngali)

Bugesera is a district in Eastern Province approximately forty kilometers south of Kigali. Most of the district was formally part of rural Kigali or Kigali Ngali Province before administrative redistricting in 2006. The climate in Bugesera is hotter and drier than in other parts of Rwanda, making it less desirable for agriculture. It also contains vast areas of swampland – home to the tsetse fly and malaria-carrying mosquitos, which result in higher disease levels in Bugesera than the rest of the country. In 1991, the region was 90.8 percent Hutu and 8.8 percent Tutsi (Republic of Rwanda [1991] 2003).

Violence against Tutsi began early in Bugesera, predating and predicting genocidal violence in 1994, as it conditioned local authority structures and gave youth *interahamwe* militias experience with killing. In March 1992, local authorities massacred several hundred Tutsi. In an attempt to rally Hutu, local authorities announced that some Tutsi had fled across the border into Uganda to join the RPF (Des Forges 1999: 108). The editor of the extremist newspaper *Kangura* also visited the area in order to spread rumors about pending *inyenzi* attacks (Des Forges 1999: 89). Hutu were encouraged to protect themselves against the enemy. An Italian nun at the Nyamata parish warned of these early massacres, and was murdered as a result.[35]

As the genocide began in Kigali, violence quickly spread to Bugesera. Many Tutsi fled to churches at Nyamata and Ntarama where they hoped for safety in numbers; sadly, these churches were the sites of some of the most gruesome massacres of the genocide. Massacres of remaining Tutsi in the region unfolded quickly and brutally. Some Tutsi in Bugesera survived by hiding in the swamps for weeks. The RPF took control of Bugesera by mid-June, sending droves of Hutu civilians to the south of the country near Butare (Huye). Others fled into Tanzania, fearing retributive killings by the RPF. Throughout the 1990s, thousands of people were resettled in the region because of its low population density (Justino and Verwimp 2008). Despite these resettlement programs in the late 1990s, Bugesera's overall population dropped from just over 914,000 in 1991 to 792,500 in 2002.[36] Today, it has one of the lowest population densities in the country, with 285 people per square kilometer (Republic of Rwanda 2011: 21). In almost all of Bugesera's sectors, women outnumber men. The overall sex ratio in Kigali Ngali in 2002 was 88.9 men per 100 women. By 2012, the sex imbalance had recovered somewhat to 94.3 men per 100 women (Republic of Rwanda

2011). Despite this, even in 2012, women headed 29.8 percent of all households in the district.

By the end of May 1994, the RPF had captured the airport in Kigali and overtaken FAR's adjacent military camp. By June, it had secured most of eastern Rwanda, and by July, it announced control of Kigali. It established control over the remaining parts of the country in the following months, although periodic attacks, massacres, and other forms of violence persisted through the end of the year. During this period, the leaders of the FAR, the *interahamwe*, and members of the Habyarimana government fled the country. Many ordinary Hutu civilians also fled because they feared RPF reprisals. By July 1994, at least 500,000 people were dead. Scholars have vigorously debated the death toll of the entire period, with estimates ranging from 500,000 (Des Forges 1999) to 1.36 million (Kapiteni 1996). The Government of Rwanda maintains the number of 1.074 million (Republic of Rwanda 2004), but has political reasons for inflating the numbers. At this point, most experts agree that the number of 800,000 is probably the best estimate, including both genocide and war deaths (Prunier 1995; Straus 2006; Verwimp 2013).[37]

One of the defining features of the end to the violence was the massive exodus of millions of members of the "perpetrator" group (i.e., Hutu). They fled to DR Congo (then Zaire) and Tanzania, and former regime elites took all of the money in the national bank with them. France's Operation Turquoise ensured safe passage for these refugees (Prunier 1995: 295–299, 312–313). Once across the border, they congregated in hastily constructed refugee camps overseen by international humanitarian NGOs. Some extremists reassembled militias, aiming to reengage in fighting as soon as possible. Conditions in the camps were atrocious; cholera broke out and the food supply was woefully inadequate (Amnesty International 1996).

The RPF established the "Government of National Unity" shortly after it took control of the country. This interim government largely followed the provisions laid out in the Arusha Accords and aimed to split power between Tutsi and Hutu, as well as between native Rwandans and returnees from abroad. Pasteur Bizimungu and Faustine Twagiramungu, both politically moderate Hutus, were appointed president and prime minister, respectively. General Paul Kagame became the vice president and the minister of defense. Government ministries were rebuilt, and members of the former opposition parties (MDR, PSD, Liberals) were appointed alongside the RPF to various positions. Aloisea Inyumba, one of the highest-ranking women in the RPF, was appointed minister in charge of Family and Women Promotion.

Despite the ostensibly multiparty government, it soon became clear that Kagame and a small group of Tutsi RPF military officers were the true power holders. Any Hutu within the government were looked on as potential traitors and were frequently placed under surveillance (Prunier 2009: 45). As time passed, the regime tightened its grip on the country. The pace of civilian arrests escalated; by 1995, government forces were arresting approximately 1,500 civilians per week (Human Rights Watch 1995). In April 1995, the new regime orchestrated massacres of several thousand people in a displaced persons' camp in Kibeho (Amnesty International 1995c; Bradol and La Pape 2017: 85–96). This led to an unraveling of the political coalition, as people within the government – most notably Seth Sendashonga, a well-respected Hutu member of the RPF – became furious at the RPF's complicity in these atrocities. Faustin Twagiramungu resigned his post of prime minister shortly thereafter and went into exile. The RPF rounded up many former members of government and executed them on the spot, often without any form of judicial process (Des Forges 1999: 709). The RPF also killed civilians – Hutu and Tutsi alike – in a series of massacres in eastern, central, and southern Rwanda likely motivated by a mix of revenge and desire to coerce the population's acceptance of its rule (Des Forges 1999: 705).

In addition to RPF-led violence against civilians, other forms of violence and insecurity continued. Genocide survivors were sometimes murdered if they had witnessed killings and could identify perpetrators in courts. Returning refugees were also vulnerable to similar anti-Tutsi attacks. *Génocidaires* hiding amid refugees in DR Congo waged periodic attacks across Rwanda's border, particularly in the regions around Gisenyi and Ruhengheri in Northern Province. Dozens of people were killed during these attacks (Amnesty International 1995a, 1996a, 1996b). In DR Congo, the influx of Rwandan refugees triggered massive insecurity and violence. Rwandan troops entered DR Congo in 1996 to clear *interahamwe* militias from the refugee camps; they eventually overthrew President Mobutu Sese Seko with the assistance of several other regional powers (Prunier 2009: 67–72). A power vacuum resulted, fomenting a chaotic and bloody war that drew involvement from perhaps a dozen other nations, including Zimbabwe, Angola, and Uganda (see Lemarchand 2009; Prunier 2009; Reyntjens 2009). Under the reign of President Laurent Kabila, security in eastern DR Congo further deteriorated. Proxy militias backed by the RPF-controlled government of Rwanda battled against civilians, local militias (*mai mai*), and Congolese army forces. Fighting reached a peak in the late 1990s, but continues in different forms to this day. All told, the ensuing violence and instability has taken millions of lives. Thus, the violence linked to the Rwandan genocide and civil war continued long after 1994, albeit in different forms.

CONCLUSION

In this chapter, I outlined Rwanda's recent history, paying particular attention to the way that gender operated to shape differences between men and women from the precolonial period to the early 1990s. I then outlined the emergence of violence in Rwanda, emphasizing that violence began in 1990 during the RPF invasion and lasted long after the oft-cited "100 days." Rwandan women were affected by this violence at all stages; they were subjected to displacement, physical abuse, sexual torture, and murder. And while this violence was primarily directed at Tutsi, many Hutu suffered greatly as well, targeted for their political allegiances and ambiguous ethnic identity by Hutu extremists, the RPF in the context of the civil war, or because of the micro-level logics of violence that often did not neatly align with macro political cleavages.

In the next chapter, I further discuss this legacy of violence as it pertains to women in Rwanda, as each wave and form of violence had different repercussions for women. Beginning with the civil war in 1990, the political and economic structures of the state began to shift, ushering in a period of massive turmoil. Certain demographic, economic, and cultural shifts precipitated by these different waves of violence shaped the way in which women engaged politically in their households and communities and as citizens of the Rwandan nation. I then explain how the violence opened up unexpected opportunities for women's mobilization in informal and formal political spaces, before suggesting how such transformations were ultimately only temporary and limited to elite women with close ties to the RPF.

3

War and Structural Shifts in Rwanda

The violence in Rwanda began in 1990, lasted into the late 1990s, and continues in the Democratic Republic of Congo to this day in a different form. Still, the most extreme turmoil occurred between April and July 1994. That period of violence unleashed a series of structural changes that had lasting implications for the role of women in Rwandan society. In this chapter, I outline the demographic, economic, and cultural shifts precipitated by the violence. In the following chapter, I examine the impact of these shifts on women's political engagement.

DEMOGRAPHIC SHIFTS

In July 1994, after approximately three months of widespread killing, the Rwandan Patriotic Front (RPF) secured tentative control over Rwanda and (mostly) ended the genocide and war. The country was in ruins: one out of every ten Rwandans was dead, 2.1 million had fled over the border into neighboring countries, and 120,000 were in overcrowded prisons (UNHCR 1994; Prunier 1995; Republic of Rwanda 2005a). Of the post-violence population of seven million people, between one and two million were internally displaced, squatting in households left empty after the slaughter of their owners, or in internally displaced persons' (IDP) camps (Newbury and Baldwin 2000; Gervais 2003). Beyond the obvious effects of massive population loss, these demographic shifts had two major components: the violence led to extensive population displacement, which included an exodus of refugees, an influx of former refugees, and the internal displacement of millions of Rwandans. In addition, the

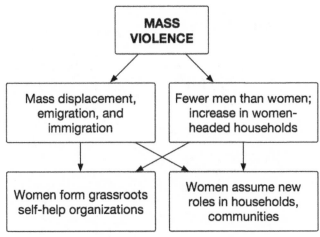

FIGURE 3.1 Demographic Shifts after Mass Violence in Rwanda

violence and resulting displacement led to a shift in the sex ratio, which led to an increase in women-headed households (see Figure 3.1).

Displacement and Population Movement

Three processes characterized population displacement during and after the violence. First, there was an enormous exodus of primarily Hutu Rwandans into neighboring countries toward the end of the genocidal portion of the violence. Second, there was a massive influx of "old caseload" refugees who returned to Rwanda from exile in neighboring countries in the years following the violence. Third, there was widespread displacement within Rwanda, which altered social networks, family structures, and reordered the way that millions of Rwandans lived their lives. All three processes had social and political consequences for the Rwandan population, particularly given endemic competition for land in the country.

Emigration

Approximately two million Rwandans fled across the border to DR Congo and Tanzania during and after the violence, often because they feared retaliation from the RPF. They crossed the border at astounding rates, some days at a rate of 10,000 an hour (Amnesty International 1996b).[1] The largest number of refugees crossed the border through

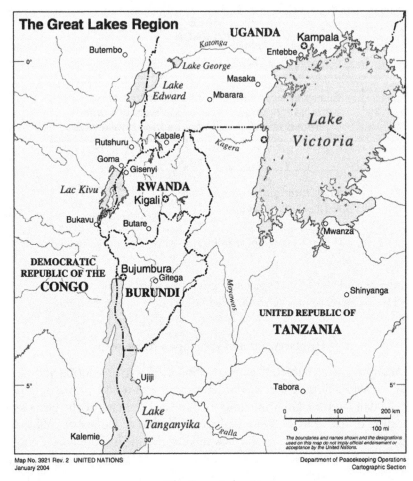

MAP 2 The Great Lakes Region

Gisenyi, the last FAR stronghold and the seat of Habyarimana's remaining government leadership. These "new caseload" refugees congregated in camps along DR Congo's border with Rwanda near Lake Kivu. The largest camps, Katale and Kibumba, hosted as many as 200,000 refugees in each (Amnesty International 1996b). Reports from the camps indicated that likely only 30,000 to 50,000 were members of genocidal militias such as the *interahamwe* (Newbury 1998: 8). Others had certainly participated in the genocide in some way, but were not central to its organization or execution.

Many women and children went to the camps. Some reports estimate that in the Goma area, 80 percent of refugees in the camps were women and children (Newbury 1998: 8–9). Other camps, however, were primarily comprised of men. For example, Mugunga, a camp located in Goma, contained an estimated 20,000 ex-FAR militants and their families (Pottier 1996: 413). Many of these refugees had left quickly from their homes, taking only those possessions they could carry. Raymond Bonner, writing in the *New York Times*, described the magnitude of this displacement:

The lines go on for mile after mile after mile, a river of people fleeing the war in Rwanda into neighboring Zaire. Men, women and children – barefoot and dirty, with bundles of firewood, rolled-up mattresses and suitcases balanced on their heads – walking, walking, walking. They lead goats on leashes, carry chickens by their legs and rabbits by their ears, and cradle baby goats. People, and longhorn cattle, and cars.[2]

Humanitarian agencies were inundated by the sheer volume of refugees. Cholera broke out, as most camps in DR Congo lacked adequate water purification systems and their sanitation capabilities were overwhelmed. Between July and August 1994, approximately 50,000 refugees in Goma died as a result of cholera, dysentery, dehydration, and violence (Eriksson 1996: 13; see also Bradol and Le Pape 2017: 47–54). Fearing disease, some refugees felt like they were "caught between two deaths" – if they stayed in the camps, they would likely die of illness if they returned to Rwanda, they feared they would be killed by the RPF.[3]

Hundreds of thousands of refugees also fled into Tanzania from western Rwanda. On May 1, 1994, a "slow-moving column of refugees from Rwanda trudged into a remote area of Tanzania ... stretching across 10 miles of roads and fanning out over the hills of elephant grass."[4] Their departure left villages empty of both people and animals. Unlike in DR Congo, the refugees in Tanzania were met by a relatively well-organized aid response, which settled them in a large, open plain just kilometers from the border with Rwanda (Bradol and La Pape 2017: 43–46). Tutsi who fled *génocidaires* also ended up in Tanzania, but they established separate refugee camps at a safe distance from those occupied by Hutu.[5]

Humanitarian relief for these refugees came in different forms. France led the initial efforts as an extension of Operation Turquoise. The United States also sent troops and aid and set up food distribution centers along the major roads between Kigali and the border with DR Congo. Humanitarian aid agencies poured in, establishing a virtual "aidland" (Apthorpe 2011) awash with funding. They concentrated first on the crisis in DR Congo, as it was the most severe and posed the greatest danger to human lives, especially as the cholera outbreak threatened to reach epidemic proportions. This focus on DR Congo, however, angered many members of the RPF, who accused the international aid industry of aiding *génocidaires*. While some refugees were certainly guilty of genocide crimes, the vast majority were innocent civilians. Nevertheless, the RPF's critique served to cast all Hutu who had fled as guilty.

By 1995, the international aid community – led by the Office of the UN High Commissioner for Refugees (UNHCR) – was strongly encouraging the return of refugees to Rwanda in order to lessen the strain on the already unstable eastern DR Congo region. However, rumors about RPF-coordinated revenge killings and massacres abounded in the camps, generating fears among many refugees that they would be persecuted or killed if they returned to Rwanda. Such fears were largely unfounded, as the RPF was desperately trying to reassure the population that it could govern and was not engaging in a widespread killing campaign. International aid agencies, however, had little credibility to dispel the rumors. Instead, organizations tried to tempt people back to Rwanda with promises of food or other goods. Women and the elderly were most likely to take advantage of these opportunities (Amnesty International 1996b). Within a few years, many were returning: the UNHCR estimated that 1.3 million returned to Rwanda in 1996 alone. By that point, these returning "new caseload" refugees were spurred by worsening conditions in the camps and by increasing violence in the Kivu region of DR Congo. As the Rwandan government aimed to dismantle the camps, militia activity increased, which presented a major threat to stability in the region (see Lemarchand 2009; Prunier 2009).

Immigration

The second wave of demographic population shifts occurred in the months following the RPF's victory, as approximately 700,000 "old caseload" refugees returned to Rwanda from neighboring countries, Europe, and North America (Amnesty International 1996b: 8). These refugees were predominantly Tutsi, although a few were Hutu who had fallen out with previous regimes. Most had fled during previous episodes of anti-Tutsi violence. Many of these returnees were better educated than ordinary Rwandans and brought with them skills, technical knowledge, and linguistic capacities that differentiated them from both Hutu and Tutsi who had grown up in Rwanda (Kinzer 2008). They also brought with them an estimated one million heads of cattle (Prunier 2009: 5).

Some of these returning refugees did not speak Kinyarwanda well, and they had learned English rather than French in schools, or had grown up speaking Swahili or other languages. What separated these refugees from the rest of the population the most, of course, was that they had not experienced the genocide. While many had lost extended family members, they typically carried a lighter psychological burden than those who had witnessed or participated in killings.

Many within this group of refugees had been in exile for decades; therefore, they did not have land or homes to return to. The Arusha Accords mandated that only repatriates who had left the country within the previous ten years had the right to claim their former property (Pottier 2006: 517). As a result, many of these "old caseload" returnees took up residence in abandoned homes left empty after the emigration or death of previous residents (Prunier 1995). Some spent weeks in transit camps before the government organized their resettlement in areas near Byumba and Kibungo (Amnesty International 1996b: 8). Adjusting to a rural, agricultural life presented serious challenges for many of these "old caseload" refugees, who had lived urban lives in exile. Wealthy returnees congregated in the capital; it was these returnees who often had close ties to the RPF. There they monopolized quality housing and wage jobs, which increased tensions between these returnees and "native" Rwandans.

To accommodate these returnees, the new regime began to resettle people into preplanned villages (or *imidugudu*). These villages typically consisted of 200 houses grouped together with centralized amenities like a well. While this "villagization" policy was initially developed to group Tutsi returnees and survivors of genocide together for their security and protection, it was later expanded to encompass the entire population (Hilhorst and Van Leeuwen 2000; Isaksson 2013). Drawing inspiration from other (failed) social engineering schemes (see Scott 1998), the government aimed to resettle the entire rural population in order to promote security, increase agricultural production, and facilitate a wholesale transformation of the Rwandan countryside (Van Leeuwen 2001). Eventually, the government planned to install roads, water systems, and other basic infrastructure in order to ensure the viability of these villages. Proponents of the policy argued that it would alleviate the land and housing disputes that stemmed from massive population shifts after the genocide. Critics at the time, however, warned that similar programs – such as in Tanzania – failed with disastrous consequences. Regardless, returning refugees were in dire need of places to live.[6]

Internal Displacement

In addition to emigration and immigration, many Rwandans were displaced within the country's borders. As the violence subsided, an estimated 500,000 people were living in IDP camps in southern Rwanda, where they had fled to find protection in the Zone Turquoise established by French troops. The camp at Kibeho – which I briefly discussed in Chapter 2 – was the largest IDP camp, hosting 100,000 people in 1995. It contained tens of thousands of civilian IDPs in addition to several extremist Hutu militias (Pottier 2002: 76). Another 500,000 Rwandans were living in other displaced persons' camps or abandoned houses across the country. Some people from northern Rwanda were still displaced from the early days of the civil war with the RPF. Only about 3.6 million people – or 45 percent of the prewar population – lived in the same place as they did before the war (Prunier 2009: 5).

For the displaced, conditions of life were often excruciating. They frequently lacked access to shelter, adequate food and water, or sanitation facilities. Umutesi (2004) and Dallaire's (2003) memoirs both describe the stench that emanated from the camps in northern Rwanda, as IDPs were forced to relieve themselves in the open fields. The ill and dying were often abandoned so that desperate camp residents could loot their remaining food and possessions. Social and familial networks that existed prior to the violence were fractured as relatives and friends lost track of each other.

Families sometimes experienced two or more processes of displacement at the same time. Scores of Tutsi families gave their young children away to Hutu friends in an effort to protect them from *génocidaires*. Then, as they became displaced from their homes or were forced into hiding, they lost track of their children's caretakers, who had often been forced to flee as part of the massive outmigration described earlier. One member of parliament (MP) described to me how she "gave [her children] away – because they are Tutsi. So for their own safety, I didn't know where they were." This MP continued to describe how she learned that they were in DR Congo. As she put it, "In that period I was very stranded. I had no hope. But I heard that they were there, so I was hopeful that I would find them. It was sad but then it gave me more hope and energy and motivation to go ahead and do something" (Interview #19, July 2012). This woman's experience was common. While life was extremely challenging during displacement, many women I interviewed reported that they met new people and connected with international humanitarian agencies. These connections inspired them to work harder to make sure their children had enough to survive while displaced from their homes. A few lucky women found jobs with these humanitarian NGOs, which significantly improved their economic situation.

Demographic Shifts Lead to Sex Imbalance

In addition to the massive population displacement, men constituted 56 percent of the dead during the violence in Rwanda. This was primarily because of the ongoing civil war, in which men comprised the majority of combatants (De Walque and Verwimp 2010). In addition, particularly at the beginning of the genocide, "mercy" was occasionally shown to Tutsi women – although frequently at the price of rape rather than death (Nowrojee 1996; El-Bushra 2000). While demographic data immediately after the violence are of poor quality, this, combined with the sex imbalance in the displaced population, created a demographic vacuum of men in Rwanda. In some urban districts, the sex ratio dropped from about 1.15 men per woman in 1991, to 0.898 men per woman a decade later (Republic of Rwanda 1985, 1991, 2002). And in some rural areas, where women had already been the majority prior to the violence, the sex ratio dropped from 0.77 men per woman in 1991 to 0.592 men per woman a decade later. In 2002, the overall sex ratio stood at 0.91, while it was just 0.87 for people over seventeen years of age (Republic of Rwanda 2003: 42; Republic of Rwanda 2011). This meant that across the country, 36 percent of households had no adult males present – up from 21 percent prior to the violence. In five of Rwanda's twelve prefectures, the percentage of women-headed households was higher than 60 percent (Republic of Rwanda 1999: 2; Newbury and Baldwin 2000: 7). This demographic shift created a practical need for many women to continue their daily activities without their husbands, brothers, or fathers present.

In addition to many widows, there were also many women-headed households because of men in exile, in jail or other detention facilities, or in military service with the RPF. Although still alive, these men's absence from the home presented similar challenges, and women assumed an identity as a sort of *de facto* widow. While official arrest data from this period do not exist, reports indicate that the arrest rate among men in certain parts of the country – in all likelihood areas with the strongest links to the former regime – was extremely high. For example, in 1995 Human Rights Watch reported that in one sector of Musambira commune, "virtually all the young men have been detained" (1995: 3). The prison population peaked at 130,000 in 1998

(Human Rights Watch 2004: 10). In the popular mindset, being arrested was equated with being guilty; as such, women with jailed husbands faced the additional challenge of being viewed with suspicion by their neighbors.

Prisons in Rwanda were grossly overcrowded and conditions were abysmal. Informal prisons (*cachots*) in police stations or administrative offices were often even worse (Amnesty International 1995a; Des Forges 1999). While in prison, men could not contribute to household income or agriculture. Nevertheless, they continued to drain household resources, as family members had to provide them with food while in jail (Human Rights Watch 2004: 10).[7] Once released, many men suffered physical disabilities and disfigurement from their time in prison (Bouka 2013: 250). Others suffered from diseases contracted or left untreated while incarcerated. These health issues impacted men's ability to work and contribute to household subsistence after their release, and increased women's domestic burden.[8]

This permanent or temporary absence of men from the household precipitated shifts in women's roles at the household and community levels – indeed, "survivors, particularly women, found that 'traditional' ways of life were no longer possible" (Burnet 2008: 384). Women of different class and ethnic backgrounds shouldered a multitude of new responsibilities. Jeanette, a genocide widow and current head of an NGO from Eastern Province in Rwanda, said that:

In the Rwandan custom, [as] a woman, even if you're educated, you were still looked after by your husband. Because before [the violence], I looked [to] my husband for everything. I might have been educated but the only thing I would think of is my kids. I would come from school after teaching and just look after my kids. So it was very hard to adjust from that to being the head of my family. (Interview #25, July 2012)

As Jeanette notes, prior to genocide, women's activities were typically confined to the household sphere and centered on childcare and the production of food. As I discussed in the previous chapter, women legally needed their husbands' permission to open a bank account, engage in profit-making activities, or enter into any formal agreement. Men typically controlled any cash income in the family unit (Sharlach 1999; Burnet 2008). Further, women were not legally eligible to inherit land from husbands or male relatives.

Contrast this to after the violence: hundreds of thousands of women now had to milk cows, replant fallow gardens, make bricks, reroof their houses, and sell anything they could to generate an income (Newbury and Baldwin 2000; Burnet 2008, 2012; Uwineza and Pearson 2009; multiple interviews). As one parliamentarian put it:

In my region ... there were some activities that were done by men, and others done by women. Like cutting down a bush; women were not supposed to do that. Or hard stone farming; the men had to go do that. But for a widow, since she had no husband, she would have to go do that for herself. (Interview #21, July 2012)

These new responsibilities eradicated the separation between "men's work" and "women's work" – at least temporarily. But they also deepened the poverty and isolation of many women. Jacqueline, a forty-six-year-old genocide widow and mother of four, described her frustration with this new division of labor:

Even just survival at home is also another hassle. It is like you become a father and a mother, so you get all of the man's responsibilities as well as the woman's responsibilities ... My agreement with my husband was him taking care of me and my kids – buying food, knowing that the kids have all of the materials that they need to go to school. This is not what we agreed on. It's not me. If the roof is off, because it was blown off by the wind, that should not have been me, it should be him. You can imagine. Now it is all my responsibility. (Interview #77, February 2013)

As Jacqueline described, widows faced tremendous challenges assuming these new roles. The overwhelming burden of these new activities forced women to seek basic economic, emotional, and legal support from others in their communities.

This absence of men was particularly challenging when it came to land and property rights. Traditionally, women in Rwanda only had rights to land through their husbands or fathers. Widows could only access land if they had an adult male child. Because of this, an enormous land crisis ensued after the genocide, as *de facto* and *de jure* widows faced pressure from neighbors and extended family members to relinquish the land they lived on. These landownership debates forced many women to join together – often with someone more educated or wealthy – to petition local government officials for official property rights (Interview #25, July 2012). As a result of this land pressure and the urgent needs faced by millions of women across Rwanda, thousands of small, informal self-help groups began forming across the country. As I discuss in more depth in the following chapter, the demographic shifts caused by violence – including massive population displacement and shifts in the sex ratio – catalyzed the formation of these grassroots organizations, which eventually served a critical role in facilitating women's increased participation in public, political life.

ECONOMIC SHIFTS

The violence in Rwanda also led to a shift in the economic needs of the population. This stemmed from the massive collapse of infrastructure, soaring inflation, the disruption of internal and foreign trade, and the corresponding emergence of critical needs for food, water, health care, and shelter. Rwanda's plummeting economy prior to and during the violence also facilitated this shift: its GDP dropped from $2 billion USD to $750 million between 1993 and the end of 1994; and its GDP per capita dropped from $330 per year before the genocide to just under $170 in 1995 (World Bank 1990–2012). Of the $598 million in bilateral aid pledged to Rwanda in January 1995, donors had disbursed only $94.5 million by June (Prunier 2009: 37).[9] As a result, the Rwandan economy was in shambles.

In addition to macroeconomic devastation, the violence ruined Rwanda's usually rich agricultural sector and destroyed infrastructure – including more than 150,000 homes (Prunier 2009: 5). Roads were not well established even before the genocide, which prohibited the smooth distribution of aid to remote parts of the country. Electricity was erratic. Crops rotted, as there was no one to tend to them. Together, this meant that food, water, shelter, and other basic necessities of life were hard to come by.

In the mid-1990s, 10 percent of households were at extreme risk of severe malnutrition or starvation. The remainder of the population struggled to find sufficient food (UNDP 2007). One study estimated that in the aggregate, the daily available calories were only a little more than one third of what was needed to meet the minimum caloric requirements of the population (Newbury and Baldwin 2000: 12). Women-headed households were particularly vulnerable, as they were more likely to be in extreme poverty than households with adult men (Republic of Rwanda 2006; Justino and Verwimp 2008: 40; Finnof 2010). Diseases – ranging from malaria to diarrhea – also plagued the population, overwhelming the already devastated health care system.

In addition, without any state-sponsored system of childcare, hundreds of thousands of orphans became the wards of anyone who would take them in (Prunier 1995, 2009). Jeanette described how:

Life changed totally. Because there were 10 of us [in my family], and only three survived ... all of the kids of my brothers and sisters, they all came to my home. Everybody was in my home. Even the kids of the neighborhood, they didn't know anyone else so I was like their mom ... I can't imagine how we survived. (Interview #25, July 2012)

As Jeanette suggests, the burden of caring for orphans fell to women, and there were an estimated 770,000 orphans under fifteen years of age in the country (USAID 2001; Republic of Rwanda 2004). As a result, women-headed households averaged between six and seven young dependents each (Republic of Rwanda 1999: 2).

Urgent needs heightened women's economic vulnerability. But unlike in the past when most women grew their own food on their own plots of land, women now found themselves receiving food through humanitarian NGOs or with cash provided by a relief organization at a commercial market. Thus, while performing traditional caregiving roles was *not* new, the need to enter public spaces to perform them *was*. In the process of securing their families' basic needs, women began expanding their social networks and interacting with foreign and local actors. This had two major effects. First, these economic needs led to a mushrooming of informal, grassroots self-help organizations across the country. Second, women's care responsibilities outside of the home led to their use of cash, credit, and loans, often for the first time. Both of these shifts are discussed in what follows (see Figure 3.2).

Massive population displacement and new economic needs sent a large number of women into public spaces to receive aid or assistance from neighbors, humanitarian aid distribution centers, newly forming NGOs, or government programs. Civil society organizations or NGOs were virtually nonexistent in Rwanda prior to the violence, especially in rural areas. However, as women were forced to seek basic material goods, they inadvertently expanded their social networks and interacted with government or aid agencies. Soon, women formed thousands of informal self-help groups across the country in order to find food, cultivate fields, rebuild homes, or locate other basic goods (Interviews with CBO founders; El-Bushra 2000: 74; Gervais 2003: 544; Smith 2010). These organizations allowed for certain burdens women shared to be distributed among the membership. Humanitarian organizations began to provide funding and organizational support to these grassroots organizations, commencing an eclectic process of organizational formalization. I describe this process in greater depth in the following chapter.

War, Women, and Power

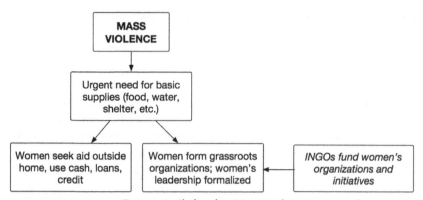

FIGURE 3.2 Economic Shifts after Mass Violence in Rwanda

Further, as time passed, many of these informal self-help organizations facilitated women's increased use of cash and credit. Prior to the genocide, it was virtually impossible for women to get bank loans, although a few women had opened accounts at Duterimbere, the country's first women's microcredit association (Newbury and Baldwin 2000; Interview #29, February 2013). While individual accounts at major commercial banks were looted during the violence, women's accounts at Duterimbere remained intact (Burnet 2008: 373). This put some women in a position to start or restart small businesses that had been destroyed. In the wake of the violence, humanitarian aid organizations aimed to expand this access to credit and loans to more women across the country. In partnership with the postwar government, these INGOs implemented programs teaching women how to apply for loans or design a small-business plan (Republic of Rwanda 1999). Interviewees described how INGOs and affiliated government agencies also distributed small grants to women to rebuild their homes, buy school supplies for their children, or pay for medication or other essentials. These small cash payments gave some women control over household financial decision-making for the first time.

The genocide and war wreaked widespread destruction on the country, ushering in a period of massive insecurity. This devastation forced women into new social roles, and pushed them to seek aid from organizations and others in their communities. Women formed groups to meet their emotional and material needs. Before long, these grassroots organizations began to formalize, particularly as they interacted with international organizations and more formal domestic NGOs that were deepening their reach into the rural parts of the country. By giving small loans and grants and encouraging women to engage in profit-making activities, these organizations helped facilitate a shift in the way women controlled wealth. As a result, these emergent grassroots organizations changed the way that economic power was distributed in society, and additionally provided an institutional blueprint for women's leadership at the local level.

CULTURAL SHIFTS

"We have suffered. The men made war, and the women suffer." – Anonymous (quoted in Kumar 2001: 28)

After the violence, women's participation in community organizations and political life became increasingly normalized. As I discuss in the following chapter, women took on leadership roles in their local communities, and some eventually ran for regional and national political office. In the first postwar election in 2003, citizens voted to approve a new national constitution that mandated women hold 30 percent of all decision-making positions. During the same election, the population elected women to 48 percent of the seats in Rwanda's national parliament – the highest percentage in the world. This reflected an extensive shift in cultural attitudes toward women from before the violence, when, as one MP put it, the political sphere was "a male domain. It was like their personal bedroom where no one else could go in" (Interview #10, July 2009). What explains this shift?

During my fieldwork, I heard dozens of women insist that the war would not have happened had women been in charge of the country. This sentiment was part of a powerful new "frame" (Goffman 1974; Benford and Snow 2000; Saguy 2013) that presented women as peaceful actors capable of helping the country move forward. Many women in Bosnia produced a similar discourse, as I discuss in Chapter 6. In short, there was a cultural reconceptualization of women as legitimate political actors after the violence, which stemmed from the fact that women were less culpable for atrocities that had occurred. In addition, women had proven their capabilities through their ability to provide care for their dependents amid unfathomable atrocity. As the key interlocutors between various state agencies, INGOs, and the population, women were well positioned to assume new public roles (Figure 3.3).

This cultural shift was made possible by a process through which women's "more peaceful" nature was juxtaposed with men's propensity for war. Across the board, elite and non-elite women I interviewed agreed that it was

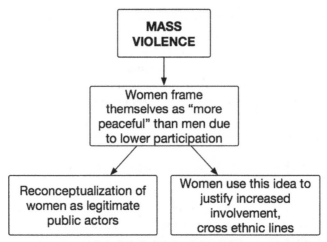

FIGURE 3.3 Cultural Shifts after Mass Violence in Rwanda

important to have women in political positions because they were more peaceful than men. One senator put it simply, "Women are peace-actors; they are the ones who carry out peace" (Interview #4, July 2009). Because of the patrilineal structure of Rwandan society, women were even considered "less ethnic" than men.[10] Such characterizations of women were tied up in nationalist representations. When the government media, officials, and documents referenced the RPF, they portrayed its members as strong, violent, powerful, and virile. In contrast, they depicted Rwandan women as "mothers of the nation" and as caregivers essential for the nation's future. While women had an important national responsibility, it was not on the battlefield; rather, it was as the biological producers of men who could eventually serve as soldiers for the nation and carry on its bloodlines.

Thinking counterfactually, one might question whether Rwandan women would have employed this framing if the genocide had not occurred. Might women have used alternative discourses in order to justify their engagement in Rwandan political life? Why not depict themselves as "Iron Ladies," as in Liberia, or as gun-toting guerrilla fighters, as in El Salvador? Why did the framing of women as "peaceful mothers" make women's presence in the political sphere palatable to the broader public? Thinking critically about the origins of such a narrative brings several historical processes and constraints to mind.

As discussed in Chapter 2, Rwanda has historically had a powerful female figure: the queen mother. During the monarchy, queen mothers wielded considerable power over the state as they ruled in conjunction with their sons, the kings. This indigenous tradition established mother-hood as a political status. However, the legacy of Kanjogera left a bitter taste for many Rwandans, as she became infamous for her ruthless savagery.[11] Moreover, she was Tutsi, and thereby for many represented Hutu oppression and servitude. Thus, for the majority of Rwandans, the queen mother was not a sufficiently compelling inspiration for the adoption of this "peaceful mother" frame.

Instead, the violence was key for this reconceptualization of women as peaceful actors. During the peak of the violence in 1994, all Rwandans perceived they were at risk. Hutu feared attacks from their Tutsi neighbors who were rumored to be collaborating with the RPF, and Tutsi feared *génocidaires*. As a result, the violence became *illegitimate* for masses of ordinary Rwandans. The perpetrators of the violence were not heroes; rather, those who planned the genocide became seen as violent extremists. It was in this context – and *because* of this context – that the idea of women as more peaceful than men became politically salient.

Further, frames are constrained and made possible by the facts at hand: in Rwanda, women were able to represent themselves as peaceful because, in reality, few women participated in killing. While some studies have highlighted exceptions (see African Rights 1995b; Sharlach 1999; Brown 2014), in general men overwhelmingly perpetrated the violence. This is perhaps most clearly evidenced by the fact that less than 9 percent of those tried for genocide have been women, and the majority of these crimes were property-theft related (Nyseth Brehm, Uggen, and Gasanabo 2017; Verwimp 2005: 306). In Verwimp's study, merely 1.4 percent of women were involved with killing (2005: 306). As Rwandan women survived the war, many began pointing to their status as mothers or as more peaceful than men in order to justify their increased presence in various public realms. They presented themselves as morally uncompromised by war and as those who "suffered the most" from the violence (Interview #15, July 2009). As such, they were more easily viewed as acceptable political actors who could assist the new RPF-led government's mission to create "good politics" and secure peace.

A final process was at play as well. As discussed in the previous section, Rwanda suffered from massive economic devastation during and after the genocide. As the primary care providers for their families, women found themselves taking on new roles in order to secure everyday essentials for themselves and their families. As women succeeded in seeking aid or small loans from humanitarian NGOs or government projects, they gained value in the postwar social context. Women's value as political

actors therefore emerged from the nexus between the population's immediate social needs and a pressing national need for a new, less-violent type
of political actor. As mothers they would provide, and as peacemakers
they would secure stability. This narrative helped lay the foundation for
the feminization of Rwandan political space.

Women employed this frame to justify their involvement in community
organizations as well as in politics. One organization's director explained
how women promoted their role as mothers to announce to the country
at large: "We are not responsible for our history, but we have just inherited a country that has been destroyed, and we need to rebuild it, because
we are mothers, and we are doing it for our children!" She continued to
explain, "When you are a mother, you don't want your child to be a refugee. You do not want your child to suffer. You do not want them being in
jail. So [women said], 'let's get together and fix this together'" (Interview
#5, July 2009).

Women I interviewed frequently told me stories about women's "more
peaceful" orientation as evidence for why women should be involved in
politics and the country's recovery. Most retellings of a story that came
up several times during my interviews highlighted the same general narrative: in the years after the genocide, militias in DR Congo kept crossing
the border in northern Rwanda in order to "finish the job" of killing the
Tutsi and to destabilize the new regime.[12] The wives and mothers of these
men were the first to protest the violence and eventually put a stop to it.
As one MP told it:

These women said, "You people. You have failed in the war – you cannot
win. Please come out of the bush. If this is not the case, we shall never shelter you anymore. When you come out we shall put you out and never give
you food." And women did it that way – and those women started reporting
even their own sons ... they'd say, "This one is a rebel!" Soon, many fighters
deserted the militias and entered rehabilitation centers, where they were dis-
armed and demobilized. Women took credit for this accomplishment, saying
they had stopped the war without using the bullet and the gun! (Interview #11,
July 2009)

Many women in politics repeated stories like this one to me by strategically using this idea of women as peacemakers to justify their presence.
According to another woman in parliament:

The shift [in women's roles] happened after the genocide, because one, women
were the ones that were bearing most of the burden of the genocide. Everybody
suffered but women suffered the most ... And they all got together and said, you

know, now there are new doors open to us. [Men] are now recognizing that we are capable. We need to take advantage of this, we need to be determined, and we need to have the will and the strength to make this happen for us. (Interview #15, July 2009)

This quote reflects another pattern that emerged in my interviews, which makes clear that the use of this framing was at times explicitly tactical: emerging women leaders recognized the benefits of casting themselves as peacemakers who were helping to rebuild the country, in order to juxtapose themselves to the men who had been responsible for the "bad politics" that led to the genocide in the first place. Such a tactic required embracing society's gendered hierarchies, in which women were charged with bearing children and preserving life, but in the process also stimulated women's increasing participation in local and national politics. Elsewhere around the world, groups of women – such as Las Madres de la Plaza de Mayo in Argentina, the Mothers' Front in Sri Lanka, and the Mothers of Srebrenica in Bosnia – have used similar arguments to justify their increased presence in political spaces.

This framing of women as different and more peaceful than men is at odds with feminist work that emphasizes gender sameness (Lorber 1994; Epstein 1997, 2007; see also Tripp 2016). Moreover, as I discussed in Chapter 1, such "affirmative" or "strategic" essentializations can be depoliticizing, as they reinforce the male/public and female/private divide. Yet scholars of Africa have complicated this feminist literature, challenging that politicians in Africa often draw on kinship ties (e.g., family or clan networks) to claim political power. While such materialist roles are deemed apolitical by much Western scholarship, Oyewumi (1997) and others have shown that African women have deployed the idea of a powerful mother for centuries to protect their interests and children (see Moran 2012 for a discussion). Tripp (2016) also showed how women's movements that emphasize women's difference with men are more likely to be inclusive of ethnic and racial difference, making them particularly powerful in postwar contexts.

The current government of Rwanda has picked up on the cultural salience of this idea of women as peacemakers and has frequently published reports or policy briefs that articulate the importance of including women in leadership positions. According to the government's logic, the entire Rwandan nation should endeavor to promote women in order to prevent a return to violence in the future. For example, one report describes women as:

bearers of life [who] can offer a special perspective and experience which will help to overcome prevailing life-destroying methods of dealing with human problems and conflicts.[13] Since military conflicts and diplomacy, which have traditionally been exclusively orchestrated by men, have failed to be a reliable system to safeguard peace, the inclusion of women in all stages of the peace process becomes imperative. (Republic of Rwanda, 2005b)

The government's attitude is infamously self-serving: its promotion of women has distracted attention from the regime's domination by a small group of Anglophone Tutsi elite that actively suppresses any form of dissent (see Reyntjens 2004, 2011; Prunier 2009; Straus and Waldorf 2011; Thomson 2013). Nevertheless, many Rwandans have become accustomed to the idea of women as legitimate political actors, which reflects a significant evolution from the pre-genocide era.

CONCLUSION

In this chapter I outlined the demographic, economic, and cultural shifts triggered by the violence in Rwanda between 1990 and 1994. Violence led to a demographic shift, due to the disproportionate death, conscription, and imprisonment of men and the massive displacement of people from their homes. This demographic shift led to the rapid formation of grassroots self-help organizations and pushed women to engage in new roles in their households and communities. Violence also triggered an economic shift, due to the destruction of infrastructure and agricultural capacity and the arrival of international humanitarian aid. This shift compelled women to seek aid from NGOs and other institutions in their communities, leading to a shift in control over household finances. Moreover, INGOs that arrived in the wake of the violence provided funding to nascent women's organizations, which formalized women's leadership at the grassroots level. Finally, the violence precipitated a cultural shift toward accepting women as legitimate public actors, as women juxtaposed their "more peaceful" nature with men's propensity for war. This reconceptualization of women allowed many to justify their increased presence in public spaces and engage in activities that crossed ethnic lines.

These shifts occurred simultaneously and often overlapped and intersected. Combined, they had profound implications for gendered power relations in Rwanda, and each helps to illustrate the processes through which war can be transformative for women. While each shift emerged from the devastation of large-scale war, they also reveal how war violence can be more than simply destructive – it can also be transformative for institutions and structures in society. This takes us to the next chapter, which describes the impact of these shifts on women's political engagement in the years following the violence. As I make clear, these shifts "set in motion change and the construction of the new" (Cramer 2006: 279).

4

Women's Political Mobilization in Rwanda

"So, I think it was a sort of choice: to be part of the solution or to be part of the problem. And my option was to be part of the solution."
   – *Judith Kanakuze (Interview #13, June 2009)*

Noémie was born in the south of Rwanda in the early 1960s (Interview #18, July 2009). She attended the National University of Rwanda and majored in sociology, got married, and became a teacher. When the genocide broke out in 1994, her husband was killed. As she described it:

I was married to a successful man. [I thought] he will give me anything, do everything for me. But after the genocide it was different because my husband was dead. And I was the head of the house. So, I had to do everything that was the same for the kids as when their dad was around. They must have [the same things] when only I am around.

Noémie recounted how she joined a widows' organization in the aftermath. For three years, she worked very hard for that organization, and as she put it, "people were really getting to know me." Soon, people in her community approached her and encouraged her to join politics. She described how she "used to really hate politics, because I thought politics was just a bunch of lies." But after the death of her husband, she felt motivated to make a difference:

So, I thought about it and was like, alright! Why can't I join politics and even help out my country? So, I joined politics and was appointed to be the [head of a sector]. By that time I was the head for three years ... And then I went to elections for the mayor ... I was the mayor for three years, and then I left the mayorship to join [Parliament].

Noémie's transition from being a teacher to a member of parliament (MP) exemplifies the way that war can serve as a period of rapid transformation in ordinary women's lives. With her level of education and status as a widow, Noémie was biographically well positioned to take a leadership role in a grassroots organization; from there, she had the network and visibility necessary to run for political office.

While Noémie ended up in Rwanda's highest legislative body, hundreds of thousands of other Rwandan women also experienced shifts in their political engagement that manifested in less formal political spaces during and after the violence. In what follows, I examine the impact of the violence in Rwanda on women's informal and formal political participation. As explained in the introductory chapter, I conceptualize informal political participation as occurring in neighborhoods and communities, through nonhierarchical forms of organization and without substantial resources. Women's informal political activities often revolve around practical gender interests and everyday struggles. While not political actions in and of themselves, as more women engage in such activities they can accumulate, leading to the formation of community organizations that can eventually have an impact on formal political processes. In contrast, the formal political realm is centralized, highly institutionalized, and resource-intensive; it consists of interactions with the state and its appendages. The boundaries between the two realms are not always clear, however, as informal political participation can culminate in formal political change. Here I analyze both, as well as their intersections.

The violence in Rwanda brought about women's mobilization in many social arenas, from the grassroots to the national political realm. Before long, women's ordinary activities in new social roles reflected a "politics of practice," whereby women's everyday efforts to establish normalcy in conditions of chaos ultimately manifested in political change (Bayat 2010). I understand these new activities as political because they represent the first stage in the broader process of political engagement. For Noémie, these everyday efforts included that she "had to do everything that was the same for the kids as when their dad was around." As I show in what follows, and in parallel to Bosnian women's experiences, millions of Rwandan women found themselves taking on new roles to improve their lives and the lives of their family members, and in the process broke cultural taboos. Testifying in local or international courts about rape and sexualized violence they had experienced was also part of this shift. These everyday actions challenged the gendered division of labor and social expectations about women's place in Rwandan society.

Next, I describe how these shifts facilitated the rapid formation of grassroots community-based organizations (CBOs) in the country. Women took the lead in establishing and running these organizations. While many organizations were "feminine" in nature and concerned primarily with advancing practical gender interests associated with day-to-day life, they also catalyzed women's increased presence in public spaces and represented new arenas for women's collective action. For Noémie, participating in a grassroots widows' organization gave her the network and visibility she needed to run for political office. Soon, many of these groups shifted from working on emergency relief to advocating for women's legal and political rights. As INGOs and government institutions attempted to reach Rwandans, they partnered with these grassroots organizations to implement programs, disperse funds, and mobilize citizens. This initiated a process of "institutional isomorphism" (DiMaggio and Powell 1983), whereby fledgling CBOs mimicked the set-up and structure of the larger and more formal NGOs and INGOs they sought funding from – a process that also occurred in Bosnia, as I discuss in Chapter 7. As their missions expanded, these organizations institutionalized a system of female leadership at the local level and eventually provided a platform for some women to launch careers in formal politics.

Finally, I conclude this case study by illustrating how the violence precipitated women's participation in formal political capacities. Unlike Bosnia, Rwanda experienced a wholesale political transformation after the war and genocide. The regime responsible for perpetrating the most egregious forms of violence was on the run, which left thousands of political offices vacant at all levels of power. The new political elite, led by Paul Kagame and the Rwanda Patriotic Front, welcomed women into the political fold. Women who came to lead community organizations and NGOs increasingly interacted with more formal institutions of power, and some – like Noémie – eventually ran for political office. Others entered formal political realms because of their close ties to the RPF party. As I described in the previous chapter, the government was supportive of women's inclusion in the political process in part because women represented a neutral, less violent type of political actor – although a more cynical explanation is that the RPF supported women's political advancement because it distracted the international community from the regime's use of extralegal violence and consolidation of ethnic power. As I explain later, this frame helped facilitate the ascent of Rwandan women in formal political roles.

A "POLITICS OF PRACTICE": EVERYDAY POLITICS

As we have seen, women took on new roles in their households and communities as a result of displacement, the loss or absence of their husbands, and the economic devastation of the violence. With approximately 36 percent of households lacking an adult male, women assumed tasks that were previously considered "men's work," from milking cows to repairing houses. They maintained traditional caregiving roles – such as finding food, caring for children, carrying water, and gathering fuel – but now had to venture outside of their homes to care for their dependents, since many could no longer subsist on their own plots of land. One parliamentarian described how:

During this reconstruction process, women themselves got very much involved. In the reconstruction process, physically, socially, they were there everywhere. So that's when I think men came to realize that also women can perform! ... Because formerly it was believed that the man would head the family; but after this, women came in and they did even jobs which we formerly believed were jobs for men. (Interview #11, July 2009)

If only a few women had assumed these new roles, such activities would not in themselves have indicated a broader political transformation. Instead, as thousands of women assumed new roles and challenged conventional gender norms, their activities accumulated and had a broader social impact.

Before long, such activities shifted conventional social expectations for women and showed men that "women can perform" (Interview #11, MP, July 2009). Rose Kabuye, who served as mayor of Kigali immediately after the genocide, described one example of how this process unfolded:

Construction is the biggest industry [in Rwanda]. Well at first the women were shy, and at first they even just did cleaning, sweeping, giving out something. But then they started climbing. And putting stone on, and doing painting, and I remember the President was surprised and he said, "the women, they put on shorts!" – when usually they wear, you know, the skirts. So that is how it started. And then later they started going into business, they took over the tiny businesses ... I mean genocide, yes, but the women became hardened, and they wanted to live, and so they have survived. And they took over roles they never had done. They became managers, they became builders, they cut grass, they did everything. (Interview #30, February 2013)

Rose describes how women took on men's roles, made cash income, and even shifted their type of dress away from traditional cultural expectations. The significance of women wearing shorts or pants arose in many of my interviews; by wearing pants, women could climb, which allowed them to repair their houses and roofs.[1] Before long, some women owned and managed their own businesses, leading many in their community to understand them as capable.

Other political elites I interviewed also suggested that women's participation in tasks previously considered "men's work" eventually culminated in political shifts. Since housing was a primary concern for millions of Rwandans, women's involvement in rebuilding houses meant that they were directly participating in the country's recovery and rebuilding project. The same parliamentarian mentioned previously also described:

[People] had to participate themselves, to contribute, maybe making bricks, providing labor. So women got involved, and you would see a woman starting to construct a house! You know? They had never done it before. And I think when the people were involved in the government, when they saw that also women can do it, that's when they said, also these women should have a share. (Interview #11, July 2009)

As this MP described, ordinary activities like making bricks or repairing a house reflected an initial step in transforming social expectations about women's status in society. Women went from being farmers and housewives to being perceived by the state and the whole population as crucial for the country's recovery. As hundreds of thousands of women participated in such activities, other forms of political action began to materialize.

NEW ACTIVITIES THROUGH CIVIL SOCIETY ORGANIZATIONS

"Civil society itself was just a band of women who organized themselves. No one gave them the positions; it was just women who showed up" – Organization director (Interview #29, February 2013)

In villages and neighborhoods across the country, women began to form informal self-help groups to distribute the burden of these new responsibilities.[2] Despite restrictions on political space in the aftermath of the violence,[3] the organization sector in Rwanda grew rapidly as widespread demographic and economic shifts created urgent needs among the population. These needs were particularly acute for women, who often found themselves assuming new roles, caring for expanded families, and controlling household income for the first time in the absence of their spouses. Organizations ranged broadly in structure and mission. Some were small, informal groups of women that lacked funding or an articulated mission to help women meet their basic material needs. Other, more formal organizations eventually helped women lobby local officials for land rights or trained women to run for political office.

Before the civil war began, merely a handful of organizations existed in Rwanda, and most were tightly linked to the Habyarimana regime; by 1997, women had formed perhaps 15,400 new organizations across the country (Newbury and Baldwin 2000; Powley 2003). By 1999, a study by Réseau des Femmes found 120 women's organizations operating at the prefectural level, 1,540 at the commune level, 11,560 at the sector level, and 86,290 at the cell level (USAID 2000: 19). As a report put it at the time, these "grassroots civil society associations tend to be small, locally based with few ties to national-level organizations, and formed by neighbors and kin living on the same *colline* (hill) who know each other" (USAID 2000). In what follows, I describe some of the different types of organizations women formed.

Support Groups

Linda (Interview #48, July 2012) grew up in a rural part of Rwanda, but in 1988 moved to Kigali with her husband. She was thirty-one when the genocide broke out. Because she was Tutsi, Linda fled the city; but her husband – also Tutsi – was killed. Trying to survive, Linda stayed in the bush for several weeks. There, her muscles atrophied because she was too scared to move and lacked food and water; she became too weak to walk. *Génocidaires* killed her family and many of her friends and neighbors. She survived, but suffers from serious physical disabilities and found herself alone after the violence. As she put it, "When you lose hope, and lose all your loved ones, you have no one to talk to." But she began to notice people in her area – mostly widows – who "came together to console themselves." As she grew a bit stronger, she began to join them, "so [I] could have people to talk to, friends." These groups were incredibly important for Linda and they helped her emotionally and financially recover. Today, Linda is a member of an income and loan savings cooperative, in addition to several larger survivors' organizations. She credits all of them with helping her survive and reclaim her life after the violence. Linda's experience suggests that emotional support organizations drew women out of the private, domestic sphere and into a more public one, eventually linking individual women's pain with larger social networks and support structures. Many emotional support groups formed organically, as women met in line to collect food from relief organizations, or in IDP or refugee camps. Women with some education or skills often took the lead and helped others in their communities to care for their kids, attain food, repair or build homes, and find schools and medical care. Like I discuss in Chapter 7 in the context of Bosnia, having tangible, immediate goals allowed women to organize around concrete problems affecting their lives. Without the social networks they had before the violence, women used organizations to make connections. In short, organizations formed because women "all had the same problem" (Interview #25, July 2012) – and they needed to survive and improve their lives.

Avega-Agahozo, Rwanda's largest widows' association, exemplified an organization that initially formed to provide women emotional support. The director of Avega described how after the genocide, a group of widows from Kigali would run into other women and say, "'Oh, you survived too!' So they took an opportunity to meet ... Women came together just to cry" (Interview #23, July 2012). According to a former director of the organization:

The first thing that we wanted to take care of and "repair" was ourselves, because everything had been destroyed. We had lost our families. We ourselves were torn apart, so we needed to take care of each other, so that was the first priority, to be able to take care of each other. The first need was emergency relief; then it was taking care of people's rights, especially the rights of women with inheritance. (Interview #40, July 2009)

Over the next few years, as this woman suggests, the mission expanded; the founding widows decided to help other women and children in their community obtain access to health care, trauma counseling, and eventually legal resources to secure their property. As the group secured funding from donor organizations, it grew rapidly. By 1999, more than 1,500 women had turned to Avega for emotional and social support.

Avega, like the majority of grassroots women's self-help organizations in Rwanda, does not identify as a feminist organization. Such organizations do not explicitly aim to challenge traditional patriarchal society or dismantle the gendered status quo; instead, they often essentialize women's roles as nurturers or as peacemakers because they are rooted in the understanding that women's primary responsibility is to preserve life (Kaplan 1982; Taylor and Rupp 1993; Stephen 1997). Regardless, these organizations reflected an emerging "female consciousness" (Kaplan 1982) centered on the shared sense of struggle to survive in the aftermath of atrocity. Further, they offered a space for the development of collective solidarity. Many women who participated in emotional support groups reported that they started to realize that their own suffering paled in comparison to the suffering of others in the group. Because of this, many indicated they were inspired to help other women, children, and their country move forward.

Income-Generating Groups

Chantal (Interview #45, July 2012) grew up as a member of Rwanda's diaspora in DR Congo. She was poor and had little access to education while abroad. She returned to Rwanda in 1996 after the war, but knew few people beyond her husband, who worked as a primary schoolteacher. She described how she would just stay at home all day with no friends. Soon, however, she noticed small groups of women meeting regularly in her area and decided to join them. By joining, she regained her faith in God, since she heard stories from survivors about what they had lived through during the genocide and war. She was so relieved that she had not experienced such suffering herself and became motivated to make a new life in Rwanda. The group soon began to collect small amounts of money from members each week in order to loan larger chunks of money to members for various projects. Soon, the group loaned Chantal enough money to buy an assortment of fabrics. Chantal enjoyed selling the fabric, so she started a business. After several additional loans from the organization, Chantal had a reasonably successful fabric business in place. Combined with her husband's income, she has been able to send all six of her children to primary school, and most of them to secondary school when money allows. Chantal is extremely proud of this, especially since she had little formal education herself. Her experience reveals how participating in a community organization allowed women to engage in wage labor outside of the domestic realm. It also illustrates how savings cooperatives offered women control of surplus income for the first time.

Organizations that were initially "for discussing ... [women's] sadness, [the] hard situation they were facing after losing their husbands," soon transitioned into income generators (Interview #35, MP, February 2013). INGOs frequently funded microcredit projects, which encouraged some women's groups to shift from self-help and emotional support to vocational-training and profit-marking activities. Women soon realized that by joining together and establishing a formal organization, they could become eligible to receive economic benefits from INGOs, larger domestic NGOs, or the government. For women to receive small grants, they usually had to be members of a community organization; and, for a CBO to be given funds, it needed to register with local authorities and develop a leadership structure. This required members to elect a president and vice president, draft a mission statement, prepare a budget, and so on. Like in Bosnia, this process of "institutional isomorphism" (DiMaggio and Powell 1983) led emergent grassroots organizations to mimic the structure of the larger NGOs they sought funding from and thereby formalized women's leadership.

From Grassroots Organizations to Local Politics

Cherise was twenty-seven and living in Western Province when violence erupted in 1994 (Interview #6, June 2009). Just before the genocide, she had gotten married and had a child. During the violence, however, her husband, parents, and most of her siblings were killed. She found herself caring for fourteen children, only one of which was biologically hers. Most were the children of her siblings who had been killed. With a degree from the National University of Rwanda obtained before the violence, Cherise found herself in a better position than many other widows. As she saw it, all women faced difficult circumstances after the war, and "found themselves in the same situation of having to fulfill responsibilities that they never thought that they would have." Cherise used her education and social network to bring together a group of other widows. Some of these women had lost husbands in the genocide, while others "found themselves alone because their husbands had participated in the genocide and found themselves in jail." Others still had husbands who were off fighting with the RPF. They began meeting regularly. Cherise described how:

The first activity was to help those who were sick. In the beginning, when we first started to organize ourselves, we were immediately needed on an emergency level to help ... and so there was emergency relief, but also trying to reunite families together, mothers and children. Those were our first activities.

Cherise helped reunite families, a task that put her in direct contact with the International Committee of the Red Cross (ICRC) and the UNHCR. Through these activities, her social network expanded. The group of women she worked with also grew, and they began working with other women's organizations to "organize around the rights of women" and eventually fight to reform the legal code that prevented women from inheriting land. As Cherise described, before long women in her community realized that "we have more in common than we had differences, and we were facing the same challenges, and we needed to get together to move forward." Working for the women's organization helped Cherise build confidence and motivated her to seek broader influence. In 1995, she started working full-time at Pro Femmes/Twese Hamwe, an umbrella organization for women's groups. She attended several INGO trainings that aimed to teach women about their political rights and how to run for political office. Several years later, Cherise was elected mayor of a large district. As she put it:

For every bad thing that happens, there can always be one good consequence. One of the positive effects of the genocide was that we could not see what was happening and just stay there, so we were faced with an incredible choice, and we had to make the decision to do something ... I entered politics, because I wanted to do something to help women.

Cherise continued describing how women were uniquely victimized during the violence, as they had watched their loved ones killed in front of them. As she explained, "we found ourselves with the heaviest burden." This motivated her to do something to help women, because, "when you help a woman, you also help a family, because most times women are less selfish than men ... I believe that I can make a difference."

Cherise's experience reveals the impact of several of the shifts discussed in the previous chapter. She found herself as the sole income earner in her household, which had inherited fourteen orphans. The suffering she saw around her motivated her to help others. Moreover, she saw women as suffering in a unique way due to their status as mothers and as caretakers of their families. Her early actions in community organizations connected her to larger and more well-connected organizations and INGOs. Eventually, she successfully pursued a career in government.

Who Joined? Who Led? Why?

While no comprehensive data exist that can shed light on the women who founded and led these grassroots organizations, my data suggest that most were Tutsi with secondary or university education. Women with some education or skills (e.g., ability to read and write, nursing, weaving) were particularly influential in helping to establish and formalize income-generating organizations (Zraly, Rubin-Smith, and Betancourt 2011: 260). At the membership level, however, organizations included women of a wide range of backgrounds – including Hutu and Batwa women. At any level, participating in these newly forming institutions brought women into public and community spaces, increasingly their visibility and linking them with new social networks, government officials, and even international actors. The women who led these organizations became well known; one study found that 50 percent of the members of two large widows' associations held leadership positions in their communities (Zraly and Nyirazinyoye 2010). Women's participation in these organizations increased the visibility of women in public spaces and leadership roles.

International Organizations Incentivize Grassroots Organizations to Formalize

While the earliest women's organizations were informal and provided solidarity and support to those affected by the genocide and war, some then shifted to income-generating activities, and before long, some began to focus on advocacy issues at the local, regional, or national levels. Land rights were the most urgent issue at hand. This more overtly political type of organization was often developed in consultation with larger organizations, INGOs, or humanitarian organizations, which provided a vocabulary and framework for speaking about women's empowerment and gender rights. For example, after 1995, INGOs often referenced the Beijing Platform of Action, which established a global agenda for women's empowerment.[4] In my interviews, Rwandan women who had founded grassroots organizations referred to these international legal frameworks as "tools" they could use to justify their activities to spouses and community members, or in conversations with members of government.

As grassroots organizations began to apply for funding from the government and from INGOs, some gradually formalized. Women who were formally self-subsistence agriculturalists or teachers or housewives found themselves with official titles like president or secretary of the organization. These formal leadership positions had profound implications for their community status, self-esteem, and ability to enter politics. For example, Odette, a genocide widow, was living in Eastern Province after the genocide (Interview #23, July 2012). She "saw so much need ... widows were really suffering; they needed houses, food, health care." In 1995, she organized a group of several other widows from her area who had lost their homes during the genocide. Together, they approached a representative of the United Nations Development Programme (UNDP) and requested iron sheets that would allow them to rebuild the roofs of their homes. The representatives at the UNDP listened and eventually provided them with the requested materials. Encouraged by their success, Odette and the group of women decided to officially form their own organization and apply for additional funding from international sources. They named their organization, wrote a mission statement, and elected Odette as president. This title granted Odette a formal leadership position in her community and gave her a credential she eventually leveraged to join a prominent national NGO.

In sum, many women realized that, in order to fully benefit from the humanitarian aid pouring into the country, they needed to be members of an organization. As I discuss in Chapter 7, a similar process occurred in Bosnia. Foreign funding helped women in Rwanda formalize local organizations and gain a voice in public spaces and leadership. INGOs prioritized housing, health care, and income-generating projects for widows and orphans, as well as organized "trainings" and paid locals to participate.[5] Through this process, many ordinary Rwandan women served as interlocutors between their communities, local government, and international funding organizations.

From Informal Organizations to Overt Political Action

Like in other countries around the globe, community organizations became the primary mechanism through which women in Rwanda could stake political claims and participate in public life. There are many examples of how organizations facilitated formal political action. Here I highlight the work of Pro Femmes/Twese Hamwe, a prominent umbrella organization for an array of women's groups, as it serves as the foremost example of an organization that bridged informal and formal political spaces.

A group of women formed Pro Femmes in 1992 in reaction to the civil war, because they felt that they were:

caught in the tide of the war, and we realized that the primary burden of it was laying on our shoulders, because it was our children who would go to war. It was our husbands who were going to war, and it was us who were left to care and deal with the consequences of that war. (Interview #5, Pro Femmes founder, July 2009)

Drawing inspiration from other women's peace movements around the world, Pro Femmes' leadership attempted to organize a public march for peace in Kigali in 1992. However, the Habyarimana government shut it down, fearing the march would add to the country's ongoing insecurity. Not to be deterred, the organizers cut out pieces of paper shaped like feet to symbolize marching women. They wrote, "We want Peace – We want this to end" on the paper feet and posted them all over the city (Interview #5, July 2009).

This early example of women asserting their political voice through the structure of an organization suggests the powerful ability of war to mobilize women's interests. Unlike Avega, which was primarily focused on social support, Pro Femmes was focused on changing women's legal rights and substantive government presence. In the aftermath of the genocide, Pro Femmes expanded rapidly, growing from thirteen member organizations in 1992 to more than forty several years later (Powley 2004: 157). As it grew, Pro Femmes gained funding from international agencies and frequently hosted consultants from the UNHCR, the UN Development Fund for Women, and other international organizations that provided inspiration and technical training to the organization's membership (Republic of Rwanda 1999; Burnet 2008; Interview #5, July 2009). In this way, Pro Femmes built capacity to serve as a broker between large international entities and rural Rwandan women's associations in its network. Through the coordinated efforts of local women's associations and well-connected NGOs like Pro Femmes, locally initiated campaigns to increase literacy, develop leadership skills, and practice family planning techniques were implemented across the country, all of which were shaped by the international community's priorities.

Pro Femmes relaunched its Campaign for Peace in 1996. As the explicit project of the burgeoning women's movement in Rwanda, the Campaign aimed to promote a culture of peace in the country amid ongoing instability (USAID 2000: 20; Burnet 2008: 374). In doing so, the Campaign reflected a shift among women's groups from emergency relief to a political agenda. The late Judith Kanakuze, one of the women involved with this effort, described how the campaign "was a novel program in which we were discussing how to rebuild society, how to rehabilitate our nation, what is the role of women, and what capacity [do] women need to be part of the solution" (Interview #13, June 2009). The program aimed to insert women's voices into national conversations about housing, refugees, and justice (USAID 2000: 20). Through the Campaign for Peace, Pro Femmes began working closely with the few women in the transitional government, as well as with the Ministry of Gender and Women in Development in the executive branch. While the campaign reinforced the association between women and peace, it also serves as an example of how women leveraged their "peaceful" identity to serve political ends.

Many of the organizations within the Pro Femmes network next turned their efforts toward land rights. Without legal rights to land or a formalized system of land certification, disputes about ownership were pervasive after the violence. Disputes escalated as hundreds of thousands of "old caseload" and "new caseload" refugees returned from neighboring countries in the mid-1990s. With more than 90 percent of Rwandans dependent on agriculture for their livelihood, access to land was vital (Gervais 2003: 546; Ansoms 2008: 2). Many returning "old caseload" refugees and landless women – both of whom were predominantly Tutsi – petitioned local authorities for access to communal land, land abandoned by its owners, or less-desirable marshland that was still considered part of the commons (Gervais 2003).

According to many women I interviewed, lobbying local officials through the institutional structure of an organization became one of the only ways women could gain formal access to land (see also Gervais 2003: 547). Centralized organizations like Pro Femmes helped coordinate many of these efforts: it convened meetings with grassroots women's organizations in order to assess women's needs and concerns in different parts of the country, and it also worked with the newly formed Forum for Female Parliamentarians (FFRP) and the Ministry of Gender to ensure policymakers heard women's concerns. Women's efforts to obtain land rights eventually manifested in a campaign run by Hagaruka, the legal advocacy organization within the Pro Femmes network. In conjunction with women in government, Hagaruka, Pro Femmes, and other civil society organizations lobbied to amend the legal code to allow women to inherit land from deceased family members, as well as to change laws on divorce, property rights, and gender-based violence (see also Mageza-Barthel 2015).

One of the key achievements of these efforts was a detailed report recommending that the Government of Rwanda include specific provisions protecting women in the constitutional referendum (Powley 2004: 157–158). In 1999, the Organic Land Law and the Succession Law were passed, granting women the right to inherit land and property for the first time (Republic of Rwanda 1999).[6] This major accomplishment of women's mobilization in Rwanda set the stage for subsequent legislation that established children's rights and protected against gender-based violence (Powley 2006; Powley and Pearson 2007), although there were major shortcomings of the law.[7]

For individual women, involvement in these NGO campaigns for peace, land rights, or other goals expanded their social networks by granting them access to government actors or institutions and connecting them to the new regime elite, and equipped them with the vocabulary necessary to speak about gender-specific issues. Some who emerged as leaders in these organizations – like Noémie and Cherise – were actively encouraged to run for political office, and others were hired by INGOs to run various development programs.[8] Indeed, participating in informal and formal civil society organizations was the most common "pathway to power" among the forty elite women in government that I interviewed. Of these women, 77.5 percent were involved in a grassroots organization before entering politics; 67.5 percent worked with a more formal NGO or INGO (see Berry 2015a). Many MPs credited their exposure to certain social issues while working in these organizations with driving their motivation to influence people at a higher level through government service.

National Women's Council

The postwar government also contributed to this process of formalizing women's mobilization. For example, the regime initiated the National Women's Council (NWC), a system of government-affiliated women's groups at all levels of government (Interview #2, Inyumba, July 2009). These councils were patterned on a similar program in Uganda, as well as on international women's councils that emerged in the 1970s. Led by the late Aloisea Inyumba, the NWC was designed as a pipeline through which women's voices at the base would be heard by the political leadership at the top. To implement the program, Inyumba dispatched a network of party officials to meet with representatives from women's organizations in each district in the country. These party officials encouraged women to organize into neighborhood councils. Each neighborhood council was then asked to elect representatives to the sector level, where further elections were held to send representatives to the district, provincial, and, eventually, national levels.

According to Inyumba, the structure of the NWC emerged in response to the bottom-up organizing efforts occurring across the country. Eventually, it served as another mechanism for connecting ordinary women to the national governing structure. Women elected to NWC leadership positions gained a formal credential, which they could leverage to launch a political career. For example, after the war, one woman became involved with Réseau des Femmes Oeuvrant pour le Développement Rural (Network of Women Working for Rural Development) and several small organizations in the Pro Femme network, and then decided to participate in the NWC. She described the importance of the NWC to her subsequent activities:

I started at the most local level [of the NWC]; I started at the cell and then I went to the sector, then I went to the district, then I went to the Parliament and so

I came here. I was still living in the rural area, so when I joined the National Council of Women it pushed me to move up. (Interview #16, July 2009)

This MP's experience captures how women's participation in community organizations gave them the network and credentials needed to later run for leadership positions. At the same time, the NWC was modeled after the hierarchically structured Rwandan state – and thereby served to embed the state into ordinary citizens' lives.

FORMAL POLITICS

While the mobilization of women in the informal capacities discussed earlier was primarily initiated by the war and genocide, another factor enabled this informal political mobilization to translate into formal political spaces. In short, in Rwanda, unlike in Bosnia, the former regime was totally displaced after the violence. Those closely tied to Habyarimana were eliminated – killed, arrested, or forced into exile. The new, RPF-led regime overhauled existing laws and institutions and implemented a political system based on the Arusha Accords. The resulting personnel vacancies at all levels of power offered opportunities for new political actors to enter formal political offices. During the nine-year transition period between 1994 and 2003, the Rwandan government – specifically the Ministry of Gender and the FFRP – worked with civil society leaders to find ways to best incorporate women into politics. At the forefront of this effort was a quota, enshrined in the 2003 constitution, mandating that women hold 30 percent of all decision-making positions. Before long, the regime looked to leaders in communities across the country to fill vacant offices at all levels.

But why was the government of Rwanda so supportive of recruiting women for leadership positions? The reasons for this are debated, but a few are particularly plausible. Most critically, despite the RPF's success at bringing the genocide to an end, in 1994 most Rwandans distrusted it and considered it the enemy because it was dominated by Anglophone Tutsi who had grown up in Uganda. Many Rwandan Hutu feared RPF revenge attacks, even if they had not participated in genocide crimes. Thus, as the RPF attempted to secure and legitimize its control, women emerged as a large political constituency that the party could safely mobilize in its ranks (see Longman 2006; Straus and Waldorf 2011; Thomson 2013; Berry 2015a). As discussed in Chapter 3, women were widely seen as less complicit in the genocide and therefore less "ethnic," in part because Rwandan society is patrilineal, meaning that ethnicity is passed

TABLE 4.1 *Women in Parliament in Rwanda*

Year	% Women in Parliament
1981	6.3
1983	12.9
1988	17.1
1994	4.3
2003	48.8
2008	56.3
2013	63.8

Notes: http://data.un.org/Data.aspx?q=bangladesh&d=MDG
&f=seriesRowID%3A557%3BcountryID%3A50; www.ipu
.org/PDF/publications/women45-95_en.pdf
Sources: UNData; IPU: Women in Parliaments 1945–1995.

down through male lineage. Thus the RPF could more easily appoint both Hutu and Tutsi women to leadership roles. In this political context, Kagame and the RPF began to vocally encourage women to join politics, often prioritizing the women who were emerging as leaders of local grassroots organizations.

While this promotion of women in government certainly was – and is – part of a broader strategy of consolidating political control, it also reflects the valued place that women held in the RPF movement since its origins in the mid-1980s in Uganda (Interviews, Rose Kabuye, February 2013; Aloisea Inyumba, July 2009). President Kagame in particular has been a champion of women's rights, describing how "the politics of women's empowerment is part of the politics of liberation more generally" (Kagame 2014). This "political will" is widely cited by politicians today as a reason for Rwandan women's advancement in leadership positions. Of course, women candidates who have challenged Kagame's leadership – such as Victoire Ingabire and Diane Rwigara – have found themselves arrested and imprisoned.

For these reasons, many Rwandan women who supported the RPF's agenda encountered opportunities to participate in political capacities that would not have been feasible before the violence; yet these women tended to be more educated than average and were disproportionately Tutsi. Of the forty women political elites I interviewed for this project, I estimate that twenty-nine were Tutsi (both survivors and returning refugees), while only eleven made no mention of their victimization during the genocide, and thus were likely Hutu. As I mentioned previously, these figures are estimates; ethnicity is illegal to discuss in Rwanda today, and therefore I was unable to directly ask my interviewees about it and did not seek to verify ethnicity through other avenues.

NGOs played a critical role in facilitating this process of incorporating women in formal political positions. For example, one MP survived the genocide and lost most of her family in the process. In the aftermath, she was desperate to join the RPF, which she saw as saving her and her older sister from a gruesome fate. This MP attended several trainings hosted by Pro Femmes that taught her how to run for office, how to be confident, and how "to know that you are able and you can do whatever you want to do, when you want to do it, as a woman." She soon ran for a position at the local government level, and won. Motivated by her success, she then described how "when I reached that position I was like I need to go higher up, to where I am now" (Interview #12, July 2009).

Vacancies at the top administrative level of the country also allowed women with long-standing ties to the RPF to assume positions of power. For example, Lt. Colonel Rose Kabuye became the mayor of Kigali City and the late Aloisea Inyumba became the minister in charge of Family and Women Promotion. As I discussed in previous chapters, both women had held prominent roles in the military and fundraising arm of the RPF during its early days and served as visible examples of women's legitimate presence in politics. Connie Bwiza Sekemana (Interview #9, July 2009) was another early member of the RPF who grew up in Uganda as a refugee. In the early stages of the RPF, she was responsible for working with unaccompanied children and others who were displaced. When the RPF took power, she rose in the party ranks and became a key part of the transition team. Through her position with the party, she worked with multinational organizations like UNICEF on reunifying families after the violence. Eventually, her work with UNICEF was integrated into a government ministry charged with reunification and resettlement, and ultimately this position was folded into the Ministry of Internal Affairs. In the late 1990s, she was transferred again to the Ministry of Land, and then in 1999 was nominated by the RPF to join the transitional parliament. Her experience, like that of many other women in parliament, suggests that closeness to the ruling party is an additional asset in linking individual women to formal political roles.

Several other women became involved in formal politics after holding high-level positions in women's organizations. Judith Kanakuze, for example, was a pioneer of women's issues even before the war and became one of the first women to transition from civil society into politics (Interview #13, June 2009). She was an early member of the transitional government and represented the NGO sector as one of three women on the Constitutional Commission. There, she lobbied for the government to incorporate the platform established at the 1995 Beijing Conference into its domestic political framework. Kanakuze became a well-respected gender advisor to several government ministries and her work to mainstream gender-sensitive protocols was key in advocating for the adoption of the reserved-seat gender quota for women in parliament.

Cooption of the Civil Sector

The transition of some women – like Judith Kanakuze – from the civil sector to government, however, was not necessarily motivated by the regime's desire to empower women. Rather, it appears that it may have been part of a broader political strategy to undermine the strongest voices outside of politics – what Jennie Burnet (2008: 378) calls an effort to "emasculate" the burgeoning women's movement. Without a strong civil society – the regime reasoned – there would be little opposition to continued RPF control, and the vibrant women's movement was among the regime's first "targets" (Rombouts 2006). For example, the leaders of Réseau des Femmes, one of the oldest and strongest women's organizations in Rwanda, resigned their positions in the organization to join the government after 2003. Their departure left the organization poorly managed and it eventually fell deep in debt (Burnet 2008: 379; multiple interviews).

The regime's strategy of coopting civil society reflects its desire to deeply embed its power infrastructure and ensure its continued control over the country (Mann and Berry 2016). Moreover, it reflects the growing gulf between the RPF, which is mostly comprised of returnee Tutsi (i.e., those who had grown up abroad, such as in Uganda), and Rwandan Tutsi (i.e., those who had survived the genocide). Rwandan Tutsi were the founders and members of survivor associations, which comprised the most active and dynamic part of the civil sector. The regime's repression of these associations – and of the civic sector more generally – increased after 2000. Human Rights Watch reported several assassinations of leaders of survivor associations, which were likely politically motivated (Human Rights Watch 2000, 2007).[9] The government has also shut down the most independent organizations in civil society, often accusing them of "genocide ideology." Outspoken human rights activities and champions, including women who were early leaders in the women's movement, have fled into exile. In short, the rapid formation of community associations and NGOs in Rwanda ultimately did not manifest in a robust civil society that could serve as an effective counterweight to the power of the state.

CONCLUSION

In this chapter, I illustrated the variety of ways that women engaged in new political roles in the aftermath of violence in Rwanda. Women became involved in various forms of "everyday politics" as they took on new roles and responsibilities in their households and communities. Such ordinary actions began to accumulate, shifting expectations about women's roles in Rwandan society. As a result of these new roles, community organizations proliferated and became an important space for women to engage with others in their communities. In doing so, these organizations instituted a system of women's leadership at the local level and furthermore connected ordinary Rwandan women with more formal NGOs, foreign donors, and government institutions. Many women who came to lead these organizations found themselves well positioned to run for political office. With the overhaul of the former regime and the arrival of a new regime committed to advancing women's leadership, today Rwanda has the highest percentage of women in parliament of any country in the world.

Yet a key question remains: was women's increased participation in informal and formal politics sustained? Moreover, have the strides women have made at the national political level fundamentally transformed ordinary women's lives? While the political class of elite women has seen rapid wealth accumulation and the extension of myriad rights, "ordinary" Rwandan women's stories illustrate a depressing paradox: despite the world's highest percentage of women in parliament, some of the strongest state-led efforts to promote women, and an entire government apparatus designed with gender equality in mind, profound impediments to women's equality and liberation are deeply entrenched and appear unlikely to dissipate any time soon (Berry 2015b). As I explain in Chapter 8, many of the gains women have made are undermined by the authoritarian nature of the state, in addition to the problematic implementation strategies of foreign NGOs. Further, as suggested earlier, while women have made important strides in many areas, wealthy, foreign-born Tutsi women have disproportionately ascended the national political ladder. As such, new forms of inequality are developing in Rwanda, constraining much of the impressive progress women made in the immediate aftermath of the violence.

5

Historical Roots of Mass Violence in Bosnia-Herzegovina

War broke out in Yugoslavia in the early 1990s as the central power structure crumbled and some of its constituent republics declared their independence. What followed in Bosnia was the bloodiest conflict in Europe since World War II. By 1995, more than two million people (out of a population of 4.3 million) were internally displaced or seeking refuge in neighboring countries, more than 100,000 people were dead, and between 20,000 and 50,000 women had been raped (Silber and Little 1997; Enloe 2000; Research and Documentation Center 2013). In this chapter, I provide an overview of recent Bosnian history in the lead-up to the violence, with a particular focus on the status of women.

Scholars have debated the causes of war in Bosnia, but most agree that "ancient ethnic hatreds" did not drive the war, and that such depictions simplify and distort the conflict's actual origins.[1] Bosnia sits at a geopolitical crossroads. Looking west, it is a short boat ride across the Adriatic Sea to Italy. Looking east, Bosnia is a gateway to the southern Slavic states, and beyond that to Turkey and the countries bordering the Black Sea. A visitor to Sarajevo today cannot help but notice the two distinct cultural traditions. As one walks east down Maršala Tita, the main pedestrian road through the heart of the city, Austro-Hungarian-style buildings stand next to modern shops, cafés, and commercial infrastructure. Bosnians of all ages pack cafés, regardless of the day of the week (perhaps a result of the high unemployment rates). An Orthodox cathedral, built in the mid-nineteenth century, towers over an open courtyard periodically filled with street fairs or groups of men playing chess on a large, open-air chessboard. Popular European clothing chains advertise the latest fashions with bold signs and blaring pop music.

MAP 3 Yugoslavia

The smooth pavement across most of downtown soon turns to cobble-stone, and, upon entering Baščaršija – the Ottoman heart of the city and the former bazaar district – the atmosphere changes. The Gazi Husrev-beg Mosque, built in 1531, stands proudly in the center of the neighbor-hood as Bosnia's most important Islamic structure and a fine example of Ottoman architecture. Just yards from the mosque is Sebilj, a wooden fountain built in 1753. While Ottoman architecture dominates this neighborhood, Catholic cathedrals and Jewish synagogues just up the street are evidence of the area's historical religious diversity. Bazaars and shops selling trinkets – many from Turkey – abound. Cafés serve Bosnian coffee. Made similarly to the Turkish tradition, Bosnian coffee consists of finely ground beans cooked in a copper pot with a long handle until the coffee rises and nearly overflows from the pot, creating a thick foam. It is then stirred and poured into a small cup, served with sugar cubes, a glass of water, and a side of *rahatloukoum* (Turkish delight). Around Baščaršija, men smoke *shisha* (hookah) and restaurants offer house-made *rakija* (a popular fruit brandy).

These dualities – the feeling of east meeting west – help explain much of Bosnia's turbulent history. The Ottoman Empire, an expansionary Sunni

MAP 4 Bosnia and Herzegovina

Islamic state based out of western Anatolia, took control of Bosnia in 1463. For the next four centuries of Ottoman rule, Bosnia underwent a series of population shifts. While religious tolerance characterized Ottoman policy, the empire actively championed Islam and approximately two-fifths of the native Slavic population – previously Orthodox Christians or (often heretical) Catholics – converted. Anyone who aspired to state service, military service, or regional trade had a pragmatic reason to adopt

Islam (Malcolm 1996: 51–69; Udovički 1997: 22; Lampe 2000: 23).[2] The proportion of Orthodox Serbs in Bosnia also continued to rise due to migration, and, by the late 1860s, Serbs comprised more than one-third of the population. The Ottoman millet system allowed non-Muslim religious communities in the Balkans a degree of religious and juridical autonomy, and thereby permitted Serb, Jewish, and Croat communities room to maintain their cultural differences. By the mid-nineteenth century, the population of current-day Bosnia was roughly divided between Bosnian Muslims at 44 percent, Orthodox Christians (Serbs) at 31 percent, and Catholics (Croats) at 17 percent. These groups all spoke the same south Slavic language, variously referred to as Bosnian, Serbian, or Croatian depending on the region where it was spoken. Neighboring territories of Serbia and Croatia were more religiously homogenous; as such, Bosnia emerged as the most ethnically diverse entity in the Balkans. Regardless of religious or national identity, traditional Balkan society was patrilineal and patriarchal. Men dominated their households, and women's primary status emerged from their role as a link between fathers and sons. Only by giving birth to a son could a woman gain status in her family and community (Milićević 2006: 269).

Orthodox Serbian resistance to Ottoman rule grew in the nineteenth century, in part because Serbs within Bosnia occupied a low position in the agricultural hierarchy vis-à-vis Muslim landholders. Croatian Catholics, residing both in current-day Croatia and throughout the region, were also disenfranchised under Ottoman rule, and joined Serbs and other minorities to protest. Peasant revolts became common throughout the nineteenth century, and Serb and Croat elites began to articulate visions of "Greater Serbia" or "Greater Croatia" and thereby announce their ambitions for greater territorial control. In 1875, Serb and Croat peasants instigated a massive revolt in Herzegovina (a region of southern Bosnia) that left 150,000 people dead or forced them to flee (Malcolm 1996: 132; Lampe 2000: 66). But the Ottoman Empire was weakening and its control over the Balkans was slowly fading.

The Treaty of Berlin in 1878 ushered in political sea changes, as European countries placed Bosnia under the control of the predominantly Christian Austro-Hungarian Empire as an "occupied Ottoman territory." As a result, tensions between Orthodox Serbs and Muslims increased, and several hundred thousand Bosnian Muslims fled to areas still under control of the Ottoman Empire (mostly in modern-day Turkey). This outmigration rendered Orthodox Serbs a plurality in the state (Lampe 2000: 6). Bosnian Muslims who remained came under Austro-Hungarian control, which made them religious minorities within the Empire and compelled them to strengthen their cultural and religious autonomy (Malcolm 1996: 136–155).

The administration implemented aggressive policies to further agricultural and industrial production in Bosnia. The agricultural project, however, was largely a disaster, and the predominantly Orthodox Serb peasantry increasingly consisted of landless sharecroppers (or *kmetovi*) and occupied disproportionately fewer positions of wage employment in the urban areas (Lampe 2000). Bosnian Muslims made up just 37 percent of the rural population, yet accounted for 91 percent of the landlords. By contrast, Serbs comprised 42 percent of the rural population, but 74 percent of the landless population (Lampe 2000: 82). As a result, Serbs became increasingly frustrated, particularly as rural education was neglected and much of the agrarian population remained illiterate.

Amid deepening antagonism between Serb leadership and the Austro-Hungarian power holders, in 1908 the empire decided to formally annex the province of Bosnia-Herzegovina. The annexation was motivated by the empire's fear that the Young Turk revolution in Turkey (the remnants of the Ottoman Empire) would instigate a movement to reclaim Bosnia for Turkey. As a consequence of this annexation, tensions between Serbia and Austria-Hungary increased, as Serb nationalists felt that Bosnian territory had been stolen from them (Malcolm 1996: 150). Organizations to fight for pan-Serb unification and/or the unification of all south Slavs developed; in Bosnia, such organizations included the "Young Bosnia" movement. This informal group was mainly composed of young Bosnian Serbs, and one of its members, Gavrilo Princip, assassinated Franz Ferdinand, the heir of the Habsburg Empire, on June 28, 1914, during a visit to Sarajevo. Ferdinand's assassination ignited World War I,[3] during which the Austro-Hungarian Empire collapsed.[4] With the end of the war, the movement for a unified federation of southern Slavs could achieve its goal: it established the Kingdom of Serbs, Croats, and Slovenes, which was later known as the First Yugoslavia (Ramet 2006). The territory of Bosnia and Herzegovina was integrated into this kingdom. Yet the federal political and economic framework of the new state was weak, and Serbia was, in many ways, at the center of political power (Djokić 2007: 41–42).

WOMEN IN THE INTERWAR PERIOD
AND THE FIRST YUGOSLAVIA

During the interwar years, Yugoslavians suffered from the global economic depression, and women were disadvantaged in many ways. They lacked the right to vote, were consistently paid less than men, and had limited access to education. In some parts of Yugoslavia in the early 1930s, including in Bosnia, women's illiteracy rate was as high as 85–90 percent (Jancar-Webster 1990: 27). In the countryside, traditional values confined women's place within the home. Women were charged with household agricultural production in the *bašča*, a small patch of land or garden close to the family residence (Bringa 1995: 53). Families were clustered in *zadruga*, a two- or three-generation family economic and social unit ruled by a patriarch, who wielded power in the household and controlled any economic surplus.[5] *Zadruga* structured the organization of agriculture, women's tasks, and the ownership of property (Jancar-Webster 1990: 27;[6] Cockburn 1998: 156). According to Jancar-Webster:

> Women were subordinated to men, working at their "women's tasks" and ensuring the harmony and smooth-working of the households. Their work was considered a separate contribution to the home, of less significance than men's. Daughters were sent out of the house at marriage, and the new bride immediately assumed the lowest status in her husband's household. Her servant status improved to the degree that she bore male children. (1990: 28)

If women left the *zadruga* to find wage employment, they found their work undervalued. Despite – or perhaps because of – women's disadvantaged position in the labor market, some women began to actively organize public protests and strikes. Women textile workers in Croatia went on strike in 1927–1928 to protest inflation and the high cost of living, and to demand a right to vote. While little historical data on strikes from this time period are available, anecdotal accounts indicate that women participated in great numbers (Jancar-Webster 1990: 36).

While leftist (Marxist) political parties had emerged in the region around the turn of the century, women's involvement in them was minimal. As the global economic crisis deepened in the 1920s, however, many Serb women in the Balkans became increasingly active in the Yugoslav Communist Party (KPJ) and the related Union of Communist Youth (SKOJ). Fearing the Party's growing strength, King Aleksander's regime outlawed it and forced it to go underground, where it developed the strategic and personal networks that would eventually foster its transformation into an organized revolution combatting German occupation during World War II. In 1928, the KPJ noted the significant contributions of women and set up women's commissions. Repression of the Party worsened as King Aleksander consolidated his power, and thus these women's organizations soon served as the primary mechanisms through which the KPJ could infiltrate legal trade unions or other organizations (Jancar-Webster 1990). Many in the core membership of these organizations were schoolteachers, students, or workers, who became experienced in organizing during the interwar period. Women's clubs, societies of academic women, women's congresses, and other similar groups flourished during the 1930s (Slapšak 2001: 164). The Yugoslavian Women's Union (Jugoslovenski ženski savez) connected women's groups from across Yugoslavia (Sarajevo Open Center 2014: 21). Because communism was outlawed, women did not talk about revolution, but rather about women's rights and issues (Jancar-Webster 1990: 25). These topics gave them gendered cover to pursue explicitly political agendas.

Muslim women affiliated with these groups in greater numbers after 1928, as hopes of democracy began to fade when an opposition politician shot five deputies in the parliament. This triggered a political crisis, and King Aleksander further tightened his grip on the country (Ramet 2006: 73). In 1929, he redesigned the Kingdom of Serbs, Croats, and Slovenes as the Kingdom of Yugoslavia (or the Kingdom of the South Slavic People), and simultaneously dismissed the parliament, abolished the constitution, and outlawed political parties. This "royal dictatorship" (Lampe 2000: 196) encouraged people to think in terms of a Yugoslav identity, rather than nationalist ones; King Aleksander aspired to erase the old regional identities from the map, and redrew territorial divisions accordingly (Malcolm 1996: 169). Yet tensions did not ease, and in 1934 King Aleksander was assassinated. Under the reign of his successors, Prince Regent Paul and Prime Minister Milan Stojadinović, inner Yugoslav tensions continued (Lampe 2000: 176–178; Djokic 2007: 106–120).

WORLD WAR II

World War II was a critical period for women in Yugoslavia.[7] The kingdom was attacked and defeated in April 1941 by Nazi Germany and its allies, and as a consequence was dismembered. Some parts were annexed by the victorious Axis powers, and Bosnia was integrated into the newly created "Independent State of Croatia," a Nazi puppet state led by the Croatian fascist Ustaše movement, which waged murderous campaigns against Serbs, Jews, Roma, and Communists. Several local Yugoslav resistance movements emerged during the war and became embroiled in defying the Axis powers (Ramet 2006: 113–150). The largest of these movements, Josip "Tito" Broz's Communist Partisans, aimed to battle the occupying powers, liberate the population, and create a multiethnic communist state within Yugoslavia. Radical Serb Četniks, who at first resisted the occupying powers, eventually collaborated with them against the Partisans and publicly called for a "homogenous Serbia" that would be "cleansed" of all non-Serb elements (Cigar 1995).[8] These various overlapping conflicts led to "a war of all against all" (Prpa-Jovanović 1997: 57) and eventually to an estimated one million deaths (Ramet 2006: 114, 161).

Several weeks after Germany invaded Yugoslavia, it turned its attention to the Soviet Union, prompting the Communist Party to enter the fray. Tito appealed to all Yugoslavians, regardless of nationality, to "unite without consideration of politics or religious convictions and in a united struggle throw out the hated occupiers from their country."[9] Tito's appeal resonated widely. For Yugoslavian women, the Communist Party offered women a chance to both defend their nation as fighters and to position themselves within a movement that articulated a firm commitment to equal economic and political rights for women – even if the Party's slogan, "brotherhood and unity," explicitly excluded them. Many women joined Tito's Communist Partisans. Barbara Jancar-Webster (1990), who conducted the first English-language study on women's participation in the Partisans, declared women's involvement "one of the most significant events in modern history. In no other country in the world have women played such a decisive part in the achievement of victory over an occupying enemy and the realization of a Communist state" (1990: 1).

Throughout the war, an estimated 5.7 million people were mobilized in Tito's National Liberation Movement, including two million women – approximately 12 percent of the prewar female population. Approximately 70 percent of these women were younger than twenty years old. Most women participants were likely Serbs, followed by Croats, Slovenes, Montenegrins, and then Muslims and Macedonians; however, no official statistics were collected. Within the military wing, the Partisans amassed a force of approximately 800,000 (Ramet 2006: 153–159). The military wing included approximately 2,000 women officers. Of the total number of participants, perhaps one million died during the struggle.

Women were motivated to join Tito's Partisans for a variety of reasons. Some had been exposed to progressive political circles in the build-up to the war and were committed to advancing the socialist cause. Many were motivated by the movement's goal to eliminate fascism. Others had joined for personal reasons, such as to avenge the death of a family member. Others had brothers, husbands, or fathers who had joined the movement, which prompted them to join as well, particularly if their loved

ones had been killed early in the struggle (Jancar-Webster 1990: 50, 159).
The Party-affiliated Antifašistički Front Žena (AFŽ, or Antifascist Front
of Women) helped organize women in the struggle by assigning them
jobs teaching literacy to the rural population or serving as recruiters for
the socialist cause (Slapšak 2001: 167; Helms 2013: 49). Thousands of
women were eager to join because Partisan life also promised camarade-
rie and provided many new experiences to participants, including exposure to music, dancing, theater, and more. Women served in all capacities
while in the movement, including as fighters, nurses and doctors, sup-
pliers, and communication specialists.[10] Discipline was strict; Partisans
were expected to uphold a code of conduct that prevented Partisans
from entering a village and asking for food, stealing, having illicit sexual
relations, or other types of dishonorable conduct (Jancar-Webster 1990:
77–78). Life as a Partisan was grueling, particularly during the freezing Bosnian winters when food was scarce and deep snow blanketed the
region. Yet Jancar-Webster cites a Partisan woman, Saša Bozović, who
stressed that the war "taught her that human beings are stronger than
they realize, with an incredible capacity to endure" (1990: 81).

TITO'S YUGOSLAVIA

As the war came to a close, Tito's Partisans were victorious in the rural
and mountainous regions of Yugoslavia. Tito emerged as the leader
best poised to bring internal peace to the Balkans. The following period
marked significant changes in women's roles, primarily as a result of
the socialist ideology in Yugoslavia that advanced social equality. Tito
banned Ustaša and Četnik extremist groups, declaring that all ethnicities
in the region had a home in Yugoslavia. Although Tito was half Croat
and half Slovene, he nevertheless situated the national governing structures in Belgrade, privileging the Serb faction within the country. Tito
was staunchly communist and initially implemented a Stalinist model of
the state, collectivizing agriculture and nationalizing industry. Yet, while
Stalin wanted Yugoslavia to become a Soviet satellite state like the rest of
the region, Tito adamantly defended Yugoslavia's independence. For this
and other reasons, Yugoslavia was expelled from Cominform in 1948,
prompting Tito to distance his policies from those of other communist
states and to join the nonaligned movement (Malcolm 1996: 194; Ramet
2006: 175–179).[11]

In the following years, Tito's version of socialism followed a traditional
Marxist model: rather than state ownership of industry, Tito promoted

a decentralized system of worker ownership of the factories and organizations in which they were employed (Jancar-Webster 1990: 163;
Woodward 1995). The Yugoslav state pushed religion into the private
realm and took political power away from the churches in order to prevent discrimination along religious grounds and to ostensibly give all citizens equal opportunity. It also forbade Muslim women from wearing the
veil, outlawed religious schools, and abolished Islamic courts (Malcolm
1996: 195). Women in the AFŽ actively led the campaign to ban religious
dress that they believed marked women as subordinate (Helms 2013:
49). The state eventually loosened these restrictions on religious freedom
in the 1950s, and the overall treatment of observant Muslims improved
over the next few decades.

In socialist Yugoslavia, questions about what it meant to be Muslim,
Croat, or Serb remained, including whether these markers indicated religion, ethnicity, or nationalism. By the census of 1953, citizens could also
register as "Yugoslav, nationality undeclared," which meant that Bosnian
Muslims did not have to declare themselves Muslim Serbs or Muslim
Croatians. By 1961, people could identify as "Muslim in the ethnic sense"
(Malcolm 1996: 198). Slowly, policies toward non-Serbs began to relax,
and a new Muslim elite emerged within the Communist Party. These
elites were secularists and led a push to recognize Muslims in Bosnia
as a nation distinct from Serbs and Croats, and in the 1970s Muslims
were officially recognized as one of the nations forming Yugoslavia.
Simultaneously, a separate movement emerged that pushed for revival of
religious Islamism (Malcolm 1996).

During this period, women of all nationalities won legal rights and
made social gains. Women were given the right to vote during the war,
which was codified in the 1946 constitution that guaranteed women's
political and economic equality (Jancar-Webster 1990: 16). The state
legalized abortion in 1952 (Ramet 1999). Like other lower-developed
countries in the Balkan region, average total births per woman began a
rapid decline, from 5.3 in 1953 to 3.9 in 1957 and then further to 1.9 in
1979 (Sardon and Confession 2004: 214).[12] Partisan leadership fought
to preserve women's status within the state structure and implemented
measures designed to ensure women's political and legal rights (Massey,
Hahn, and Sekulić 1995: 362). Male and female partners could jointly
own property, the state mandated universal health care and childcare,
and mothers and fathers had joint authority over their children. Former
Partisans also implemented a gender quota to ensure a minimum percentage of women in the national legislature.

A key priority of Tito's leadership – and of Marxism more broadly – was to promote women's incorporation into the paid labor force under the logic that gender inequality emerged entirely from women's exclusion from wage labor. The state thus implemented policies mandating equal educational opportunities for men and women, with the idea that men and women would be equally prepared for the same types of employment (Massey et al. 1995: 363). While women comprised approximately 27 percent of the industrial labor force in 1939, this participation increased to 47 percent in the years immediately after the war (Tomšić 1980). Like in the United States, however, this dropped to around 25 percent in 1954, as preference was given to male veterans and women were once again relegated to the household sphere. In addition, women were perpetually underpaid in Yugoslavia and were the first to be laid off during economic downturns (Ramet 1992: 114). Moreover, women held few positions of managerial or political authority – for example, only 17 percent of workers' council members and 6 percent of workers' council presiding officers were women (Morokvasic 1986; Cockburn 1998: 158).

Tito's aspirations of economic gender equality did not come to fruition; instead, women were concentrated in service and education fields, held jobs with less prestige and pay, suffered poorer working conditions, and experienced widespread gender segregation within various professions (Woodward 1985; Massey et al. 1995: 375). In addition to labor inequality, women in Yugoslavia – like women in other socialist countries – faced the "triple burden" of paid employment, housework and childcare, and political and community responsibilities (Massey et al. 1995: 364). Thus, while in many ways the entry of large numbers of women into paid employment represented a shift in women's roles from the private to the public realm, like elsewhere, it did not eradicate women's subordination (Einhorn 1993: 63; Gal and Kligman 2000). Moreover, women's "emancipation" was always part of the male-dominated Party's agenda for achieving a workers' state, rather than a project initiated by women themselves (Tomšić 1980; Jancar-Webster 1990).

Mid-1970s: Feminist Movement Emerges in Yugoslavia

Women leaders in the Partisan movement generally viewed women's struggles as indistinguishable from the struggles of workers and citizens as a whole. As dedicated Party members, many of these women believed that "women's issues" had no independent existence, and instead must be seen as a necessary part of the process of establishing and growing a socialist state (Jancar-Webster 1990). Yet, in the late 1970s, an academic feminist movement emerged in Yugoslavia – and elsewhere around the world – and insisted that "women's issues" deserved separate consideration. In the region, this movement began in Zagreb, Croatia, and soon spread to Belgrade and Ljubljana (Benderly 1997; Slapšak 2001; Bagić 2006). In 1978, an international feminist conference in Belgrade inspired the formation of feminist groups across the region (Bagić 2006: 144). The movement had less strength in Bosnia (although, as I discuss in Chapter 7, this began to change during the war in the 1990s). It gained strength and direction by defining itself both through the unique contributions women Partisans made during World War II, as well as by building on burgeoning Western feminist thought and networks. These efforts were aligned with the workers' movement, but also demanded their own unique identity. Feminists began reframing women's role in the Partisan struggle as exploitative and designed to serve male military purposes. This nascent movement demanded that women's wartime role be put in broader perspective (Jancar-Webster 1990: 178).

Emerging feminists in Yugoslavia had read Western feminists, including Betty Friedan, Simone de Beauvoir, Mary Daly, and Carol Pateman (Jancar-Webster 1990: 178). Women with means could freely travel around Europe with a Yugoslavian passport, allowing them to network with like-minded women's groups in other countries. "Feminist libraries" began to emerge, along with reading clubs (Cockburn 1998). It was largely an intellectual movement, and feminist critiques of Marxism sprang up (see Jancar-Webster 1990 for a review). Members of the movement began to argue that the critical question for women was not stratification between classes – as classic Marxists would articulate – but rather a gendered stratification *within* classes, where men have historically subordinated women to their interests (Jancar-Webster 1990: 178).

In the 1980s, this movement began to implement projects aimed at spreading these ideas more broadly. A key initiative was the establishment of SOS hotlines for victims of domestic violence in Belgrade, Zagreb, and Ljubljana. Yugoslav feminists aspired for these hotlines to both assist individual victims of abuse and raise awareness about violence as a social problem that reflected women's subordinate status within society (Bagić 2006). Lesbian groups also formed during this period. With the rising prominence of nationalist political leaders, however, many of these feminist initiatives began to experience sanctions and backlash.

BUILD-UP TO THE WAR

By the 1960s, Bosnia's economy had fallen behind the rest of Yugoslavia. Bosnia's national income was 20 percent below the national (Yugoslav) average in 1947, and by 1969 dropped to 38 percent below the national average. In the 1970s, with the exception of Kosovo, Bosnia had Yugoslavia's highest infant mortality rate and illiteracy rate, and the highest percentage of people whose only education consisted of three years of primary school (Malcolm 1996: 202; Kalyvas and Sambanis 2005). Many Orthodox Serbs left Bosnia in favor of the more cosmopolitan cities of Zagreb or Belgrade, slowly shifting the ethnic plurality of the country back toward Muslims (Lampe 2000: 335). The international oil crisis in the 1970s prompted a sharp increase in unemployment. The proportion of unemployed women steadily rose; by the 1980s, 55 percent of women in Bosnia were unemployed.

In part because of these economic challenges – in addition to a decentralizing trend throughout the country – nationalism was revived in the 1970s and 1980s. As men lost the ability to provide for their families, many experienced a form of "economic emasculation," prompting backlash against communist agendas and those that had benefited from them – including women (Milićević 2006). There was a corresponding resurgence of traditional values. Islam became more visible and popular, and Orthodox Serb nationalism was revived.

Visions for a "Greater Serbia"

Tito died in 1980. From 1982 to 1986, former Partisan Milka Planinc served as the first and only woman prime minister of Yugoslavia (and the first woman to govern a communist country). As of the 1986 elections, women held 24 percent of the seats in Yugoslavia's National Assembly and comprised 17 percent of municipal representatives. These levels were much higher than global averages at the time, reflecting the Communist Party's continued commitment to gender equality (Cockburn 2001: 22). In the years that followed, the rising star of Serbian leader Slobodan Milošević fomented ethnic nationalism in Serbia (Woodward 1995; Gagnon 2006). In 1986, the Serbian Academy of Arts and Sciences published the "Serbian Memorandum," which proclaimed the validity of Serbia's quest for territorial integrity – in other words, it encouraged the establishment of a state in which all Serbs, and only Serbs, could reside. It argued that communists had deliberately drawn the borders of Yugoslavia's various states to fragment Serbs from each other; only by redrawing the map and uniting Serbs in a common territory could Serbs thrive (Cigar 1995: 23). Milošević tapped into the genuine economic grievances of many of his countrymen, funneling their discontent to his own political ends. A "political ethno-kitsch" washed over Serbian popular culture during the late 1980s, and in newly popular "turbo-folk" music, soccer clubs, media, and other Serb-dominated spaces, a nationalist form of patriotism emerged that emphasized Serbs' status as victims and their shared destiny as a nation (Udovički 1997; Milićević 2006).

Milošević's approach was explicitly chauvinistic, and the nascent Yugoslav feminist movement had an increasingly difficult time being heard in the midst of his new focus on "traditional values" (Ramet 1992: 115). Women's identities and bodies were enlisted to serve nationalist ends; a woman "patriot" was someone who could regenerate the nation through motherhood (Cockburn 1998: 161). Reproducing the nation became a prominent theme in political rhetoric. This was particularly the case in Serbia, as higher fertility rates among (Muslim) Albanian women stoked fears that Muslims were demographically taking over.[13] To make matters worse, in the late 1980s moral panic ensued in Serbia about (Muslim) Albanian men raping Serbian women, which inspired nationalist rhetoric about women as the guarantors of an ethnically pure bloodline (Cockburn 1998: 162; Slapšak 2001: 174). Serb nationalists blamed urban, educated Yugoslav women for failing to produce large families that would further expand the Serb nation.

A speech by Milošević in 1989, commemorating the 600th anniversary of the Battle of Kosovo, rallied supporters and renewed attention to the possibility of establishing an independent Serb nation, through force if necessary.[14] Over the next few years, Milošević consolidated power, as "a wildfire of nationalism" swept Serbia (Ramet 2006: 363). Economic strife continued and inflation reached 800–900 percent (Ramet 2006: 363). In this context, the radical Serb Četnik movement was revived, using the old slogans, flags, uniforms, and dress from the World War II era. As the Soviet Union and other Communist regimes collapsed in Eastern Europe, independent political parties emerged in Yugoslavia and began to challenge the dominance of the Communist Party (Malcolm 1996: 215). The Communist Party across all Yugoslav republics suffered many setbacks in the first multiparty elections in 1990, and a host of nationalist political parties emerged as winners of the elections in different parts of Yugoslavia. In September 1991, the independent Belgrade weekly magazine *Vreme* published details of a Serb plan to annex portions of Bosnia (Ramet 2005: 11).

Women also experienced political setbacks with the disintegration of socialism. In the 1990 elections in Bosnia the women's quota was abandoned, and women were elected to merely 2.9 percent of the seats in the legislature, and 5 percent in the municipal assemblies – down from 24 percent and 17 percent respectively from the 1986 elections (Cockburn 2001: 22). The proportion of women in the Serbian Parliament decreased from 23.5 percent to 1.6 percent (Milićević 2006: 271). This followed trends in the rest of the socialist world, as the fall of the Soviet Union and other socialist countries ushered in a massive decrease in the participation of women in politics (Gal and Kligman 2000).

One exception in this trend was Biljana Plavšić, the nationalist Serb representative in the tripartite Bosnian presidency before the war. In fact, Serb nationalist political parties often had women's branches, many of which grew in strength in the prewar era. The Movement of Women for Yugoslavia, for example, was a militarist women's organization. Most members were women relatives of high-ranking men in the Yugoslav National Army (Jugoslovenska Narodna Armija, or JNA) or other Serbian forces. Sometimes called the "women in fur coats," this group organized to rally people for war and to demand the punishment of people who deserted the army. Biljana Plavšić led another pro-war women's organization, the Central Circle of Serbian Sisters (Kolo Srpskih Sestara). These nationalist women's organizations were pronatalist, encouraging Serb women to replace any Serb men lost in the war with 100 new ones (Zajović 2013: 80). Childbearing became a form of national defense.

WAR BEGINS

In June 1991, Croatia and Slovenia declared their independence from Yugoslavia, citing Serbia's territorial aggression. In Croatia, the conflict escalated into a full-scale war between the JNA, controlled by Belgrade, its local Serb allies, and Croatian independent forces. The UN implemented an arms embargo in September 1991 for the entire region in hopes of preventing the further spread of conflict; nevertheless, arms began pouring into Bosnia. While the war in Croatia raged, Bosnia held a referendum on independence from Yugoslavia; more than 99 percent of those voting (63 percent of those eligible to vote) voted in favor of independence, while Bosnian Serbs mostly boycotted the referendum.[15] On March 3, 1992, Bosnia officially declared its independence. Despite various efforts that sought to peacefully resolve Serbia's territorial aims, war became imminent. Within Bosnia, Serbs, Croats, and Bosnian Muslims each formed paramilitary groups and defense forces. When the United States and the European community recognized Bosnia-Herzegovina as a sovereign state in the beginning of April 1992, Serbian forces launched a coordinated assault. Their goals were simple: to reclaim much of Bosnian territory for Serbia, and to expel all non-Serbs from the land.

The military attack on Bosnia was perpetrated by a series of different actors. Like in Rwanda, these actors included the official state military, as well as paramilitary and irregular troops controlled by political elites. In Bosnia, the Yugoslav National Army (JNA), under control of President Milošević and the government in Belgrade, was primarily comprised of seasoned career military officials, mostly from Serbia, and a mix of conscripted soldiers from across the Balkans. In May 1992, the JNA officially withdrew from Bosnia. With its remnants, including all the heavy weaponry, Radovan Karadžić and his Serb Democratic Party (SDS) founded the Bosnian Serb Army (Army of Republika Srpska). A host of paramilitary forces and irregular militias also operated during the war, many linked to criminal networks. Nearly every political party appears to have had a paramilitary group on its payroll (Woodward 1995: 254).

On April 6, 1992, Serb snipers opened fire on a peace demonstration in Sarajevo.[16] Karadžić promised a swift victory, even stating that the war might be over in six days. To achieve that goal, his troops launched a campaign of terror across the country. Shelling and attacks started in several places, including in Banja Luka, Bosanski Brod, Foča, and Mostar (Malcolm 1996: 235). Paramilitary groups began to pillage villages, rape women, kill men, and terrorize the population. Many of their atrocities were fueled by alcohol and a hypermasculine drinking culture. The strategy was designed to get Bosniaks or Croats to leave Serb-controlled parts of the country on their own. "Arkan's Tigers," a mafia-linked criminal organization commanded by Željko-Arkan Ražnatović, was particularly notorious for its brutality. Ražnatović was a criminal who was wanted by Interpol for organizing surveillance and assassinations of Yugoslav émigrés in Europe during the 1970s and 1980s (Ramet 1992: 261; Malcolm 1996: 266; Mann 2005: 404). His group of "Tigers" was comprised largely of soccer hooligans. In northeastern Bosnia, the Tigers took control of cities like Bijelina and Banja Luka. They essentially functioned as mercenaries: Serb political parties employed them to wreak terror by leaving dead bodies in the streets, cutting utility services, and roaming the city with rocket-propelled grenade launchers and other heavy weaponry

(Malcolm 1996: 236; Mueller 2000). They targeted Muslim leaders, wealthy business owners, and intellectuals, summarily executing many of them in public, as they aimed to eliminate threats to their control and to instill fear in the non-Serb population (Silber and Little 1997). Other paramilitary groups – such as Mirko Jovic's "White Eagles" – waged similar campaigns of terror on the non-Serb population. Within weeks, Serb forces controlled approximately 70 percent of Bosnia.

In Rwanda, paramilitary and irregular militias similarly terrorized on the population, but ultimately aspired to kill all Tutsi within the country's borders as Tutsi civilians because synonymous with the RPF. In contrast, Serb paramilitary and irregular military units were primarily focused on driving non-Serbs from Serb-controlled land it was a campaign of etničko čišćenje (ethnic cleansing) designed to force Muslims and Croats to flee (Mann 2005: 395).[17]

Nationalist politicians also employed these paramilitaries to convince Serb civilians in Bosnia that their Muslim and Croat neighbors posed a threat – echoing the tactics of Hutu extremists in Rwanda. Politicians and extremist media sources used narratives harkening back to Serb persecution during World War II, and Serb authorities even dug up mass graves from World War II as evidence of the persecution Serbs had faced at the hands of their Croat and Muslim neighbors in the recent past (Malcolm 1996: 237; Ramet 2005). In myriad social arenas – including sports, newspapers and radio, and even folk music – Serb leadership expressed the sentiment that Serbs had been persecuted throughout history and were the "Jews of the Balkans" (Ramet 2005: 17). Media distortions of Serbs as victims were common. For instance, Serbian television aired video of Serbs killing Croatians, but declared that the videos were instead of Ustaše atrocities against Serbs during World War II (Mann 2005: 400). Serb elites were vocal about their concerns of an Islamic jihad, and they disseminated the idea that Bosniak elites were marking non-Muslims for death. Rumors even circulated that Muslim Bosnians had drawn up "death lists" of Serb citizens, prompting many ordinary Serbs to support the paramilitaries' brutal tactics (Mann 2005: 398).

The war throughout Bosnia took on profoundly different local dynamics – strictly speaking, it was a series of distinct conflicts featuring different alliances and actors at different points in time (Moore 2013: 42). According to Michael Mann, "Those who were good at violence rose to the top in all the communities when ethnic war erupted" (2005: 418).

This meant that some regions of the country experienced particularly heavy violence, while others were virtually undisturbed. Sarajevo, for example, was subjected to a siege that lasted for years, while other parts of the country experienced rapid ethnic cleansing over the course of a few days or weeks.

In addition to Sarajevo, two regions that experienced heavy violence serve as the focus of the research in subsequent parts of this book. In the northwest, the Krajina region around Banja Luka was home to many Muslims, but was deemed an essential part of the territory linking Serb-controlled regions of Bosnia to Serbia. In the northeast, the Drina Valley region was also deemed politically important because it bordered Serbia. Both experienced high levels of violence during the war, with death tolls second only to Sarajevo (Moore 2013: 43). Non-Serbs who lived in these areas were subject to especially brutal treatment by Serb authorities. As the war broke out, they were fired from their jobs, harassed, profiled, and assaulted. Random episodes of violence frequently broke out. Military units and paramilitary groups – often drunk, loosely organized groups of opportunistic marauders – did the vast majority of the killing, although some civilians occasionally joined in (Mueller 2000). Fearing that Serb persecution would only worsen, hundreds of thousands of non-Serbs in these regions turned over their houses, money, and property in exchange for safe passage to Bosnian army–controlled parts of the country or to neighboring Croatia.[18]

Siege of Sarajevo

The war in Sarajevo featured remarkably different dynamics than in other parts of the country. Before the war, Sarajevo boasted an educated, secular urban population of approximately 500,000. It is estimated that as many as 40 percent of all marriages in the city were between mixed nationality couples (Dizdarevic 1993: 6).[19] Many Americans had been introduced to the city during the 1984 Winter Olympics, as they watched Katerina Witt and Scott Hamilton take home gold medals in figure skating for Germany and the United States, respectively.

Most accounts of the war's beginnings in Sarajevo indicate that, up until the shelling started, most citizens did not believe that war could ever occur in their multiethnic, secular city, where Serbs, Muslims, and Croats had lived together as neighbors for centuries. Sarajevans organized peace protests, where they carried pictures of Tito and banners displaying his "Brotherhood and Unity" slogan (Udovički and Štitkovac

1997: 182). Radovan Karadžić, the president of the newly established Bosnian Serb Republic, had warned Sarajevans in 1991 that if Bosnia were to declare independence, he would attack, adding that "the hell in Bosnia-Hercegovina will be one hundred times worse [than in Croatia] and will bring about the disappearance of the Muslim nation" (quoted in Udovički and Štitkovac 1997: 179). Nevertheless, many Sarajevans poked fun at Karadžić's provincial roots in Montenegro – he was regarded as a backward *seljačina*, a pejorative term for villagers or peasants unfamiliar with city ways – and thereby did not take his threats seriously until the attacks began (Silber and Little 1997: 226). Alija Izetbegović, the Bosniak president, was certain that Karadžić and Milošević were just posturing. As such, few defense systems for the city were initially put in place.

Nationalist Serb forces surrounded Sarajevo in April 1992 and began a siege of the city that would become the longest siege of a capital city in modern history, totaling 1,425 days. Located in a valley between steep mountains and hills, Sarajevo is geographically vulnerable to military attack. Serb forces dug into the mountains and foothills surrounding the city and the rugged terrain granted the attackers superior artillery positions (Andreas 2008). Journalists from all over the world widely covered the siege, and Sarajevo's existing infrastructure could accommodate foreign reporters. For instance, the famed Holiday Inn – located in the heart of what was to become known as "sniper's alley" – became a hotbed of international journalism.

The siege began with six weeks of daily shelling. Izetbegović and other Bosniak political elites organized the new Army of Bosnia-Herzegovina with the Sarajevo Corps, in addition to the Green Beret paramilitary, which was comprised of ordinary men and local gang members. However, the UN arms embargo prevented these defense forces from acquiring heavy weaponry. As a result, criminal gangs played a key role in the city's defense, especially in the first few weeks of the siege (Burg and Shoup 1999: 138; Andreas 2008). Mušan "Caco" Topalović, a former rock musician, became the commander of the Bosnian army's 10th Mountain Brigade, which ruthlessly defended Sarajevo against Serb forces – while also engaging in smuggling, racketeering, rape, and murder (Mann 2005: 418; Moll 2015).

During the bombardment, Serb forces fired thousands of shells and mortar rounds indiscriminately on Sarajevo's skyline, hitting historic buildings, infrastructure from the 1984 Olympics, and the towering apartment complexes built during the socialist era. No structure was spared.

Food supplies and links to the outside world were soon cut off. Prominent buildings like the library, the post office, the town hall, and Hotel Europa were set ablaze. Shelling was seemingly at random and designed to force the population's flight, although Bosnian forces refused to allow people to leave the city if they could feasibly assist in its defense. They feared that if they allowed free flight, nobody would remain to defend the city (Human Rights Watch 1994c). A black market cabal sprang up, regulating food rations within the city and keeping prices (and demand for deutsche marks) high (Silber and Little 1997: 254). The UNHCR directed relief operations in the city, which were far from sufficient to sustain residents' well-being. Sarajevo's residents found water at the Sarajevo Brewery, which happened to sit upon a large underground spring, and – risking sniper fire – walked there from all across the Bosnian-controlled parts of the city. The Bosnian army eventually constructed a tunnel under the frontline that allowed food and medical supplies to be transported into the city. This tunnel became the city's lifeline throughout the siege.

Destroy and Create

During the siege, there were many examples of resistance, previewing some of the war-caused shifts I discuss in the following chapters. When militaries erected barricades throughout the city, women set up "counter-barricades," where they served traditional Bosnian food like *čevapcici* and *burek* as a way of rejecting the war (Udovički and Štitkovac 1997: 182). People of different ethnicities in frontline neighborhoods like Dobrinje or Butmir joined together to defend their homes. An underground art scene emerged, and theater performances – often poking fun at the absurdity of war – were popular. Artists created public art installations made from cars, buildings, and other machinery destroyed by aerial shelling. A vibrant nightclub scene flourished, reflecting an escapist attitude common among Sarajevans. People would drink and dance all night until it seemed safer to go home in the light of morning (Gjelten 1995; Maček 2009, multiple interviews). Sarajevans even produced a satirical "Sarajevo Survival Guide" in 1993, which humorously captured the plight of the city's residents. Written in the style of a Michelin travel guide, it purported to give readers tips on how to survive during the siege. The guide poked fun at the shortage of food in the city, noting, "Combined with rice, and well seasoned, everything becomes edible. Each person in Sarajevo is very close to [being] an ideal macrobiotician, a real role-model for the health-conscious, diet-troubled West."

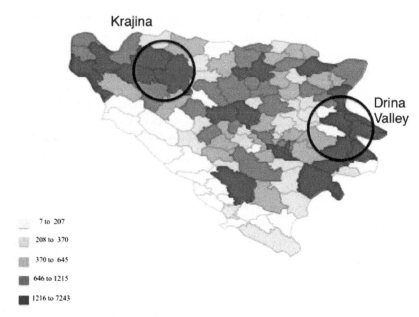

FIGURE 5.1 Rates of Killing by District in Bosnia-Herzegovina with
Focus Regions
Map courtesy of Nyseth Brehm (2014)

On February 5, 1994, a mortar shell landed on a packed market in
downtown Sarajevo, killing sixty-nine civilians and wounding more than
200 others. This event came at the close of a month in which shelling
had been particularly destructive, as a school and a stadium of soccer
fans had already been hit (Burg and Shoup 1999: 145). As a result, the
United States intensified its pressure on NATO to intervene. Before long,
NATO issued Serb leadership an ultimatum: implement a ceasefire and
establish a buffer against heavy weapons around the city, or risk NATO
air strikes (Malcolm 1996: 255; Silber and Little 1997: 313–315). When
another mortar attack on August 28, 1995 killed thirty-seven people at
a market in Sarajevo, NATO finally decided to launch massive air strikes
against Serb military installations (Malcolm 1996: 266). After two weeks
of continuous bombardment, General Ratko Mladić gave in and withdrew most of his heavy weaponry from the zone around Sarajevo. The
longest siege in modern history was nearly over. When the war finally
ended with the signature of the Dayton Accords in December 1995, more
than 11,500 people had perished within Sarajevo.

Bosanska Krajina

The dynamics of war outside Sarajevo were very different. The Krajina region was essential to the Serb military strategy, as it was home to Banja Luka, the second largest city in Bosnia. As such, it was host to some of the bloodiest violence during the war. Prior to the war, the region was comprised of approximately 44 percent Serbs, 40 percent Bosniaks, 7 percent Croats, and 5 percent "Yugoslavs" (Socialist Republic of Bosnia and Herzegovina 1991). This translated to an estimated 550,000 Bosniak and Croat citizens. As the site of massive ethnic expulsions and killings during the war, by June 1994, fewer than 50,000 of these non-Serbs remained (Human Rights Watch 1994d). By 1997, this number had decreased to fewer than 20,000 (Amnesty International 1997).

Ethnic cleansing in the region was much more bureaucratically organized than in Rwanda. As Serb forces took control, every municipality opened a "Bureau for Population Exchange." Non-Serbs had to register their land and property at these offices, often surrendering all claims to their belongings as a prerequisite to submitting a request for permission to leave the area (Silber and Little 1997: 246). In general, Serb authorities only granted women and children permission to leave (Human Rights Watch 1994d). Serb leadership often asked non-Serbs to sign an oath of loyalty to the Serb leadership. In cities like Prijedor, authorities required non-Serbs to wear a white armband in public and to hang white towels from their houses to signal that a Bosniak or Croat family lived there. Non-Serbs were also placed under a curfew and were forbidden to gather in groups, drive cars, or congregate in public places (Power 2003: 250). Tabiha, who lived in a town near Prijedor, explained, "if you did not wear [a white armband], and you went outside, they would catch you. If you were not Serbian and you did not wear it, they would beat the hell out of you or kill you" (Interview #52, May 2013; see also Human Rights Watch 1992).

A campaign of terror throughout the region began in earnest in April 1992. Paramilitary groups went door to door and tormented the population – several months of killing near Prijedor and the surrounding area left an estimated 5,000 people (almost all men) dead. Militias razed mosques and Catholic churches, attempting to symbolically purify the land for new Serb inhabitants. Over the course of a few days in May 1992, Serb forces killed hundreds – if not thousands – of people in Kozarac, a predominantly Bosniak town. One witness to this massacre described how "blood ran red in the streets."[20] Many Bosniaks and

Croats did all they could to escape the region. Some left with no warning at all, grabbing their most valuable possessions and traveling on foot to Croatia or south to Travnik, a town controlled by the Bosnian army. Those granted formal permission to leave could travel by bus or train, so long as they had the financial resources to pay for exit tolls and tickets. Others decided to stay put, feeling that the risk of death was preferable to leaving their homes and property. Croatia eventually shut the door to further refugees, trapping many non-Serbs in the Krajina region. Non-Serb men who remained were often sent to work in labor camps where they were effectively used as slave labor, and others were sent to the concentration camps (Human Rights Watch 1994d). Roy Gutman, the first journalist to document the existence of the camps during the war, revealed their horror to the world. In an article for *Newsday* on August 2, 1992, Gutman wrote:

In one concentration camp, a former iron-mining complex at Omarska in north-west Bosnia, more than a thousand Muslim and Croat civilians were held in metal cages without sanitation, adequate food, exercise or access to the outside world. (Gutman 1993: 44–45)

Besides Omarska, several other detention camps gained notoriety, including Trnopolje and Manjača, which were largely transit camps, and Keraterm, another concentration camp (Udovički and Štitkovac 1997). Serb forces set up many more small, temporary detention centers throughout the country. Some estimates put the number of camps in the country as high as 677, although most of these were small, temporary detainment facilities like schools or houses. Camps became the site of myriad atrocities, including murder, torture, and the rape of men and women. In many camps, prisoners were starved and forced to wallow in their own excrement (Human Rights Watch 1992).

Unlike Nazi death camps, these camps were not designed to exterminate non-Serbs, although many people were killed in the camps. Rather, they were designed to dehumanize the population and to prevent men of military age from picking up arms against Serb forces. Gutman's reports were instrumental in bringing international attention to the camps and later won him a Pulitzer Prize. A British television crew and the *Guardian*'s Ed Vulliamy were also able to capture images of emaciated prisoners in Trnopolje and Omarska, prompting widespread condemnation and shifting international opinions toward favoring military intervention (Power 2003: 276; Vulliamy 2012). The images of these camps led the UN Security Council to rally the international community against the war, which ultimately compelled the Serb leadership to shut down the camps (Gutman 1993: 63; Power 2003: 270–272).

The violence in the Krajina region died down by 1994; by that point, most non-Serbs had been expelled from the region. Many non-Serbs who were pushed out of cities like Prijedor and Banja Luka settled in territory controlled by the Bosnian army, such as in Sanski Most or further south in Travnik.

War in the Drina Valley

The region around the Drina Valley in northeastern Bosnia also experienced intense violence during the war. The Drina River flows between Serbia and Bosnia and has provided a territorial border between the two states for centuries. Serbian nationalists and folklore, however, refer to it as the "backbone of the Serbian national body" (Bećirević 2014). The goal of "Greater Serbia" included expanding Serbian territory across the river. The towns of Zvornik, Vlasenica, Bratunac, Foča, Višegrad, and Srebrenica are all in this region. While the Srebrenica massacre is well known, much of the violence that unfolded in this region was also brutal and severe (Bećirević 2014).

The offensive in the Drina Valley began immediately after Bosnia's declaration of independence, as the JNA cut off travel on the major roads in the region. Non-Serbs were ordered to turn over their weapons, and the violence then followed a predictable pattern. Paramilitary groups – including Arkan's Tigers, the White Eagles, and Serb territorial defense units – supported the JNA in attacking Zvornik. Bosnian army guerrilla forces retaliated, particularly in the Tuzla-Zvorik and Bratunac areas (Burg and Shoup 1999). Serb citizens were sheltered, while non-Serbs were targeted for looting and sporadic murder. Violence escalated as houses were burnt down and non-Serbs were indiscriminately killed. Arkan's snipers shot at people from the roofs of tall buildings, generating fear and uncertainty (Bećirević 2014: 91). After Serb forces took control of a city, they installed a local government that discriminated against Bosniak (Muslim) residents, confiscating their property or forcing their expulsion. Similar patterns of violence occurred in other towns and cities in the region. Concentration camps in Foča, Sušica, and elsewhere mirrored those in the Krajina region, as non-Serbs were detained in miserable conditions, subjected to serial rape, forced labor, torture, and even death (Bećirević 2014: 122).

The Drina Valley is infamous for the slaughter of 8,000 men and boys at Srebrenica in July 1995. As Serbian forces gained control of much of the territory in the region, Srebrenica and the towns of Žepa and Goražde became Muslim-controlled enclaves within Serb territory. Srebrenica is a small town built around a silver mine, located approximately nine miles from the border of Serbia. In the beginning of the war, the town had been the site of an early Serb defeat at the hands of a local Bosniak militia (Burg and Shoup 1999: 133). As a result, the area had become a safe haven for approximately 40,000 non-Serbs within ever-expanding Serb territory. Bosnian territorial defense units, led by Naser Orić, had periodically used the enclave for hit-and-run raids against Serb forces (Silber and Little 1997: 346; Burg and Shoup 1999: 140). In 1993, Philippe Morillon, the UN force commander, visited Srebrenica and declared it a UN Safe Zone, although such safety could not be militarily enforced under the UN's commitment to neutrality.[21] Serb forces surrounded Srebrenica for most of the war, and thus those stuck in Srebrenica lived in a precarious state of hunger and violence. They depended on aid deliveries from the UNHCR, although conditions deteriorated as the war continued.

On July 6, 1995, Serb forces under the command of General Mladić began aggressively shelling Srebrenica, and took control over the enclave on July 11. The Dutch UN peacekeepers were put in an untenable position, as they were charged with protecting the civilian population but forbidden from using force against the advancing Serb forces. The UN also refused to allow air strikes to thwart the Serb takeover. The 40,000 Muslims who had been living in the enclave sought to escape, and more than 20,000 – primarily women, children, and the elderly – went to the UN base at Potočari, a small town adjacent to Srebrenica. But the UN peacekeepers let only a portion of these escapees on the base, and some days later expelled them again. The Serb forces who had reached Potočari took away the men, and eventually loaded the women, elderly, and young children onto buses that took them to Tuzla. Serb forces selected women from the crowd and raped them in a nearby battery factory.[22] While many had gone to Potočari, approximately 15,000 men abandoned Srebrenica through the forest, fearing they would be killed when Serbs took control of the area. This group passed through minefields on the way to Tuzla, where they hoped to find safety. But Serb forces began to hunt down those who had escaped and to systematically kill them. In the days after July 11, Serb forces rounded up an estimated 7,000 to 8,000 of these men, loaded them onto trucks, and then brought them to different spots where they were summarily executed (Silber and Little 1997: 345–350; Power 2003: 391–405). This massacre was ultimately revealed to be the largest massacre on European soil since World War II. The massive losses in the Drina valley region meant that a huge number of Bosnian women lost multiple male relatives – sons, brothers, husbands, and fathers. I discuss the impact of these demographic losses in Chapters 6 and 7.[23]

Additional War Dynamics

In addition to the conflict between Serbs and non-Serbs, there was also a more limited conflict between Croat and Bosniak forces, although it is not a focus of the analysis that follows. Franjo Tudjman, the president of Croatia, conspired with Serbia's Milošević early in the war to divide Bosnia into Croat and Serb portions. The Croat part of the state, called Herceg-Bosna, encompassed much of Herzegovina and western Bosnia. There are debates in the scholarship about who was the aggressor of the violence in this region (see Ramet 2005 for a discussion). Most of the fighting on this front occurred in the Lašva Valley (to the north and west of Sarajevo) and in the Neretva Valley near Mostar. In this region, the Bosnian-Croat army (Hrvatsko Vijeće Obrane or HVO), controlled from Zagreb, and other Croat leaders claimed that much of the southern part of Bosnia (most of it in Herzegovina) belonged to Croatia. Bosniaks were told to go to Iraq or Turkey (Mann 2005: 409; citing the Blaškić trial, September 26, 1997). In Mostar, Croatian forces bombed the city in an attempt to partition it between Muslim and Croatian sides. The town's Turkish quarter was destroyed in the shelling, as was the famous Old Bridge (Stari Most) – widely considered the most impressive and beautiful structure in the Balkans (Udovički and Štitkovac 1997: 194).

Croat and Bosniak forces both committed violence and looting during this phase of the conflict. Croat forces committed several large-scale massacres of Muslims, such as in the Ahmići massacre in April 1993, during which Croat forces killed an estimated 116 Bosniaks and destroyed Bosniak-owned houses and mosques (Mann 2005: 413). In September 1993, Bosniak forces massacred an estimated sixty Croats in Uzdol and elsewhere in the area (Cigar 1995: 137). Overt hostilities between Muslims and Croats ended in 1994 when both sides signed a ceasefire agreement that put plans in place for a federation between the two parties.

SEXUALIZED VIOLENCE

Like in Rwanda, in all the war's varied fronts, rape and sexualized violence were systematic. While women were particularly targeted for sexualized violence and received the bulk of the media attention devoted to the issue, many men were subjected to it as well (Žarkov 2001).[24] Sexual violence followed nationalist ideologies that saw the violation of female bodies as the ultimate defeat of the Muslim nation (Brownmiller 1994; Mostov 1995; Skjelsbæk 2006). Serb forces used rape as a formal military tactic sanctioned by their commanding officers (ICTY testimonies; Amnesty International 1993). Non-Serb women of all ages were targeted, including pregnant women and some middle-aged women; however, attractive, young, wealthy, and educated women were the most frequent targets (Gutman 1993; Mostov 1995). Militias sometimes forced men to rape their wives or mothers while the rest of their family watched as an attempt to emasculate them and their male relatives, who were helpless to intervene. Forced pregnancies were another strategy, as non-Serb women were detained in rape camps, impregnated, and then released after their pregnancies had progressed to the point that abortion was no longer possible (Helms 2013: 58). With these war rapes, Serb forces aimed to damage women's future ability to serve as mothers of the Bosnian nation, as any children born of rape would be Serbs. This horrendous campaign was an essential part of the military strategy aimed at terrifying non-Serbs into leaving Serb-controlled parts of the country.

The most egregious perpetrators of sexualized violence were Serb paramilitaries, who often wore long beards and dressed in the style of World War II Chetnik militias. They displayed *kokarda* emblems on their clothes: the classic crest features a two-headed eagle and four stylized "Cs" symbolizing the extremist slogan, "Only Unity Saves the Serbs" (*Samo Sloga Srbina Spasava*, or in Cyrillic, Само слога Србина спасава). Many accounts of rape reported by Human Rights Watch and during the ICTY hearings characterized these men as dirty – sometimes covered in blood – and intoxicated. Moreover, some women reported that rapists took small white pills before the rapes, supposedly to enhance their virility. Serb leaders like Milošević and Karadzić rejected reports that their militias engaged in systematic rape of non-Serb women. They responded by blaming Muslim women for being temptresses who seduced men into their beds, and alleged that Muslims were selling Serb women to be slaves in the Middle East (Cigar 1995: 93).

The use of sexualized violence as a tactic in the Bosnian war had important implications for the treatment of women in the war's aftermath, particularly as evidence about mass rapes in Rwanda emerged around the same time. International agencies and journalists who learned of the widespread rape of women began focusing extensive resources and attention to this issue (Slapšak 2001: 174–175). Roy Gutman, in particular, wrote dozens of stories in *Newsday* recounting graphic rapes that survivors had described to him. These stories were sometimes accompanied by an image of various "victims" – poor, displaced, crying Muslim women. Titles of these photographs reprinted in his book (Gutman 1993) included "Tuzle: Distraught, hurt, angry. Rape victims from Brezovo Polje" or simply "Rape Victim from Brezovo Polje." Such depictions immediately brought an international gaze of pity to women in Bosnia. Pope John Paul II even chimed in, urging women who became pregnant from rape to accept their children, rather than seek an abortion (Nikolić-Ristanović 1998: 236). This international involvement positioned women as agency-less victims who needed to be saved, with no control over their situation. International journalists were not alone in exploiting the image of raped women to sell newspapers. Bosnian politicians also referenced widespread sexual violence in their appeals for international military assistance, and even the Bosnian ambassador to the UN declared in 1993 that "Bosnia-Herzegovina is being gang-raped" (quoted in Helms 2013: 82).

Such depictions undoubtedly contain some truth. And yet, as I show in Chapter 8, these depictions are not neutral; they were political – and ultimately depoliticizing – for women. The overwhelming focus of this attention was on rapes perpetrated by Serbs against non-Serbs, implicitly ignoring the hundreds (if not thousands) of episodes of sexualized violence that did not conform to the macro-level logic of the war. Moreover, women who were identified as raped were stigmatized, shunned, and effectively banned from their communities. "Rape victim" became their foremost identity in the eyes of the West and its humanitarian aid interlocutors (see Mertus 1994; Cockburn 2001). By 1998, raped women were eligible for financial support from the Bosnian government – to receive funds, they had to register as rape victims and meet several other requirements. Many of these women, however, articulated their experience not as victimization, but rather as surviving.[25] Focusing on rape victims created a perverse hierarchy of victimhood, in which women who had experienced sexualized violence were elevated above those who had not. Moreover, the global media depicted Bosniak women as the *most* victimized, while Serb (and sometimes Croat) victims of sexual violence were deemed *lesser* victims. This was due to the debate over genocide, in which rape was conceptualized as directed only against Muslims. In Chapter 8, I discuss various reasons why this focus was problematic and shaped the way women could organize in the aftermath.

By the end of the war in 1995, fighting had left approximately 100,000 dead. Ninety percent of the dead were men, 80 percent were Bosniaks, and 60 percent were combatants (Research and Documentation Center 2013).[26] An estimated 1.2 million people emigrated from Bosnia to seek refuge in neighboring countries, and an additional one million people were displaced within Bosnia's borders. Monetary damages caused by the war were estimated at $50–70 billion (World Bank 1997).

The violence in Bosnia came to an end with the signing of the Dayton Accords on November 21, 1995.[27] The agreement provided a new constitution, promised the safe return of refugees, and outlined a plan for the presence of international peacekeeping troops to oversee the peace (International Crisis Group 2000). It also assigned 60,000 international troops under NATO command to supervise the peace agreement's implementation (Malcolm 1996: 270). Dayton also made Bosnia a signatory to all major international human rights treaties, including the Convention on the Elimination of All Forms of Discrimination Against Women (CEDAW)), and moreover granted the international community the legal framework to intervene in Bosnia in response to certain crisis situations.

Most significantly, the accords established a consociational state in Bosnia that divided the country into two entities: 51 percent of the territory of Bosnia was included in the Muslim–Croat Federation, while the other 49 percent was codified as Republika Srpska. Sarajevo remained intact and was included in the Federation territory, although several outlying suburbs were carved out as part of Republika Srpska. Each entity was given its own parliament, executive branch, police force, army, and bureaucratic institutions. Overseeing the union was a weak central state government, which consisted of a rotating tripartite presidency with Serb, Croat, and Bosniak representatives. In addition, the agreement prescribed the central state a parliament and a council of ministers. The vast majority of laws and policies, however, would be determined within the two entities. Ultimately, this created five levels of government in Bosnia: state, entity, canton, city, and municipality. Ethnic and regional quotas were implemented in state institutions at all levels of government.

The Office of the High Representative (OHR), appointed by the internationally led Peace Implementation Council, was charged with overseeing the implementation of this new system. At the beginning the OHR had few powers of enforcement, and was charged with monitoring and

MAP 5 Dayton Divisions of Bosnia-Herzegovina

advising the implementation of the accords and mediating between the various nationalist parties. In 1997, the Peace Implementation Council granted the OHR new powers – known as the Bonn powers – allowing it to dismiss elected officials who blocked the implementation of the Dayton Accords. During subsequent multilateral conferences, foreign countries pledged reconstruction and recovery assistance (Evans-Kent and Bleiker 2003).

Ultimately, the entire structure of the Dayton Accords was premised on the false understanding that "ancient ethnic hatreds" had driven the war. As others have shown, this depiction simplifies and distorts the actual origins of the conflict (Woodward 1995; Silber and Little 1997; Lampe 2000). But, by resting on this assumption, Dayton proposed that the solution to the conflict lay in the separation of different ethnic groups, granting Serb perpetrators of the war their goal of an ethnically pure territory, even if it remained within Bosnia.[28] Dayton did not satisfy any party to the conflict and christened a political system that was virtually unworkable, as it required consensus between diametrically opposed political groups. It also established that only Bosnia's three "constituent peoples" – Serbs, Croats, and Bosniaks – can stand for election to the presidency and the upper house of parliament (McMahon 2004; Bjorkdahl 2012). This definition excludes, for example, Roma and Jewish people, who also live in Bosnia, and has thereby thwarted Bosnia's accession to the European Union in recent years.

The only truly punitive measure included in the Dayton Accords was that people indicted by the International Criminal Tribunal for the Former Yugoslavia (ICTY) could not hold public office. Through 2016, however, the Tribunal indicted only 161 people. Moreover, the power granted to the OHR threatened to usurp the legitimacy and power of local political institutions (Bougarel, Helms, and Duijzings 2007: 9; Moore 2013). Throughout the next decade, the OHR was an extremely important player in Bosnia's political landscape. In general, the political system became exceedingly bureaucratic and inept at raising taxes or rents from the population, as "grey economies" emerged and criminal and dysfunctional patrimonial economic structures persisted. The dysfunction allowed war entrepreneurs to capitalize on the chaos, and they secured their gains through the emphasis on privatization that accompanied the postwar era (Pugh 2002; Andreas 2004). Vertically integrated enterprises, controlled by political parties, linked the welfare of supporters to economic empires that consisted of hotels, casinos, restaurants, banks, tobacco, forestry, telecommunications, energy, water companies, and more. In short, Dayton codified a political system in which political elites control rents and government revenues for their own gain (Pugh 2002: 471).

Women were completely shut out from the negotiations in Dayton (Bjorkdahl 2012; Cockburn 2013a). This was despite the fact that many women's organizations emerged during the war, as I discuss in the following chapters. Dayton did not include any provisions to promote women or to secure their presence in postwar governing institutions. As such, "the Dayton Peace Agreement did not diminish, but rather affirmed, patriarchal nationalism as a dominant ideology and social system in postwar [Bosnia]" (Cockburn 2013a: 27). This exclusion of women from the peace process came at an extraordinary cost to the possibility for long-term peace and security in Bosnia.

In the years since, Bosnia's political system has been mired in corruption, stagnation, and inefficiency. Nationalist leaders of Republika Srpska continue to antagonize the Bosniak population by using inflammatory nationalist rhetoric and hate speech, and persistently claim that they want to secede from Bosnia and become independent. Milorad Dodik, who came to power in 2006 in Republika Srpska, has constantly sought to destabilize the state by undermining the Dayton system and threatening secession. Today, non-Serbs face unflagging discrimination within Serb-controlled areas, while Serbs face pervasive discrimination in the Federation.

The literature on postwar Bosnia is extensive, but it has largely been dominated by analyses of Dayton and institutional and electoral issues (Bougarel et al. 2007: 13). The separation of various nationalities into distinct territorial spaces has preoccupied scholars, producing studies of political quotas and the fraught political party system. There is considerably less research "from below" on the legacy of war for ordinary Bosnians (see Clark 2010; Helms 2013; and Moore 2013 for exceptions). To understand how the war impacted ordinary Bosnians – particularly ordinary Bosnian women – it is essential to return to the specific shifts caused by the war. This is my goal in the next chapter.

6

War and Structural Shifts in Bosnia-Herzegovina

The war in Bosnia – and elsewhere in former Yugoslavia – represented a profound disjuncture with the past. It marked an end to the idea of Yugoslavia, a multiethnic state in which national identities were subsumed under a supranational one, and the beginning of massive structural and institutional destruction. Of course, the persistence of patriarchal values and nationalist political parties suggests there was also much continuity with the prewar era. In this chapter, I outline three transformative shifts that resulted from the war as they related to women's political engagement in the aftermath. In the next chapter, I turn to the impact of those three shifts on women's political mobilization.

DEMOGRAPHIC SHIFTS

When the Dayton Accords brought the war in Bosnia to a close in 1995, approximately 100,000 were dead, one million had fled across the border, and another one million were internally displaced (UNHCR 1998; Research and Documentation Center 2007). This meant that approximately one-half of the prewar population was displaced from their homes. The manifestations of this demographic shift were twofold: first, the war led to a shift in the population distribution, based on the emigration and internal displacement of nearly half of the country's population. Second, the disproportionate death, displacement, and conscription of men led to shifts in the sex composition of the population, which led to an increase in women-headed households (see Figure 6.1). Like in Rwanda, these two population shifts led to massive changes in the demographic composition of many parts of Bosnia. One difference from

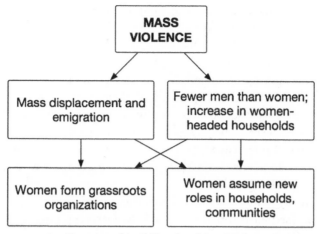

FIGURE 6.1 Demographic Shifts after Mass Violence in Bosnia

Rwanda, however, was that there was no influx of returning refugees from abroad.

Displacement and Population Movement

Emigration

During the war, more than one million Bosnians (approximately 27 percent of the prewar population) fled the country and sought refuge in neighboring states (UNHCR 1996). Bosniaks comprised the largest number of these refugees (610,000), followed by Bosnian Croats (307,000), Bosnian Serbs (253,000), and others (23,000) (International Crisis Group 1997: 10). The majority of these refugees initially fled to Croatia, before being granted temporary or permanent asylum in twenty-five different countries around the world. Bosniaks and Bosnian Croats often fled to Croatia first, while Bosnian Serbs were more likely to flee to Serbia or Montenegro, before traveling on to other destinations. The largest number of refugees fled during the first months of the war; by the end of October 1992, 650,000 Bosnians were already in Croatia.[1] The majority of these refugees were women, children, and men over fifty-five years of age (Meznaric and Zlatkovic 1992: 4). To get to Croatia, they used whatever savings they had to catch buses and took with them whatever they could carry – valuables, food, and little else. While women and children were allowed to enter Croatia and claim refugee status, Bosnian authorities usually forced men of fighting age to return and fight for Bosnia (Meznaric and Zlatkovic 1992: 4).

As fighting escalated, Croatia established the Office for Refugees and Displaced Persons to handle the influx of refugees. This office required people entering Croatia to produce letters of sponsorship from relatives or friends abroad that guaranteed them a place to stay. In June 1992, Croatia closed its borders; afterward, Bosnians lacking this letter of sponsorship were turned away as they attempted to cross (Meznaric and Zlatkovic Winter 1992). The wealthy were most able to flee, as they were more likely to have business or family abroad. Some without letters crossed the border illegally.

While many refugees first fled to neighboring countries, they were eventually resettled through the UNHCR. Germany hosted the largest number of Bosnian refugees, followed by Croatia, Sweden, Canada, the United States, and Australia (International Crisis Group 1997). This refugee resettlement process was lengthy and precarious. For many, it took several years to achieve permanent status in any one place (Eastmond 2006). While the Dayton Accords encouraged repatriation, government inefficiency and ongoing hostilities in Bosnia complicated and slowed down this process, and many refugees elected to stay abroad. By 1996, only about 88,000 refugees had returned to their homes within Bosnia (International Crisis Group 1997: 11).

While displaced, some refugees in Croatia began to organize health care, education, and various other activities within the camps. These organizations brought refugees together in new social networks as they collected information about deceased and missing persons, facilitated the distribution of aid, coordinated lectures and social activities, and orchestrated communication between refugees and their families (Interviews #8, #22; Mertus 2000). Women were at the forefront of these efforts, as they comprised the numerical majority in the camps and took on caregiving roles for those beyond their immediate families. Many of the informal organizations and networks that formed in these camps were eventually formalized as official organizations that continued to operate after their members had returned to Bosnia.

Internal Displacement
Bosnians driven from their homes found their way to IDP camps, or to refuge with friends or family members. Many of the displaced congregated in towns and cities, resulting in the increasing ethnic homogenization and urbanization of the population (UNHCR 1998). Once

Croatia closed its borders, tens of thousands of the displaced began congregating in Bosnian border towns like Capljina, Ljubuski, Posusje, and Livno, swelling their numbers far beyond capacity. Some had survived treacherous journeys across Bosnia's mountainous regions to escape the violence and were dismayed when they discovered they could not leave the country. Stuck, and often without travel documents or money, these people took shelter wherever possible. Conditions of life for the displaced were abysmal, and shelter was always in short supply (World Bank 1996; International Crisis Group 1997). Writing in the *Los Angeles Times* in November 1992, Carol Williams described the scene at these border towns:

Old women, children and furloughed fighters, exhausted by their dangerous exodus, sleep on the trampled grass. Desperate mothers rummage through cartons of donated clothing for their children; others cluster around aid workers doling out food. The ground is littered with empty cans and crushed containers. There is a pervasive stench of human waste ... they spend their days wandering the town's few commercial streets to ogle goods they cannot buy, scurrying at the sound of each general alert siren to bomb shelters and to log lean-tos designed to stop shrapnel. At night they bed down on blankets and cardboard at hastily converted public buildings, like the day-care centers no longer needed because most industry has been shut down by the war.[2]

This description echoes many others from the period. Although the general standard of living in Bosnia was far above that in Rwanda and there was little risk of starvation or the widespread outbreak of disease,[3] the displaced were nevertheless subject to prolonged periods of insecurity, hunger, and homelessness.

These processes of displacement had significant impacts on gendered social life. Before the war, social activity in Bosnia (particularly in rural areas) was largely gender-segregated. Women visited with neighbors and friends over coffee or after work, while men met over politics, in bars, or over sports (Bringa 1995; Helms 2013). These forms of social activity were highly localized, as women's social networks were confined to their neighborhoods or villages. Within the household, women's roles were further constrained by social expectations that they would defer to their husbands and remain silent about physical abuse in the family. As millions of people were uprooted from their homes, these social networks and socially prescribed gender roles were disrupted. Women established new social networks with others in refugee camps and in displaced persons' centers, or simply with new neighbors as they found themselves relocated to different regions of the country. Some women accessed the Internet and email – a new phenomenon at the time – which allowed them to communicate and spread information via their networks (Slapšak 2001: 181). In these situations of displacement, women discovered that they faced common struggles with other women. IDP camps, which were often constructed in schools or other large municipal facilities, became a physical space for building solidarity, particularly among trauma survivors.

Dr. Branka Antić-Štauber, founder of the women's health NGO Snaga Žene (Power of Women), described how many women created new bonds of sisterhood and friendship while in the displaced persons' camps:

> Even in the refugee camps women do not want to separate because they bond very strong, they have this common problem that keeps them together and they really feel sad when some of them are leaving. They talk about it, they talk about how they are sad because the government wants them to go to their places because they will separate at that time … It's extremely important in this group that they bonded, they share the same problems. They realize that they have strength as a group and now they don't want to be individuals, they want to act as a group. (Interview #78, July 2010)

As Dr. Antić-Štauber describes, women were reluctant to return to their homes after the war, where they feared retriggering psychological wounds and general insecurity. These new solidarity networks and friendship groups were critical in facilitating the formation of organizations discussed in the next chapter, and eventually reflected a form of women's political mobilizing unique to the postwar period.

Demographic Shifts Lead to Sex Imbalance

According to the 1991 census, Bosnia's population was 49.8 percent male (2,183,795) and 50.2 percent female (2,193,238). At least 93,000 men were killed during the war (representing 90 percent of the war dead; Research and Documentation Center 2013). The first census after the war was not conducted until 2013 because of the fraught political tensions within the country and the potential for census data to bolster or undermine various nationalist political strategies. Thus, official figures for the sex ratio immediately after the war do not exist; the best estimates are that there were 0.92 men/women (i.e., 92 men for every 100 women). The 2013 census, however, gives us some additional clues. The 2013 sex ratio across the country is estimated to be 0.95 men/woman. But it is particularly imbalanced among older generations – in other words, those who were in their mid-forties during the violence. Among Bosnians older than sixty-five years, the sex ratio is 0.63 men/women (Census Bureau of Bosnia-Herzegovina 2013).

The loss of men during the war in Bosnia compelled many women to engage in new roles in their families and communities in similar ways as in Rwanda. Women whose husbands, brothers, or fathers were killed, incarcerated, or displaced in various regional armies became temporary or permanent heads of their households (Mrvic-Petrović and Stevanović 2000). Temporarily heading households was especially common, since between 400,000 and 500,000 Bosnian men were conscripted during the war (Bougarel 2006; Staveteig 2011). By 1996, between 200,000 and 400,000 of these men were still in the process of being demobilized (World Bank 1996: 12). Refugee families were especially likely to be incomplete, because women and men were often separated during campaigns of ethnic cleansing, and authorities often only permitted women to cross international borders. Even in areas of the country that remained under Bosnian control, men joined territorial defense units or regional armies to fight, or sometimes left the country or went into hiding to avoid military duty.[4] Some men also stayed behind to defend their property or houses from attacking forces, while women left for the safety of nearby refugee camps or safe zones. In permanently incomplete families, men were killed (or died from other causes during the war). These widows faced additional challenges of locating their loved ones' bodies and fighting for justice, as will be discussed more in the next chapter.

The Institute for Pedagogical Research conducted one of the few studies on family incompleteness during the Bosnian war. It found that 92 percent of all families had both a father and a mother prior to the war. After families were displaced, however, only 50 percent were complete. Of these, 80 percent were missing the father or "head of household" (Mrvic-Petrović and Stevanović 2000). Widowhood also increased: before the war only 2.3 percent of women between the ages of thirty-five and thirty-nine were widows, while after the war this number jumped to 7.4 percent. The percentage increased further in the older age cohorts: among those aged forty to forty-four, the percentage of widows jumped from 4.2 percent to 11.1 percent; whereas in the age group from forty-five to forty-nine, the percentage of widows increased from 7.3 percent to 13.1 percent in the war's aftermath (Staveteig 2011: 86).[5] Survey reports also indicate that this demographic sex imbalance was particularly pronounced in areas of the country that had seen high rates of killing of men, including the areas around Srebrenica and Prijedor. In these areas – and in the communities where the non-Serbs "cleansed" from these areas had settled – there were high numbers of women-led families (UNICEF 2009).

Like in Rwanda, many of my interviewees also indicated that beyond an actual demographic loss of men, there was a more symbolic loss of men's capacity as well. This was because "men experienced a sort of collapse" (Interview #64, June 2013) – they turned to alcohol, became depressed, and gradually retreated from communal or family life after the violence (Wings of Hope 2013). Psychologists and INGOs studied war's traumatic impact on various groups after the war, including on refugees, rape survivors, children, and ex-combatants. Overall, the best estimates suggest that between 18 percent and 38 percent of the population suffered from PTSD during or immediately after the violence (World Bank 1996: 13; Nelson 2003: 308).[6] At least six of the women I interviewed indicated that the war left their husbands or fathers physically or psychologically injured, and one widow indicated that she was unlikely to marry again given the mental instability of any available men.[7] Approximately 200,000 men were wounded during the war, which may have compounded war-related trauma (World Bank 1999; Walsh 2000). Several women I interviewed suggested that their husbands' drinking made it difficult for them to work. At least a dozen of my interviews suggested there was a high rate of prescription drug usage in Bosnia; one said that people take drugs "to kill all the emotions inside" (Interview #38, May 2013). Another referred to the country as a "Prozac nation" (Interview #35, May 2013). This symbolic loss of men's capacity also contributed to a sense in many families that women needed to take on new roles in order to help their families survive.

ECONOMIC SHIFTS

In addition to demographic shifts, Bosnia underwent massive economic shifts both before and during the war. In 1990, per capita income in Bosnia was $2,365 (in current U.S. dollars). As Yugoslavia's political institutions fractured in the early 1990s, the regional economy also fell apart. The outbreak of violence in Croatia and Slovenia disrupted the flow of goods between states and eventually across the region. Serbia implemented a boycott of goods coming from countries that had declared independence. In 1991, Serbia and Croatia imposed an embargo on goods and foodstuffs going into Bosnia in order to destroy the Bosnian economy, force the country to capitulate, and partition its territory into Croat and Serbian parts. This was particularly devastating because the country depended on food imports. To counter this embargo, the Bosnian government prohibited Bosnian firms from selling a lengthy list of domestic products to Serbia or Croatia, including major exports like coal, iron, chemicals, lumber, or poultry (Woodward 1995: 264, 277). Bosnia's exports to Western markets also ceased. By 1991, 22.8 percent of Bosnians were unemployed (International Labor Organization 1991; Kalyvas and Sambanis 2005: 207). Women were particularly vulnerable during this time, and more likely to be laid off from work than their male counterparts (Interviews #24, 52, 2013; Andjelković 1998; Cockburn 2001: 26).

During the war, the economic crisis deepened. GDP per capita dropped to $378 in 1994 – the most severe economic collapse of any country since World War II (World Bank [1994] 1997: 3). Unemployment jumped to 90 percent (Cockburn 2001: 25). Farm production fell to just one-third of the population's need, 70 percent of farm equipment was destroyed, and 15 percent of farmland became inaccessible due to landmines (World Bank 1999, 2001: 1). Fighting caused factories to close in many areas, and the military occupation of certain cities and regions completely cut off some areas from supply routes. The fighting destroyed utilities, leaving many people without heat, food, or fuel. Moreover, fighting damaged or destroyed as many as 60 percent of houses (approximately 500,000), creating an urgent housing shortage (World Bank 1996; International Crisis Group 1997; Cockburn 2001).[8]

Widespread looting also occurred during the war. Nothing was off limits: irregular forces and paramilitaries, including some "weekend warriors" from Serbia, would loot land, livestock, houses, televisions, cars, cash, jewelry, farm equipment, appliances, and more. Major crime syndicates partnered with corrupt officials to traffic narcotics, weapons, fuel, and other goods (Pugh and Cooper 2004: 154). In some towns, non-Serbs sold everything they owned to pay for transportation out of their besieged villages (Cigar 1995: 83). Soldiers set up roadblocks to confiscate goods being delivered or shipped around the country.[9] War profiteers emerged, and protagonists of the war often collaborated to support trafficking opportunities that benefited both sides (Pugh and Cooper 2004). Black market economies sprung up as aid workers and people on all sides of the conflict collaborated for financial gain. Many women survived as small-scale traders in these underground economies, although men were much more likely to profit (Cockburn 2001: 27; Pugh 2002).

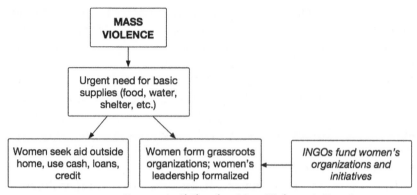

FIGURE 6.2 Economic Shifts after Mass Violence in Bosnia

Impact on Women

Women's unequal status prior to the war soon paled in comparison to the degree of disadvantage they faced during the violence. Merima, the founder of a women's organization in the Krajina region, described how women "had to take care of the whole family and other things. They had to pay bills, they had to contact the rest of the family that was outside of Bosnia. And they had to live with this fear that they may lose their father, their brother, or their son" (Interview #56, May 2013). In Sarajevo, Bosnians faced a massive shortage of basic supplies like food and water. Residents relied on meager rations from UN aid shipments, small windowsill gardens, and scavenging edible wild plants. Transportation systems stopped working, electricity was intermittent, and fuel for cooking fires became increasingly scarce as citizens slowly cut down the city's trees. Social services – such as the system of pensions, invalid insurance, childcare, schools, and other forms of social protection for vulnerable groups – ceased to exist (Cockburn 2001: 27).

With men of fighting age in charge of defending the city, many women found themselves responsible for finding food, shelter, and health care for themselves and the children and elderly who were now in their care. Women took significant risks with their lives to fulfill these responsibilities, such as walking across town to find water or firewood under the risk of being shot by a sniper or hit by a mortar shell. Ismeta Dervoz, a member of parliament, recounted how "Every day in Sarajevo so many people were killed ... and we had four years without any essential needs for human life – without electricity, without heat, without food, without medical supplies, without anything" (Interview

#2, April 2013). According to Ismeta, this pushed many women into new, often physically demanding roles as the economic providers for their families, as they cut firewood and slugged water across the city. She described how this chore often fell to her mother:

I remember from my building, and it is 10 stories, just one man who was a doctor, and three women would go out every day for work. And every day you can see it is just the women who go out to try to find something to eat, to go for water. The women showed unbelievable strength in Bosnia-Herzegovina – courage. My mother was at the time sixty-two years old, and she went with the neighbors every night to one hill here in Sarajevo to try to find some wood for the fire to cook something during the day. Sixty-two years old, she was! (Interview April 3, 2013)

This gendered division of labor – men fighting, women providing for their families – was typical of most Bosnian families during the war.

The satirical Sarajevo Survival Guide residents produced in 1993 contained astute reflections of these gender dynamics. For instance, it described "The Modern Sarajevan Male":

He has accreditation [ID], weapons, a good car, and a complete uniform. The owner of a bullet-proof vest is regarded with respect. One who doesn't wear a uniform has an ax in his right hand for cutting down trees, and a series of [water] canisters on his left shoulder. His image would be complete with a mask against poison gas.

This depiction captured the association of men with fighting and rugged military defense of the city. Contrast that with the description of "The Modern Sarajevan Female":

She cuts wood, carries humanitarian aid, smaller canisters filled with water, does not visit a hairdresser nor a cosmetician. She is slim, and runs fast. Girls regularly visit the places where humanitarian aid is being distributed. They know the best aid-packages according to their numbers. They get up early to get water, visit cemeteries to collect wood, and greet new young refugees. Many wear golden and silver lilies as earrings, as pins, on necklaces.

While intended to be humorous, such depictions encapsulated the gendered division of labor during the siege: women maintained their roles as caregivers, while men were charged with defending the city. While emotionally and physically difficult, this division of labor pushed women into new social roles that eventually became the basis for new forms of collective action. Moreover, many women I interviewed explained how fulfilling traditional caregiving roles during the devastating environment of war cultivated a moral sense of political conviction. They came to see previously mundane tasks of finding food and caring for others as part of a personal rejection of the war, which they did not want and did not believe in.

Outside of Sarajevo, massive displacement and the disproportionate death and imprisonment of men left many rural women with the burden of caring for their families alone. Like in Rwanda, this meant that, among the rural poor, women took control of household finances for the first time, as they had to "take all of the roles that men had" to account for the absence of their partners (Interview #67, June 2013). In addition, and like in Rwanda, many women needed to deal in cash daily and spend their savings on food, as they could no longer grow their own. These women often lived on the margins of society, economically and psychologically struggling from the consequences of war.

The war affected a devastating financial toll for nearly all displaced people. People spent savings and valuables on the transportation required to leave the city, "exit tolls," or food. Black markets became one of the few ways to get decent food, as well as medicine, which was also scarce and primarily available only through illicit channels. This loss of savings on new expenses was one of the primary reasons people moved into collective shelters (Mrvic-Petrović and Stevanović 2000). Others moved in with family or friends, and those with more resources rented apartments in parts of the country where they were displaced.

Women Form Organizations

Civil society organizations or NGOs were virtually nonexistent in Bosnia prior to the violence, in large part because the state provided most services (Walsh 2000).[10] As the state fractured, women faced enormous pressure to assume new responsibilities and secure basic material supplies. Many began to collaborate with friends, neighbors, and strangers to help each other in their time of collective need. Svetlana, a Serb who remained in Sarajevo during the war, hinted at how new economic responsibilities established solidarity among women:

Women were exposed to all sorts of new challenges. They had to find water [and] food, they had to find firewood outside, they had to do the washing. It created a sense of *survival solidarity*. And people who you wouldn't normally interact with or be friends with were all of a sudden your closest friends. Because it was a time with no lies. Everything was straightforward; nobody presented any false sense of themselves. (Interview #3, April 2013)

As Svetlana mentioned, this "survival solidarity" bonded women together and led to the formation of community organizations in order to respond to "the twin crises of destitution and trauma" (Cockburn 2001: 87). Dubbed "kitchen table" organizations, these loose organizational structures established a new model of social organization during crisis.

Approximately one-quarter of the women I interviewed in Bosnia were involved in founding small, informal groups in their communities that aimed to assist others in finding their loved ones, securing basic goods like food and clothing, accessing trauma counseling, or developing small income-generating activities.[11] An individual woman with some training, resources, or contacts – or simply a particular vision – often initiated an organization's formation. Soon, many of the founders of these emergent organizations realized that they could receive funding from international humanitarian agencies and INGOs – and indeed some were motivated to form organizations because of INGO initiatives. To do so, they were encouraged to register with the local authorities, which required them to collect thirty signatures and name their organization. Bosnians joked that anyone who could gather the signatures of twenty-nine of their friends and relatives could become an NGO (Helms 2013: 90).

Foreign donors flooded Bosnia with development aid and humanitarian assistance. Donor support averaged $1 billion per year for the first five years after the war, and the World Bank lent $860 million between 1996 and 2001. International donors used local organizations as implementing partners who could assist in the distribution of goods, and saw the development of local organizations as a way to build civil society, and thereby democracy. In the aftermath of the Cold War, encouraging the growth of democratic institutions was paramount for many Western donors. Grassroots organizations were seen to promote ethnic tolerance and support for democratic reforms (Helms 2013). As donors saw civil society as a neutral "third sector," where the multiethnic state could flourish and potentially undermine the nationalist political leadership, community organizations soon became the primary service providers in the country.

Estimates of the number of organizations in Bosnia after the war vary widely, from 1,500 to upward of 8,000 (Simmons 2007: 175; IBHI 1998). By 1997, international funding for these women's initiatives began to dry up. In response, many organizations transitioned from caregiving organizations to income-generating entities. This gave some women control over surplus income for the first time, particularly if their husbands were dead or unable to find employment after the war. Thus, as women's organizations continued providing essential services to the population, they additionally began to make profits of their own, which facilitated a shift in the way economic power was distributed in the country. I discuss this process of organizational growth and formalization more in the next chapter.

The war reduced per capita GDP to about 20 percent of its prewar level. Industrial production fell by 90 percent (World Bank 1996: 14). By 2000, 46 percent of Bosnians in the Federation and 75 percent of those in Republika Srpska lived in poverty. More than two decades later, most of the population still subsists on foreign remittances, foreign aid, undeclared earnings, and back pay or pensions for demobilized soldiers, widows, and other victims of war (Pugh 2002: 472). Pensions, however, barely cover the cost of living. As a result, many Bosnians work in grey or shadow economies, which emerged during the war alongside war profiteers and mafia-linked trading networks. In the early 2000s, Bosnia's informal/grey economy was estimated at about $500 million annually (Pugh and Cooper 2004).

CULTURAL SHIFTS

As the number of community organizations mushroomed during the war, the "third sector" emerged as a parallel power structure to that of the state. NGOs and their local implementing partners provided essential goods and services that a state might normally provide. Women's presence at the helm of many of these organizations made them well-known public figures in their communities. This growing acceptance of women in more public leadership roles reflected a departure from traditional, conservative, and patriarchal Balkan norms. For many Bosnian women – particularly poor, less educated, rural women – participating in organizations involved in issues related to peacebuilding, refugee return, or income-generating activities represented a departure from their prewar social roles. Like in Rwanda, the war allowed Bosnian women to construct a "frame" that legitimized their presence in public because of their identity as mothers and status as "more peaceful" than men during the war (Goffman 1974; Benford and Snow 2000). Women were generally seen as less complicit in the violence, and many began to publicly claim that "this was not our war" (see Hunt 2004).

Women could in part construct this nonviolent, antiwar frame because the dominant narrative of the Bosnian war depicted women as victims – particularly as refugees and victims of sexual violence (Mertus 1994). Elissa Helms put it succinctly:

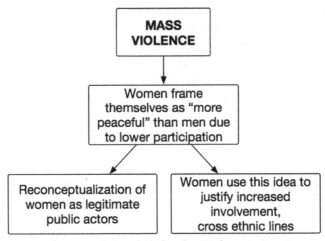

FIGURE 6.3 Cultural Shifts after Violence in Bosnia

Mention women and Bosnia and your first association is likely to be one of two iconic images: distraught women in headscarves and traditional Muslim dress fleeing ethnic cleansing, their ragged children and a few belongings in tow; or the shamed and silenced young Muslim victim of rape and forced pregnancy, doubly victimized by her attackers and then by her own patriarchal community. These were the images that flooded the world media during the war and that have been instrumentalized in various political discussions of the region ever since. (Helms 2013: 25).

Such depictions essentialized and depoliticized women, portraying them as helpless victims of a war in which they were simply caught in the middle. And yet such depictions also positioned women outside of the political realm. As in the case of Rwanda discussed in Chapter 3, the "affirmative essentialization" (Helms 2002, 2013) of women as more nurturing or peaceful than men allowed Bosnian women to juxtapose their own inherent "peacefulness" with men's propensity for war. Against the background of the suffering caused by violence, this discourse served to politicize women's daily activities; it gained traction because women implicitly recognized themselves in the frame.

Many women I interviewed emphasized that women's ability to empathize and provide "motherly care" made them important peacebuilders in their communities. Such essentialist depictions complicate feminist frameworks premised on women's sameness with men. Yet feminist activists, like Svetlana Slapšak, note that during extraordinary situations like war, women's movements have the chance to move fast and make progress when they "link their politics to pacifism" (Slapšak 2001: 180). Given the corrupt and immoral perception of politics in Bosnia, such apolitical depictions offered women an opening to advocate for various causes on the basis of their status as "moral victims" (Helms 2013).

Women's organizations thus played an important role in crafting these essentialized depictions of women's victimhood in order to distance women from the illegitimate, male-dominated realm of politics and war. In organizational documents and mission statements, "mothers" could affirm some sort of space within the nationalist political discourse. Women could claim – as some did and still do – that the war never would have happened if women had been in charge of the country. As one politician put it:

Women are, as biological creatures, capable of giving birth and rais[ing] their children, and by the very nature have the gift that men do not have. Women have a higher level of empathy and are more capable to do everyday life work. During the war, in unbelievable conditions, women managed to do their everyday work that they used to support their families and the whole society. They were crucial in rebuilding society and cleaning the mess that was created by the "war games." (Interview #64, June 2013)

Women's victim status rendered them innocent of the "war games" this politician mentions, and conferred upon women a sense of moral legitimacy.

This distinction between women's peacefulness and men's propensity for war continues to be a salient narrative today. Throughout my fieldwork in Kozarac, I observed multiple women wearing t-shirts that said, "I won't raise my kid to kill your kid." As one of many examples from my interviews, Munira Subašić, the director of Mothers of Srebrenica, explicitly posited the biological origins of women's inherent peacefulness:

Every mother is just a mother, no matter what her ethnic or religious background. When I realized this, that I could talk to any mother, I understood that all mothers suffer, and that we could overcome obstacles and talk in ways that politicians cannot, and that through this dialogue we can rise above and progress. (Interview #60, June 2013)

Other women reiterated this narrative. One MP stated that "women are more sensible and they can create a better society if they are involved in politics … because we can create a better society for our children because we have a sense for negotiation, we are not violent" (Interview #74, July 2010). Another MP described how she believed that "women are just on a higher evolutionary level than men. There is scientific evidence that there are more connections between the left and the right hemisphere" (Interview #32, May 2013). She continued by emphasizing that women were the first ones to cross ethnic boundaries after the war, and attributed this to the idea that "all women developed this kind of sensitivity if they had kids."

Crossing Ethno-National Divides

In addition to believing that women are biologically predisposed toward peace, many of my interview respondents suggested that women were better positioned than men to speak to people from different ethnic and religious backgrounds during the war. Anti-nationalism, in essence, became a grounding identity for women's activism. Women's organizations argued that it was easier for women to interact with members of a different ethnic group than men because they had not engaged in the fighting themselves (see also Hunt 2004; Kleiman 2007; Cockburn 2013a; Helms 2013; see also Tripp 2015). Moreover, their status as mothers made them more capable of empathizing with others' suffering.

My interviewees provided many examples of instances when women were able to cross ethnic lines more easily than men.[12] Explicitly feminist organizations, such as Women in Black and Medica Zenica, organized antiwar conferences all over the region and formed an initiative called "Women Activists Cross Borders," which brought together women from all areas to travel in a bus around the region. The goal of the project was to show how women from different backgrounds could transcend newly established borders and begin to build peace (Spahić Šiljak 2014). For instance, Sabiha Husić, the director of Medica Zenica, stated:

> It was during the war that women really started to think in another way; okay, how can we help each other; how can we help other women; where are we; where is our position; what can we do differently. In very hard times, however, women of different religions and backgrounds started to communicate with each other. For example, women from Zenica [predominantly Bosniak] started to speak and to send messages to women from Banja Luka [predominantly Serb] or from Vitez [predominately Croat] ... it was so good that we started as women to rebuild our bridges again. (Interview #73, June 2013)

Women also bridged ethnic divides by founding informal self-help organizations in their communities or while displaced in refugee or IDP camps. In just one of many examples, in the village of Grahovo, Croat and Serb women formed the Women Citizens' Association (Funk 2015). Led by Danka Zelić, a practicing Catholic dedicated to peacebuilding in her community, the organization's mission was simple: to bring neighbors together, regardless of their ethnicity. The association introduced livestock programs, daily production initiatives, and even fish farming into the region, and all property of the program was registered in women's names in order to promote cross-ethnic female solidarity (Spahić Šiljak 2014: 41; Funk 2015: 5). This cross-ethnic women-led collaboration also occurred in the business sector; Nermina Ćemalović, a former electrical engineer who now sits in parliament, described how she came up with the idea to organize an exhibition of industry products in spring 1995 in order to foster dialogue between different ethnic groups in her hometown of Zenica. The exhibition was a success, and according to Ćemalović, "It was the first event organized between Croats and Bosnians [during the war]. They were surprised" (Interview #50, May 2013).

CONCLUSION

In Bosnia, many women were able to engage in important political activities while still situating themselves outside of the political realm, largely because they reframed their presence in terms of peace, motherhood, and nonparticipation in the war. Against the background of devastating violence in both Rwanda and Bosnia, being "peaceful" legitimized women's presence in public; their victimization during the war and subsequent efforts to rebuild the country rendered them assets to the recovery process and less likely to enflame ethnic animosities. Although this narrative relied on an essentialized understanding of gender difference, it was an important initial step in reconceptualizing women as legitimate public actors. Yet such a framing raises questions about how sustainable women's gains will be if premised on such gendered essentialisms.

We have seen throughout this chapter how violence precipitated demographic, economic, and cultural shifts in Bosnia in the 1990s. Massive population displacement, sweeping economic needs, and a reconceptualization of women's roles propelled many women to engage in new activities in their communities. While the gendered division of labor and patriarchal norms remained in place, these new activities ushered in processes of political mobilization that departed from the past. In the following chapter, I analyze the impact of these demographic, economic, and cultural shifts on women's participation in informal and formal political capacities.

7

Women's Political Mobilization in Bosnia-Herzegovina

"Yes, women do have power, more than people would expect. And it is important to show them where the power lies and to empower ones who don't recognize it."

– *Merima (Interview #56, May 2013)*

Sabiha Husić was twenty-two years old and living in Vitez – a city in central Bosnia – when the Croatian army (HVO) violently expelled her and her family from their home. They ended up in Zenica as refugees. Before long, her father was wounded and her brothers were called to fight in the Bosnian army. Sabiha found herself responsible for the well-being of her family and for keeping them together (Interview #73, June 2013; see also Spahić Šiljak 2014: 3–9). While in the refugee camp in Zenica, she felt motivated to help others and began working with refugees who had experienced trauma. Through a friend, Sabiha connected with women refugees who had experienced wartime rape, and soon dedicated herself to this cause. The refugee community in general was predominantly comprised of women, children, and the elderly. Men had been "cleansed," recruited to fight in the military, or killed. Sabiha wanted to "mobilize women so that we start to do something concrete," feeling that "we cannot only sit and listen to news and wait to see what will happen."

Sabiha began working with Medica Zenica, an organization recently formed by Monika Hauser, an Italian gynecologist, to treat women survivors of war violence (Cockburn 1998: 174). Over the next few years, Medica became a highly respected organization and one of the most essential service providers in the country; it collaborated with international feminist networks and received foreign visitors and funding from various countries and foundations. Sabiha described how participating in the organization shifted her mindset from caring for women's medical needs to more holistically caring about their human rights. Together with others at Medica, she worked with local religious leaders to destigmatize rape. Eventually, the group's efforts prompted the imam of Zenica to issue a *fatwa* that urged people to respect women who had been rape victims (Cockburn 1998). Today, Sabiha is Medica's director; she is a widely known and respected human rights activist and champion for women's issues. She often speaks publicly about UN Security Council Resolution 1325, the landmark UN resolution aimed at increasing the number of women in the prevention and resolution of conflicts.[1] She and the Medica team work with other NGOs to advocate for women's political representation, educational opportunities, and promotion in business.

While Sabiha ended up as the director of one of Bosnia's foremost women's organizations, hundreds of thousands of other Bosnian women also experienced shifts in their public engagement as a result of their experiences during and after the war. In this chapter, I examine the impact of war-induced demographic, economic, and cultural shifts on women's political engagement. Unlike in Rwanda, the end of the war in Bosnia did not bring about a regime change; instead, the Dayton Accords divided the political system into two consociational entities with a loose national federation overseeing the divided state. Alma Čolo, a member of parliament, described how "the men stayed who were engaged in politics and the army" (Interview #74, July 2009). There was little room for women in politics.

Ordinary Bosnians perceived formal politics during and after the war as chauvinist, corrupt, nationalistic, and – perhaps most critically – male. "Politics is a whore" (*politika je kurva*)[2] became a widespread refrain. Politics also often "happened" over *rakija* at bars, an exclusively male space. In interviews and in more informal social settings, women in Bosnia today repeatedly expressed their awareness of the lack of openings in the national political scene after the war. Women were shut out, both formally and informally, as the postwar political elite emerged as the same people responsible for the war in the first place.

Yet, while there was a widespread condemnation of the formal political realm, in what follows I describe how the war catalyzed a shift in many women's everyday engagement in public spaces and with government institutions. Women I interviewed expressed a deep sense of moral conviction that the war was wrong, which motivated them to make changes to their everyday routines that could secure a better life for themselves and their children. As women applied for passports, appealed for restitution for lost property, or even sought verification of marriage documents to claim benefits after the death of a spouse, I argue that they engaged in a "politics of practice" that reflected a change in women's roles after the war. This shift included testifying about rape and sexual violence in court, and such acts began to accumulate as tens of thousands of women faced similar circumstances.

Women also increased their engagement in informal political spaces by founding and participating in civil society organizations. Given the widespread disdain for politics in Bosnia, the organization or NGO sector became a key site for political activities in the aftermath of the war. "Humanitarian" became a buzzword that differentiated some women's NGOs from the more political activities led by organizations partnered with international actors – such as the Organization for Security and Cooperation in Europe (OSCE), the Office of the High Representative (OHR), and the UN. This label situated women's organizations squarely within women's traditional domain and allowed them to stress their independence from political parties. Yet, like in Rwanda – and as Clemens (1993, 1996) found in relation to women's associations in the United States in the late nineteenth century – framing these organizations as apolitical allowed women to politically mobilize in novel and eclectic ways. Many women-led organizations advocated for the return of refugees, justice for survivors, or ethnic reconciliation – all distinctly political issues (Cockburn 2001; Helms 2002, 2013). As a result, they provided essential services that the state would normally provide (e.g., health care) and thereby gained status in their communities, while avoiding political complications and pushback.

The war also brought another shift in women's political activities: an increase in women's defiant or resistant actions in public spaces. Their actions were defiant in that they challenged patriarchal expectations about what women could or could not do in public, often visibly and vocally deriding the established political order. Unlike in Rwanda, where public space was tightly controlled, women in Bosnia had few constraints on their ability to protest in public. These protests occurred before the war, but took on new meanings and dimensions during the violence and in its aftermath, particularly as public spaces became increasingly intertwined with chauvinist, nationalist political rhetoric. These activities reflected a middle ground between informal, everyday political activities and more overt, deliberate forms of formal political action.

I conclude this case study by analyzing how the war impacted women's participation in the formal political realm. Unlike in Rwanda, Bosnia did not experience an upsurge in women's formal political representation immediately after the war. The war did, however, impact some individual women's decisions to enter politics in the years that followed. Moreover, women's organizations that emerged after the violence advocated for the adoption of various measures to increase women's presence in government and secure gender-sensitive legal reforms. While today the percentage of women in parliament is still not much higher than it was during the socialist era, there is a growing acceptance of women in government. Moreover, anti-nationalist parties like the Social Democratic Party (SDP) and progressive parties like Naša Stranka, have made progress toward positioning women in important political roles.

A "POLITICS OF PRACTICE": EVERYDAY POLITICS

"Our pain organized us" – Nura, Widow (Interview #68, June 2013)

Like in Rwanda, Bosnian women took on myriad new roles and responsibilities in their households and communities as a result of widespread displacement, the loss or absence of male family members, and a decrease in economic capacities and resources. Establishing normalcy under the conditions of upheaval required new forms of action. Women, as caretakers for their families, were particularly likely to adapt. As an architect in Sarajevo put it:

Women tend to find ways to adapt to new situations without thinking about their individual benefit. I've seen refugee women in camps who have been university professors, who now go out of the camp and clean other women's houses because they want to make sure the children are dressed well when they go to the local school, so that no one makes fun of them. (Interview #63, June 2013)

Because thousands of women faced similar circumstances of displacement, economic scarcity, trauma, and loss, shifts in women's day-to-day responsibilities – including shifts in the social prestige of the work – were widespread. Such shifts were particularly salient for Bosnians who were displaced from their homes, who lost male family members, or who testified in court about their wartime experiences. Because of the patriarchal, conservative society like Bosnia, as women in these situations struggled to improve their lives and the lives of their family members, their daily survival activities became part of a broader political transformation. For Bosniaks in particular, working to live amid violence designed to cleanse Muslim culture from the land became a distinctly political endeavor.

Women without husbands were the most likely to take on new responsibilities, such as tending to and maintaining the home and land, negotiating permission to travel with government or international aid officials, or finding ways to earn money. This marked a departure from the prewar era, when, as one NGO founder put it, "women were kind of protected by their husbands. If they wanted something to happen they would tell them" (Interview #22, April 2013). Nineteen of the 109 Bosnian women I interviewed for this project lost husbands or sons during the war, and each described how this loss motivated her increased participation in public life. In these families, women often took on new activities related to the survival of their dependents; they also faced the additional logistical and emotional burden of finding out when, where, and how their loved ones had been killed.

One type of activity that rapidly increased during and after the war was women's interactions with various government institutions and multinational aid agencies. Before the war, men typically represented their families in interactions with state institutions (Bringa 1995). During the war, women whose husbands were off fighting, in prison or concentration camps, or dead had to assume this role. Women had to register their property or marriages and apply for social support payments. In order to receive letters of sponsorship and valid travel documents allowing them to leave Bosnia during the war, families had to navigate a complicated and divided government bureaucracy (Interview #6, April 2013; see also Mertus 2000).

Ajla, for example, was a young mother living in Sarajevo during the war (Interview #34, May 2013). Her husband was killed in combat while fighting for the Bosnian army. Ajla's daughter was just two years old at that time and suffered from a series of health problems during the siege. It became apparent that her daughter needed surgery. Ajla described how she "had to be a father and a mother at one time" and began searching for ways to get her daughter out of the country to have the necessary surgery. She had to apply for travel permissions and documents and then enlisted the help of a larger NGO for financial support. Her daughter was able to have the surgery in Germany in 1995, and Ajla described how "during the war I realized how tough I am. During that time you realize how strong your will is to survive, to keep on going – it really did make me stronger." By surviving the siege and securing health care for her daughter, Ajla gained a new political consciousness that motivated her to become involved in women's organizations and eventually politics.

Several of the widows I interviewed mentioned that, in order to apply for federal financial assistance or their husbands' pensions during or after the war, they had to produce documents showing they had been married. This required them to navigate the divided government bureaucracy and to appeal to local officials to find their personal records. Many also registered with the International Commission of Missing Persons (ICMP) to provide DNA samples and dental and medical records of their missing loved ones. These mundane tasks facilitated everyday interactions with government and multinational institutions, which began to accumulate and shift women's social networks. Some women joined together in small groups or aligned themselves with grassroots organizations that could help. As discussed in what follows, widows and mothers' organizations provided support for women as they navigated this bureaucratic process and eventually encouraged women to demand accountability and justice from the government. After the war, campaigns to ensure widows received pensions became a national political debate about whose deaths were deserving of compensation. By pressuring government institutions for such pensions at the local level, many women unknowingly joined part of a broader political fight.

For women whose family members had been killed, these routine interactions with government became more regular and contentious. Hajra Catic, the founder of the NGO Žene Srebrenica (Women of Srebrenica), described how interactions with the state eventually morphed into more overt forms of protest (Interview #19, April 2013). For example, after "the bulk of [her] family was killed during the war," Hajra worked with other women to search for her husband and son, who she hoped were alive in concentration camps. She described how "We went from one [government] institution to another. For two or three years we were trying to find them." This process involved filling missing persons reports with the ICMP, coordinating with the Red Cross to see if they had been displaced as IDPs or refugees in the region, and talking to untold numbers of Bosnian politicians from different political parties. Eventually, however, authorities discovered mass graves in the area where her husband and son had last been seen. At that point, "we realized that all of them were killed. Then we started looking for their remains, and of course, we put pressure to arrest the people who did this genocide." Hajra's experiences reveal how the loss of male family members motivated women to pressure local leaders to arrest perpetrators of the violence and to demand justice. This process of mobilization connected women to others in similar circumstances, expanding their social networks and cultivating a sense of shared solidarity. While Rwandan women joined grassroots organizations to gain official documentation of their land rights, Bosnian women pressured the government to find missing loved ones and to identify their remains using DNA technology. In each case, the war catalyzed changes in women's engagement with formal institutions and agents of the state.

Women's participation in these new capacities was, in many ways, an unexpected result of the patriarchal mentality that considered women less capable (Slapšak 2001: 191). Before the war, women – particularly women from poor or religious families – were socially marginalized and discriminated against. Yet, when faced with the daunting tasks of surviving and caring for children, especially in the absence of their husbands, Bosnian women turned "handicaps into advantages." This led to what activist Svetlana Slapšak called the "spontaneous creation of a kind of women's market of information and services" (2001: 191). This "market" consisted of women taking over the tasks most essential for a "normal" life – finding food, water, shelter, health care, and so on. Such everyday tasks were essential for survival and thereby for maintaining Bosniak lives in the face of a political project aimed to destroy them.

Testimony as Politics

Testifying in national or international courts became another element of everyday politics, as seemingly atomized women told similar stories of their abuse and suffering to strangers in public settings. The UN established the International Criminal Tribunal for the Former Yugoslavia (ICTY) in 1993 to "try those individuals most responsible for appalling acts such as murder, torture, rape, enslavement, destruction of property and other crimes."[3] Women activists were instrumental in creating the court and in ensuring that sexual violence was treated as a systematic war crime, rather than as a by-product of war (Mertus 2004). Situated in The Hague, Netherlands, away from the ongoing war, the ICTY eventually charged more than 160 people. Thousands of women became involved in this international justice project when they testified as part of ICTY proceedings, either at the ICTY offices in Sarajevo or in The Hague. Given that a courtroom is a "theater of power" (Cole 2010; Koomen 2014), giving testimony – especially about rape or other personal experiences – became an explicitly political act with profound consequences for both national and transnational justice initiatives.

For many women, testifying was a terrible experience. At the beginning of the court's tenure, one witness described being housed in the same hotel as the family of the defendant, and suddenly running into the defendant's supporters in the hall (Interview #47, May 2013). Another reported that she requested something to eat after being kept waiting all day to testify, only to be brought a sandwich with a bill that she was unable to pay (Interview #68, June 2013). Others reported that they were asked to testify without being given appropriate clothing, so that when they arrived at the court they were embarrassed and ashamed by their poverty (Amnesty International 2009).[4] Such experiences deepened trauma and provoked insecurity among those willing to testify. As awareness grew about the court's shortcomings, many women's organizations in Bosnia began lobbying for reform (Mertus 2004; Engle 2005). They pushed for the inclusion of gender expertise and gender-sensitive protocols at all stages of the prosecution; eventually, the court implemented measures to increase the protection of survivors and witnesses of gender-based crimes, setting new standards for gender-inclusiveness in international law.[5] In fighting for these reforms, many Bosnian women's groups were connected to international actors and networks. For several women I interviewed, the act of giving testimony and then lobbying for these legal reforms left them with a deeply felt political mission for justice. Collectively, Bosnian women's testimonies helped change the international legal standard and establish rape and sexual violence as a war crime, as a crime against humanity, and as part of genocide (see Stiglmayer 1994; Engle 2005; Oosterveld 2005).[6]

NEW ACTIVITIES THROUGH CIVIL SOCIETY ORGANIZATIONS

Beba Hadzić, a school principal before the war, was displaced from her home during violence in the Drina Valley. She described how she had a normal life before the war, but then, in May 1992, "Serbians ... put us in trucks and took us out of town, and then ten days later they put us in trucks again like cattle and took us to slaughter, and then I became a refugee" (Interview #22, April 2013). She described how she was shocked to find herself asking the Red Cross for food and shoes – she had been wearing flip-flops when militias arrived at her house. Beba took shelter with hundreds of other refugees in a school in Tuzla. There, she brought together a group of women who did not know the fate of their male family members. They realized that while their husbands were gone, "they had to take responsibility for the family, to find shelter for them, to find food for them ... They had to be in charge at this time."

To offer these women something productive to occupy their time, Beba decided to form an organization. She studied Bosnian law to figure out how to go about this process. After she had registered the organization, Beba appealed to Oxfam for materials to launch a knitting project. At first, they gave her 300 kilos of wool, and the women were really happy and encouraged by the project. Beba approached Oxfam again:

The next time they gave me 4,000 [kilos]. The first project started at three schools ... We created socks and sweaters for school kids. After three weeks we had created sweaters and it was created from that group of women. Oxfam was surprised and everyone was very happy ... [the] next contract was for 44 schools and we got a car and everything. It was a huge project.

Eventually, Beba's organization – which she named BOSFAM to represent a large Bosnian family – grew and founded more than a dozen centers where women produced handmade garments and crafts. While it started as an emotional support group, today BOSFAM sells the goods made by women in the organization to the public. Beba recognized the importance of the group for women's solidary and survival during the war, acknowledging that:

There were a lot of bad moments during the war of course. But there were of course some great moments as well. Having this great group of people that works together creates a special kind of connection, and that is one of the greatest moments of this time. This is what helps the person to go through it; you learn new things and you don't think about the war.

While organizations like Beba's were virtually nonexistent before the war, between 1,500 and 8,000 organizations emerged during and after (Simmons 2007: 175; IBHI 1998). As discussed in Chapter 6, organizations formed in large part to meet the urgent needs created by violence. They were particularly likely to form in Bosniak (Muslim) areas – including Zenica, Tuzla, Mostar, and Sarajevo – because they were often established where there were large numbers of people in need of aid. These organizations were essential for creating pockets of stability within the crisis of war, as they helped people communicate with displaced family members, transfer money and goods, resettle after displacement, and find jobs, emotional support, housing, financial support, medication, and much more.

As discussed in the previous chapter, many organizations developed and formalized with the help of INGOs or other funding agencies, which linked individual women like Beba to international institutions like Oxfam. These interactions encouraged women's organizations to mimic the missions and structure of larger organizations and to elect individual women to formal leadership positions – a process that DiMaggio and Powell

(1983) termed "institutional isomorphism." More than 100,000 foreigners from various UN agencies and more than 200 INGOs were reported to have been part of the humanitarian operation in Bosnia (Andreas 2008). These individual actors brokered connections between emergent grassroots organizations and more formal international humanitarian agencies. This influx of international funding led to new distribution networks for critical goods and services, and also provided well-paying jobs for some locals.[7] Many INGOs – such as Kvinna til Kvinna from Sweden or Medica Mondiale from Germany – adopted local implementing partners, and thereby helped local organizations grow and formalize as funding increased. A $5 million grant from the United States in 1996 launched the Bosnian Women's Initiative, which aimed to coordinate NGO efforts working to empower women (Cockburn 2001: 32). This funding further facilitated the formation of community organizations.

Strategic Use of Humanitarianism

Many women's organizations that formed during this period strategically used women's importance as caregivers to justify forming the organization. For example, Srcem do Mira (Through Heart to Peace) is a small women's organization based out of a large yellow house in Kozarac, a town currently located in Republika Srpska just outside of Prijedor. Before the war, 90 percent of the town's 24,000 residents were Bosniak (Sivac-Bryant 2008). The town experienced high levels of violence during the war and a massacre in May 1992 left hundreds (maybe thousands) of residents dead. Most of the survivors were sent to concentration camps and hundreds of Bosniak homes were razed. Some residents fled to Croatia, where they congregated in refugee camps.

While in a refugee camp near Zagreb, Majda[8] saw many women from the region around Kozarac who were eager to do something to improve their lives (Interview #8, May 2013). Because she was well known in her community before the war, Majda organized a meeting with about twenty refugee women from different walks of life – doctors, lawyers, hairdressers, seamstresses, housewives, and farmers. None had ever participated in a community organization and they did not know how to write a proposal for funding. But, according to Majda:

We sat down and they wrote their goals for what they were trying to accomplish. There were women who had children and those children had to go to school. So they wanted to talk about how they were going to go to school and where. And if they were sick or needed medical attention [how they would get it].

The group of women identified its strongest skills. With a hairdresser in the group and several talented tailors, they decided to open a small hair salon in the refugee camp and to establish a sewing group that could make clothing to sell. The group became a place where women "could come ... and work."

After the war, Kozarac was incorporated within Republika Srpska. As a result, few Bosniak residents were eager to return (see also Sivac-Bryant 2016). Many, including Majda, returned to Sanski Most, a nearby city just across the border in the Bosnian–Croat Federation. Soon, however, Majda and several other women in her group decided to return to their hometown. Many lived under tents until their homes could be rebuilt. Despite constant harassment from the local Serb population, other displaced Bosniak residents followed. Former Serb army leaders dominated local government in the area around Kozarac and in nearby Prijedor; many were widely known to have committed atrocities. Local authorities erected memorials to Serb victims of war, but denied that crimes against Bosniaks occurred and prevented survivors from erecting their own memorials.[9] Nearby concentration camps, like Trnoplje, lay in ruins. Majda noted how people in the area constantly felt threatened or unsafe. "You have to live here and feel it," she said, "The people who were in the Serbian army who did bad things, they now have high positions and a good reputation. They are like heroes."[10]

Srcem do Mira became a pillar of the returnee population. But at the same time, the organization purports to be apolitical – Majda emphasized to me during our meetings that it is a "humanitarian" organization primarily run by and for women. Even the organization's name, Through Heart to Peace, reflects an essentially feminine logic. At the jubilee anniversary of its founding in May 2013, members and supporters of the organization heralded its mission to promote *"ljbuv, tolerencja, and mira"* (love, tolerance, and peace). Handmade paper doves and flowers decorated the event – "feminine" touches designed, in the words of one attendee, to show how "you can't hold beauty back" after the destruction of war.[11] Such a framing of Srcem do Mira's mission is in part strategic, as it situates the organization outside of male-dominated political channels, allowing it space to maneuver without significant pushback from the local Serb authorities.

In reality, Srcem do Mira has been a leader in a highly contentious political project: the resurrection of a vibrant Bosniak community in the middle of a Serb-dominant region that, according to popular lore, has one of the world's highest numbers of convicted war criminals per capita (Sivac-Bryant 2008). The organization frequently brings its members and supporters to former concentration camps, drawing the attention (and ire) of the surrounding community and quietly demanding that Serbs acknowledge the crimes that occurred. The town is now widely known as one of the most successful returnee communities in Bosnia (Sivac-Bryant 2008, 2016). Framing the organization as apolitical was gender-conservative, and yet it strategically allowed the organization to engage in the contentious process of minority refugee return (see also Helms 2002: 25).

Organizations like Srcem do Mira often judiciously adopted the label "humanitarian organization" to differentiate themselves from organizations with ties to nationalist political parties. Adopting the humanitarian label allowed women's organizations to operate without controversy, as powerful men largely saw them as nonthreatening and merely extending women's traditional caregiving roles. At the same time, these organizations engaged in explicitly political goals, such as working toward ethnic reconciliation, refugee return, transitional justice, or rights for the displaced. Therefore, through traditional roles, these organizations have provided a platform for their leaders and members to interact with international actors, funding networks, and other institutions of power.

These "humanitarian" organizations allowed women who had not previously engaged in any type of political activities to join together toward some purpose or goal. Dr. Branka Antić-Štauber described how the urgent needs created by war eventually allowed ordinary women "to have some political power because they are together in a group" (Interview #23, July 2010).[12] As Dr. Antić-Štauber suggests, participating in an organization – regardless of mission – became a form of political engagement in itself. While before the war few women engaged in public or political life, Branka Rajner, the director of a human rights organization, described how "these unfortunate circumstances [of war] … were a catalyst for [women] being politically engaged" (Interview #72, May 2013).

In the years since the war, the humanitarian sector in Bosnia has emerged as a parallel power structure to the state. Organizations like Medica Zenica, Vive Žene, and BOSFAM became the primary service providers in the country (see Walsh 1998; Mertus 2000; Bagić 2004; Helms 2013). Some of these organizations became implementing partners of the UNHCR, which connected them to the resources and bureaucratic network of the United Nations (Walsh 2000). Through expanded social networks, connections to international sources of funding, and official leadership titles, women who participated in these organizations gained power in their communities that could extend beyond the civic realm.

Feminist Advocacy Emerges

Some organizations that formed to address the acute needs of women during war morphed into explicitly feminist organizations. For example, Žene Ženama (Women to Women), founded immediately after the war by feminist activists from different ethnic backgrounds, was initially designed to aid women refugees in Sarajevo who needed urgent economic, medical, and psychological care (Kleiman 2007).[13] But the three women who formed the organization had experience in feminist networks – including in the Women in Black movement – and ultimately aimed to create a space where they could advocate for women's human rights in all spheres of private and public life. One of the founders, Jadranka Miličić, described how as women of different ethnic backgrounds, they knew that they were making a political statement simply by working together (Interview #61, June 2013). They therefore used the influx of foreign funding to develop trauma counseling programs as well as an organizational structure dedicated to broader women's empowerment initiatives.

Medica Zenica is another example of a service-providing, "humanitarian" NGO that morphed into a political, feminist organization. Initially designed to provide care for survivors of sexual violence, Medica soon became a holistic treatment center, providing refuge, hot meals, and general interpersonal support and solidarity to women in the region. Many women who became involved in Medica found that their work as doctors, nurses, therapists, or support staff catalyzed a shift in their own political consciousness (Cockburn 1998; Interview, Sabiha Husić, June 2013). Meliha, for example, worked for Medica as an anesthesiologist and, prior to the war, was completely apolitical. After joining Medica, however, she stated, "it's not enough to be a doctor. You have to be engaged in a political sense too. Through the project I've met a lot of women who are in the women's movement and I've found my place in it" (quoted in Cockburn 1998: 191).

Medica Zenica and Žene Ženama reveal how women's organizations linked humanitarian wartime needs to a broader political project. By espousing a clear feminist mission and networking with international feminists and feminist organizations, staff members and clients of both organizations were exposed to discourses on antimilitarism and patriarchy (Interviews Sabiha Husić, June 2013; Jadranka Miličić, June 2013). The organizations struck a balance between providing necessary services to vulnerable women and advocating for the importance of women's needs in a public, political way. As the years passed, both organizations began to engage in initiatives aimed at changing Bosnian women's legal rights. Medica led a coalition of women's groups to advocate for the Bosnian government to enforce the 2003 Gender Equality Law and the 2005 Law on Domestic Violence (Spahić Šiljak 2014: 33). Žene Ženama appointed itself the domestic monitor of the government's plans to implement CEDAW, the Millennium Development Goals, the Beijing Declaration, and UN Resolution 1325. Both organizations participate in the yearly "16 Days of Activism against Male Violence against Women," which they coordinate in collaboration with several government institutions. As such, these organizations have become leaders in the fight for gender equality, and their staff and leadership have a national (and sometimes even global) platform from which they can engage women's rights issues.

RESISTANCE AND DEFIANCE: BRIDGING INFORMAL AND FORMAL POLITICS

"We did not want this war, we refuse it." – Women in Black, Belgrade, 1991

War also opened spaces for a third form of women's informal political action: resistance to and defiance of patriarchal norms and social expectations. These forms of resistance were more overt and public in Bosnia than in Rwanda because of greater political tolerance of such forms of political dissent. I thus include them here in a distinct section. Women began engaging in public resistance before the war as the possibility for violence increased. On June 2, 1991, a group of parents – primarily mothers of soldiers conscripted by the Yugoslav National Army (JNA) – broke into the Serbian parliament in Belgrade and demanded their sons be released from military duty. They issued a statement that read:

We refuse that our sons become the victims of senseless militarists. It is not clear what are the goals for which we should sacrifice our sons. Our sons have been deceived: they have to participate in a war for which they are not the least bit responsible, in a war that has not even been declared. That they should give their lives for imperialist purposes is the project of politicians. It is a disgrace to win a fratricidal war. (Mothers of the Soldiers of Belgrade, July 20, 1991, quoted in Zajović 2013: 88)

The following day, busloads of protestors traveled to Ljubljana, Slovenia in an attempt to bring their sons home (Cockburn 1998: 166). These women only had one weapon in their hands: "little photographs of their sons" (Ugrežić 1994, cited in Nikolić-Ristanović 1998: 234). A mass demonstration followed in Sarajevo, and the protestors once again interrupted parliament to demand their sons be released from military duty. By August 29, an estimated 100,000 people had gathered in Zagreb to protest the war (Cockburn 1998: 166). Mothers angry about the conscription of their sons replicated this model around the region throughout the war, and similar episodes of protest occurred in smaller cities as well. In Prijedor in 1992, a large group of women gathered and attempted to steal the list of men to be drafted for military service (Interviews, Majda #8, May 2013; Tabiha #52, June 2013). Majda, who participated in these early protests, described how women rallied because "they did not want to send their brothers and sons and husbands to kill innocent people." Branka Rajner emphasized how these protests represented women's way of influencing politics through the civic sector. As she put it, "That's how women do politics" (Interview #72, June 2013). These activities indicate the extent of women's activism in the early phases of the war. As the war progressed, these actions continued, but their focus shifted. Many of the early protestors came from the educated elite: women who had networks or exposure to feminist thought. As the war progressed, more and more ordinary women participated in various forms of visible political protest.

Women in Black

Women in Black (Žene u Crnom) was at the forefront of women's public activism during the war. Originally founded in 1988 by Israeli women protesting Israel's occupation of the West Bank and Gaza, the Women in Black model of silent protest spread throughout the world through feminist networks during the 1990s. The Women in Black model brings women together in a public square or in front of an important building or monument to protest war by standing silently dressed in black. The movement is oriented by a staunchly feminist, antimilitarist, antipatriarchal, nonviolent philosophy, and is guided by the moral imperative "Not in our name!" and the slogan "Always disobedient!"

The group began in the Balkans as a support group for like-minded women opposed to the war and to the regime in Serbia (Spahić Šiljak 2014: 76). Jadranka Miličić, an early member of the movement, described the first meetings as "fifteen girls in a café bar with just enough money for two cups of tea and one coffee" (quoted in Spahić Šiljak 2014: 76). Women in Black held its first protest in the Balkans in Sarajevo on September 27, 1991, in response to Serbia's threats of violence. Its subsequent protests primarily took place in Belgrade, although its members also traveled around the region and set up chapters in Zagreb and Ljubljana. Every Wednesday at 3:30 P.M., members gathered in a public place to protest. Many protests were held at Trg Republike (Republic Square), the historical heart of Belgrade and the site of many of the most notable events in Serbia's recent political history (Athanasiou 2013; Spahić Šiljak 2014). Members wear black, because, as Staša Zajović, the movement's cofounder, noted, "Wearing black is testifying about war while the war is still going on, and about crimes while they are being committed; it is intervention in reality and exposing what is being denied in the public sphere, in the City Square" (Zajović 2013: 30). Women in Black protestors were self-conscious about the power of their bodies in the center of a male, public space, and saw it as an act of defiance against the patriarchal political order (Mostov 1995). They selected public sites like Trg Republike to bring attention to their rejection of war, patriarchy, hegemonic nationalism, and militarism, positing the female body as a medium for protest, and declaring the link between military war violence and domestic gender-based violence. Zajović described:

By exposing their bodies in the Square, members of Women in Black inscribe their bodies in the history of anti-war resistance, "kidnapping" the space from the dominant discourse and from those who promote it in public spaces, acting subversively against patriarchal traditional symbols. (2013: 34)

Beyond protests, the group's pamphleteering and volunteer work with refugee populations soon prompted pushback, ridicule, and retaliation by authorities and nationalist groups, who began to refer to the activists as "witches" and "traitors." Serbian authorities arrested some members for their involvement; for example, Jadranka Miličić was arrested three times during the war (Interview #61, June 2013). Nevertheless, Women in Black and other feminist groups were unfazed and organized solidarity trips during which women from Serbia would travel to Bosnia to stand with their Bosnian sisters against the war. Jadranka described meeting with seven other Serbian women during the war and frequently traveling to Sarajevo. These pan-Balkan feminist movements were the most vocal and visible political resistance against the war as it was ongoing, as they disobeyed formal restrictions on citizen travel and provided feminist women a forum for condemning a male-dominated war machine.

Women in Black activists continued regular protests after the war ended. As information about the Srebrenica massacre emerged in 1996, they pointed to it as "the paradigm of Serbian crimes" (Zajović 2013: 16). In the years that followed, they used Srebrenica as a way of shaming nationalist Serb leaders, demanding justice and truth-telling within Serbia. Srebrenica became a rallying point for many of the movement's new forms of protest; for example, in July 2010, the organization brought together activists from across the Balkans to collect thousands of pairs of shoes representing the men and boys killed during the massacre. They demanded that a permanent monument be built in Belgrade to commemorate the atrocity. This type of protest put Women in Black activists in contact with artists, theater activists, and other feminist organizations.

Women in Black continues its public protests, publications, and activities in Bosnia to this day. Moreover, many of its early members have gone on to launch additional feminist organizations. As mentioned earlier, Jadranka Miličić went on to found Žene Ženama (Women to Women) and then Fondacija CURE in Sarajevo. Žarana Papić, a professor at the University of Belgrade, went on to found Glas Razlike (Voice of Difference), an organization that promotes women's political rights. Svetlana Slapšak helped found the activist organization Balkan Women against War and established the feminist magazine *ProFemina* in 1994 in Belgrade.[14] These various initiatives have played important roles resisting the hegemonic masculinities, corruption, and nationalism that have dominated the Balkans since the wars of the 1990s.

Mothers of Srebrenica

The Srebrenica massacre in July 1995 sent tens of thousands of civilians from the Drina Valley region to take refuge in Tuzla and other cities in Bosnia under the control of the Bosnian army. At first, the women, children, and elderly who had been allowed to leave the Srebrenica UN Safe Zone assumed that their male relatives would follow close behind. Months went by and many still waited for news. As the war came to a close, it became increasingly clear that many of their male family members had been killed. In early 1996, reports started emerging about the extent of the atrocities committed in Srebrenica. Women I interviewed conveyed a sense of shock after realizing that their loved ones were dead; many had assumed they had been detained in concentration camps and would return any day.

The realization that 8,000 men and boys had been killed provoked disbelief, grief, and soon, outrage. Women began to organize. Kada Hotić, for example, a founding member of the NGO Mothers of Srebrenica, was a factory employee before the war. She lost her husband, son, and many other family members during massacres in the Drina Valley region. She described how women's lives transformed after the loss of their family members:

[Serbs] began genocide ... In my family, it was my son, my husband, his brother, and later on I realized that fifty-six of my family members had been killed. We had questions. Where are the people we love? Are they imprisoned? Are they alive? What was their destiny? We did not have a lot of answers. (Interview #49, May 2013)

In the aftermath, she joined with other women from the Srebrenica region to find the bodies of their loved ones and to pressure the government for aid. Believing that "protests were the only way to be heard," Kada began to organize with other women. Most women from the region were not well educated – they were primarily farmers or factory workers, and few had more than a couple years of schooling. Unlike Women in Black, what emerged was not a feminist movement: at no point did mothers of those killed articulate a commitment to abolishing patriarchy or recognize a shared oppression of women. Instead, it was a "mothers' movement," organized around mothers' and widows' shared grief. Nevertheless, the mothers' movement in Bosnia was a form of political awakening for thousands of Bosnian women as they demanded that politicians reveal the location of their loved ones' bodies and used DNA technology to identify their remains. As such, it was similarly political and resistant to entrenched cultural expectations that women would be passive victims and that their physical bodies would largely remain in the private realm. Instead, women leveraged their identities as victims and as mothers to engage in self-described "disobedient" activities in public spaces.

One early protest began when a group of women from the movement stormed the Red Cross offices in 1996.[15] Women were furious – as one journalist put it, "these women could tear you apart" (Interview #67, June 2013). They demanded the Red Cross pressure the police for truth about their loved ones' whereabouts, the exhumation of bodies from mass graves, compensation for the surviving relatives of those killed, an international investigation into what happened, and the arrest and prosecution of those responsible (Interview #69, June 2013). They also demanded accountability from the UN and particularly from the Dutch peacekeepers charged with securing the UN Safe Zone around Srebrenica. Similar protests continued over the following years. The mothers met in public spaces with pictures of their missing loved ones, demanding some sort of accountability and justice. Mothers organized annual commemorations on July 11, the anniversary of the massacre, in which the bodies identified in the previous year would be buried with public rituals of grief and prayer.[16] In part because of the mothers' actions, what happened in Srebrenica slowly became revealed to the world. Such protests and public displays of grief helped to define these women as "pure victims." These "victim groups" became an important political constituency for the divided postwar government and for international actors. Women in the group understood the power they wielded, because "There is no politician who is brave enough to come in front of a mother who lost her five sons and tell her, 'I don't care what happened to you,' because he is going to lose all of the elections forever" (Interview #67, June 2013).

By 1999, the global community formally recognized Mothers of Srebrenica. Because of its status and self-professed identity as a non-feminist mothers' organization, Mothers of Srebrenica has reinforced essentialist notions of women as more peaceful than men and has positioned its own power as derived from the suffering the women experience in relation to male relatives (husbands, sons, fathers). It does not aim "to disrupt the old script that each conflict leaves behind men in the power and women in tears" (Simić 2009: 229). Its identity as a mothers' organization emerged in part from relationships it developed with other mothers' groups around the globe, including Las Madres de la Plaza de Mayo in Argentina. When I visited the organization's office in Sarajevo in 2013, pictures of other mothers' groups lined the walls. A special plaque from Las Madres is featured, along with pictures of various leaders of the organization posing with leaders from around the world.

In the years since the war, Mothers of Srebrenica has organized protests, events, and seminars to further its quest for justice. Most of these actions have been less defiant than the organization's initial protests, although it continues to disrupt traditional expectations of uneducated, rural women's roles in society. Its mission has often placed its members in contact with international organizations like ICMP, as it exhumed graves and used DNA technology to determine the identities of the victims. Members have appealed to former President Bill Clinton and other international leaders who they feel are morally responsible for failing to protect their loved ones during the massacre, and they have become adept at

utilizing the media to spread information about their cause. As Munira
Subašić put it, "At the beginning of the war we were just housewives
and we were raising kids and our husbands were in charge of providing food for us … [Today] every powerful person that comes to Bosnia
wants to talk with us" (Interview #60, June 2013). Indeed, in the middle
of my interview with Munira, she pulled a crumpled piece of paper out
of her purse – it was a letter hand-signed by former U.S. Secretary of
State Hillary Clinton, who reached out to her in 2011 after the arrest of
General Ratko Mladić.

Munira has become a subversive (and controversial) representative
for the Mothers. In 2013, she flew herself to the United Nations headquarters in New York City and sat in the audience for a speech given by
Serbian President Tomislav Nikolić. The UN had barred her from talking at the meeting on international criminal justice, and in response, she
stood up during Nikolić's speech wearing a t-shirt that read, "Srebrenica:
Justice is slow but it's reachable" and held a sign that read, "Republika
Srpska – Genocide." She was quickly removed from the UN hall, but the
commotion surrounding her removal led to a well-attended press conference at which she was still wearing the shirt.[17] Some people in Bosnia
celebrated Munira's disruption as an example of the public defiance
required to garner any attention for the lack of justice today. Several
weeks later, Nikolić publicly apologized for Serbia's role in the "crimes"
committed in Srebrenica (although he stopped short of calling the massacre "genocide").[18]

Mothers of Srebrenica has also employed less obvious yet comparably
subversive tactics. For example, Kada Hotić described how every July
11 members of the organization travel to Srebrenica to bury the remains
of those identified in the previous year. Shortly after the war, they had
requested access to a large plot of land in Srebrenica for a memorial
and burial site. Yet the Republika Srpska government did not grant them
access, and even "laughed at [them] when [they] proposed the idea."
Regardless, they continued to bury people there every year "right under
their noses" (Interview #49, May 2013).

Of course, due to the Mothers' aggressive tactics and successful fundraising efforts, some Bosnians are suspicious of the group. During my
fieldwork, I often heard rumors that Munira and Kada had profited from
their jobs running the organization (I never personally saw evidence of
this). As a result, similar NGOs have also emerged led by different widows or mothers of those lost in the Srebrenica massacre. As I discuss in
Chapter 8, these groups frequently compete for funds. One such group is

Žene Srebrenica (Women of Srebrenica), a group located in Tuzla and led by Hajra Catic, who lost her son and husband during the war. Despite the disagreements between the two groups and constant battles over funding, they both utilize defiant or subversive tactics to advance their cause. For instance, Vedrana, a member of Žene Srebrenica, described how the war made her "loud." She said:

Before the war I worked in administration and I didn't have to be allowed to complain, I had things to do at work and then I went home to be a housewife. And now women are, and me as well, we are louder. We have to fight for ourselves because men are killed. And someone has to take care of us. And now we have to take care of ourselves ... And everything is on us because we're alone. And we are loud because we are in danger, women are in danger in this society. (Interview #69, June 2013)

On the 11th of every month, Žene Srebrenica organizes protests in the town center of Tuzla in which dozens of women – and a few men – gather, carrying the images and names of their loved ones who were killed. I joined them in June 2013 and spoke to many of the participants, who indicated that such a form of public protest would have been inconceivable before the war. Now, as several put it, they have nothing to lose.

FORMAL POLITICAL PARTICIPATION

Having illustrated three ways that women engaged in informal types of politics as a result of the war, I now turn to the final forum of women's political engagement: the formal political realm. The Dayton Accords ended the military conflict and divided the country into two self-governing entities. This thwarted a re-allocation of power at the state level, as Dayton allowed the same political actors involved in the war to remain in power. These included alleged war criminals like Slobodan Milošević, who remained president of Serbia after the war, and Bosniak politicians like Alija Izetbegović, who served as president of Bosnia during the war and then joined the country's rotating tripartite presidency after. In the years since, a "political-business-criminal nexus" (Bassuener 2012) has masqueraded as a democratic party system, profoundly limiting the democratic process and discouraging ordinary Bosnians from taking part in politics as a career. Citizens widely perceive the ruling (male) elite as pursing its own self-enrichment. Like in other countries transitioning from socialism to free-market economics, political elites and their well-connected friends took control of many business opportunities, and became linked to mafia-run smuggling rings, transporting weapons, drugs, and people throughout the Balkan region (International Crisis Group 1998).

As I discussed in Chapter 5, the Dayton Accords completely excluded women at every stage of decision-making or policymaking in the aftermath (Cockburn 1998; Björkdahl 2012). In the first postwar elections, women were elected to merely 2.4 percent of the seats in the federal Bosnia-Herzegovina House of Representatives, and no woman was elected mayor of a municipality (Cockburn 2001: 23).[19] Therefore, this peace settlement did not upend gender norms at the national political level, but rather fossilized those of the past.

There was, however, a swell of advocacy among women's activists and organizations to increase women's legal rights and political representation after the war. With support from organizations like the OSCE and the National Democratic Institute, women's organizations spearheaded a series of national campaigns – such as the USAID-funded "There Are More of Us: Let Us Vote" campaign – to educate women voters about the new electoral system and raise awareness about the importance of women's leadership (Cockburn 2001: 23).[20] As a result of these efforts, the Provisional Election Commission introduced a 30 percent quota for women on electoral lists in 1998. In the following elections, women were elected to 21 percent of the seats in the federal House of Representatives. While there was a perception that many women who gained seats were pawns of powerful male elites, many of the women I interviewed instead described being motivated to engage in politics because of their war experience.

For example, parliamentarian Alma Čolo was inspired by the shift away from communist politics during the war and described her motivation to get involved as follows:

I entered politics in 1993, during the war … As a lawyer I worked in one office in the Ministry for Foreign and Trade Policy. And when the war started, I was there. And this building was destroyed, and we went to the presidency building and worked from there. I entered in politics because my friend was the president of the City Council of the [SAA] Party. He is a doctor, and he wanted – he asked – for me to help them establish that party in Sarajevo, which was under the horrible circumstances [of siege]. Without water, without electricity, [without] anything that is necessary for normal life. And I'm here now. (Interview #74, July 2010)

For Alma, the war physically pushed her to work out of the presidency's office, where she expanded her social network and eventually made the connections necessary to launch a political career. Others, like Tatjana Ljujić-Mijatović, a former university professor who became a member of Bosnia's presidency during the war, experienced

TABLE 7.1 *Women in Parliamentary Assembly in Yugoslavia (Bosnia post-1991)*

Year	% Women
1945	6.3
1950	8.4
1953	3.5
1958	6.5
1963	17.4
1969	13.6
1974	10.3
1978	11.4
1982	10.2
1986	10.2
1990	4.5
1996	2.4
1998	21.4
2000	9.5
2002	14.3
2006	14.3
2010	21.4
2014	21.4

Sources: For Years 1998–2010: www.parlament.ba/Content/Read/279?title=Saziv-2010.–2014. For 2014: Bosnia- World Bank http://data.worldbank.org/indicator/SG.GEN.PARL.ZS?end=2016&locations=BA&start=2001&view=chart. For Early Years: IPU: Women in Parliaments 1945–1995 www.ipu.org/PDF/publications/women45-95_en.pdf

similar shifts in their careers during the violence (Aganović, Miftari, and Veličković 2015).

Other politicians described how the circumstances of war motivated them to become politically active. This was particularly apparent in interviews conducted with current politicians in mixed marriages or from mixed national backgrounds. Besima Borić (Interview #10, April 2013), a former member of the Federation parliament and a high-ranking member of the Social Democratic Party (SDP), was politically active before the war. As she put it, however, her "serious" political life began after, as she recognized the tragedies that so many people had faced and felt compelled to do something. She was raised secular in a partisan family and identified as Yugoslav before the war, although her ethnic heritage is Bosniak (Muslim). With children from two different mixed-ethnic marriages, her family represented all of the ethno-national groups within Bosnia. As ethnic nationalism intensified during the war, Besima felt motivated "to make some positive change. I believe if I do good, I do good for my kids, and then I do good for my country, then it is good for everyone." She described the war as an awakening, since she began to think about what it meant to kill other human beings on the basis of an ethnicity that she had never seriously considered before. She emphasized that women who came from mixed families, like her own, had an easier time crossing ethnic lines after the war. As she put it, "Women were the first ones who had a normal conversation with two MPs who were on the other side of the war. In '96 and '97 – and this was a big deal – women talked and worked together, women from two entities." By joining the multiethnic SDP, she rejected the nationalist political parties that dominated the postwar movement.

The sense of conviction or resilience that Besima reflected was common among female politicians who had survived the war. Ismeta Dervoz, a member of the national parliament, survived the siege of Sarajevo while working as a public broadcaster for a radio program. Every day during the siege she painted her nails red, applied lipstick, pressed a clean white shirt, and donned high heels. The act of dressing up, she suggested, helped her maintain her identity and resist the chaos of war that unfolded around her. Continuing to work during the siege gave her motivation to survive. As she put it:

When you are alive at the end of the day, you must feel that you are [a] human being. You must be useful to yourself and the others, of course, if you can, and I found all of this in my work ... We worked sometimes seventy-two hours or eighty hours in a shift, because it was impossible for somebody to come [relieve us], so I stayed sometimes three or four days in the radio television building, and I worked twenty-four hours, but it was wonderful because all of the colleagues (technicians, journalists) worked as normally as possible ... We did not want to be involved in any propaganda, in any situation in which we could maybe be put on some side. We were on one side. We were the citizens of Sarajevo under siege, of course. (Interview #2, April 2013)

Ismeta's experience suggests the power of everyday politics and resistance in catalyzing more formal types of political engagement. During the war, Ismeta described how she refused to be a victim; she did not believe the war was legitimate. She was expressly anti-nationalist and felt a conviction to spread information to the citizens of Sarajevo – regardless of ethnicity – who were under siege. She understood that all citizens of Sarajevo were victims because of the violation the siege caused to "our dignity, our human rights, our lives." Her position as a broadcaster connected her to many foreign journalists during the war. Through these connections she managed to organize a Bosnian delegation to attend the Eurovision[21] competition in Ireland in order to "send a message to the world that we are not savages, [that] we are people who have rights to live, to work, to be alive, and to do the best that we can in our profession." Ismeta's determination succeeded; she traveled to Ireland with Bosnia's Eurovision delegation during the war. After the war Ismeta described how she became motivated to fight for "a much better situation in Bosnia" through formal politics.

Other women I interviewed described how the end of the war and the ensuing political stagnation motivated them to enter formal politics. A Serb member of parliament married to a Bosniak man noted, "When the war stopped, things started developing slowly, and then I got my motivation to start in politics" (Interview #29, May 2013). Because of her mixed marriage, this member of parliament suffered greatly during the war, as her husband was conscripted to fight with the Bosnian army. Her house was hit many times by mortar shells and gunfire. She was hopeful that things would improve in the aftermath, but soon became discouraged. She decided to join politics so that her children would not suffer from the same exclusion and nationalist tension she had faced.

One former minister was widowed during the war and left to raise her young children on her own. In the aftermath, she described to me how she discovered that a friend in Australia had been sending her money, but that she had not received it. She approached a newly forming political party to gain assistance with locating the missing aid and, as a result, ended up joining the party "to take matters into my own hands." She also became involved with two organizations after the war that aimed to support wounded soldiers and their families. Her decision to enter politics after the war was a form of "rebellion" against the nationalists who had killed her husband. As she put it, "I thought about it, and I decided that the loss of my husband should not be my end. I grew stronger and decided to fight. I did not let myself go with the flow. I had the support of my friends, so that is how I managed to fight against that. That was my rebellion" (Interview #16, April 2013).

While the national effort to include more women in formal political roles strengthened after the party-list gender quota was adopted in 1998, a 2000 legal reform shifted the political system from a closed- to an open-list proportional representation system. This shift reduced the effectiveness of the quota (Aganović, Miftari, and Veličković 2015; IDEA 2017). Nevertheless, in the 2006 elections, the number of female candidates on party lists for parliament surpassed the required 30 percent threshold for the first time (Kleiman 2007). As a result, the number of women in parliament increased as well, to just over 18 percent in the Republika Srpska National Assembly, 21 percent in the Federation parliament, and 14 percent in the federal parliament (Kleiman 2007; Inter-Parliamentary Union 2008). Many of these gains, however, were superficial: political parties put forward women with little political experience, or wives or daughters of the party elite. As such, many became the pawns of the male-dominated political establishment and failed to advance women's substantive representation (Cockburn 2001: 23).

Nevertheless, women in these formal political positions found they began to have more substantive power while in office. Many have succeeded in working with civil society organizations to pass legislation aimed at helping other women survivors of war. For example, the Law on Gender Equality of Bosnia-Herzegovina was passed in 2003, prohibiting discrimination based on gender. Subsequent 2005 laws in the Federation and Republika Srpska granted women protection from gender-based violence and access to legal resources (Kleiman 2007: 12). Organizations like Medica Zenica and Žene Ženama were essential in coordinating women's advocacy efforts for these legislative victories. For instance, a campaign in 2006 called "For the Dignity of Survivors" was led by a coalition of women's organizations, with Medica Zenica at the forefront. This initiative aimed to pressure the government to recognize rape survivors as civilian victims of war so that they would be entitled to financial compensation: a small monthly pension from the government. The campaign eventually succeeded when SDA politician Nermina Kapetanović lobbied the speaker of the House of Representatives to sponsor the bill (Helms 2013: 207). This bill's passing reflected the commitment of some women in government to support those who suffered most from the war.

CONCLUSION

This chapter outlined Bosnian women's mobilization after war in both informal and formal political spaces. The loss of men and the widespread displacement of the population in Bosnia led many women to take on new roles in their households and communities in order to survive. Women-headed households were particularly vulnerable, and therefore they joined together with others to find basic supplies. Women represented their families and navigated government institutions in order to secure various permissions and reparations after the war. They also gave testimony about their experiences to local and international courts, publicly speaking about sexual violence and thereby challenging cultural expectations of silence and shame. Economic destruction and the loss of income also pushed women to seek aid from humanitarian agencies and to find new ways to earn money for their families. This led to the rapid formation of community organizations, which worked with international humanitarian NGOs to distribute essential supplies. Women took on leadership roles in these nascent organizations in part because they framed themselves as victims of the war and thereby as noncombatants; this enabled them to cross ethnic lines and to engage in contentious processes like refugee resettlement, while depicting their work as inherently apolitical. Women's framing of their organizations as "humanitarian" juxtaposed them with the "political" organizations working on state building, refugee return, and disarmament at the national level, which allowed them room to engage in contentious political issues without significant pushback from political elites. Women's involvement in community organizations reflected the "quiet encroachment" of the feminized civil sector as a parallel power structure to that of the state's ethno-nationalist masculine culture. While formal politics remained – and remains – male dominated and defined by a corrupt, patrimonial logic, some individual women have been motivated by their experiences during the war to get involved. Today, the number of women in Bosnian politics continues to grow.

Yet, although the war was transformative for women's engagement in politics in many ways, women's power in Bosnia remains highly curtailed. As I discuss in the next chapter, intimate partner violence is common, as is sexual harassment and overt gender discrimination. Political elites and the media ridicule feminist organizations, and communities harass and stigmatize rape survivors. I show how many of the current restrictions on women stem from the the structure of the political settlement, the involvement of the international community, and a revitalization of patriarchal violence in the wake of war.

8

Limits of Mobilization

In the previous chapters, I illustrated the various ways violence shaped women's political lives. In both Rwanda and Bosnia, women engaged in a "politics of practice" that shifted their everyday activities: they joined community-based organizations and entered public spaces in previously unimaginable ways. In Rwanda, the government passed landmark legislation supporting gender equality, so that by 2003, Rwandan women held the world's highest percentage of seats in parliament and key positions in government ministries, the national judiciary, and local government. Without an overhaul of the political elite in Bosnia, few women assumed positions in the national government; nevertheless, Bosnian women gained power and positions within civil society, which emerged as a parallel power structure to the state. Both cases, then, tell a story about the unexpected opportunities war can sometimes present for women. While acknowledging the devastating consequences of violence, this book has shown war as a liminal period, in which structural changes interact with women's resilience, strength, and agency.

Yet, looking back over the past twenty years, have these shifts in women's roles endured? If not, what processes have intervened to undermine or limit women's mobilization or postwar gains? This chapter begins to address these questions. While there were many barriers to women's progress in both cases, here I focus on three processes in particular that emerged prominently in my data. The first involves how the political

An article adapted from this chapter was previously published: Berry, M. E. (2017). Barriers to Women's Progress After Atrocity: Evidence from Rwanda and Bosnia-Herzegovina. *Gender & Society* 31(6): 830–853.

settlement impacted – and often impeded – women's mobilization. In Rwanda, the RPF victory initiated an authoritarian regime that eliminated dissent and tightly controlled civil society. In Bosnia, the Dayton Accords established an unworkable political system that divided the state into two semiautonomous, ethnically defined entities. In both cases, political elites mobilized ethnically defined social groups and privileged certain groups (1) as those "most victimized" by the violence, creating *hierarchies of victimhood* that fractured civil society and undermined women's organizing.

(2) The second process regards how international actors shaped women's mobilization in the aftermath of war. In both Rwanda and Bosnia, international actors – especially in the humanitarian sector – intervened with sweeping projects designed to aid postwar recovery. While largely altruistic in motive, these efforts sometimes undermined emergent grassroots organizations, as they implemented projects and policies that had little support in the local context and that inadvertently reinforced the hierarchies of victimhood established by the state.

(3) These first two processes are not mutually exclusive, and underlying both is a third: the reinvigoration of patriarchal norms and practices in the aftermath of war. While the gender order was in flux during the war, and women made many social and legal gains in the aftermath, women's progress in both Rwanda and Bosnia was undermined by an uptick in gender-based violence. While this violence stemmed from the traumatic legacy of war, here I argue that it was also likely a reaction to women's gains and increased autonomy during the war, which threatened men's masculinity and power. Thus, women's political, social, and legal gains have been undermined by a *patriarchal backlash*, in which violence has extended beyond the theater of war and into women's daily lives.

The discussion that follows aims to temper any superficial readings of the previous chapters that would suggest war is in any way good for women. While war facilitated some fluidity in the gendered social order and opened unexpected opportunities for women to engage in new social and political roles, interference from the state, international actors, and/ or patriarchy can limit or undermine these opportunities. Thus, this chapter questions the extent to which postwar mobilization and formal, institutional rights can be harnessed for genuine intersectional emancipation.

THE POLITICAL SETTLEMENT

In the aftermath of any episode of large-scale armed conflict, bargaining between elites, internal actors, and external interveners determines the political, social, and economic direction the postwar state will take. Such "political settlement" processes are profoundly consequential for women's lives, although most work in this field has devoted little attention to their gender dynamics (Di John and Putzel 2009). Rwanda and Bosnia are remarkably different in terms of the reach of the central state into citizens' lives. In Rwanda, the state has historically wielded great power over its population through compulsory labor programs, well-organized military and civilian defense forces, and a hierarchical state structure (see Newbury 1988; Prunier 1995). In Bosnia, the crumbling Yugoslav federation had weak control over many parts of the country; the state even lacked a coercive apparatus like a Bosnian military or police force (see Malcolm 1996; Ramet 2006). As a result, the state was largely inconsequential to ordinary people's daily lives. Despite these differences, women in both countries mobilized in similar ways, shifting political power constellations in the process.

But once women's mobilization was under way, the state shaped and constrained women's actions. Most importantly, the structure of the post-violence political settlement – namely, regime change in Rwanda and the fragmentation of the country into two semi-autonomous entities in Bosnia – profoundly impacted the ability of women's grassroots mobilization to manifest in sustainable gains. As the RPF consolidated power in Rwanda, it eliminated political opposition and public dissent. It also began a total transformation of the country by outlawing any discussion of ethnicity as part of its emphasis on unity and reconciliation (Purdeková 2015). Embodying James Scott's (1998) concept of a "high modernist" state, the regime prioritized development and modernization above all else as it endeavored to make the population "legible." To do so, it began a complete reorganization of the rural population, and "cleaned up" urban areas to ready them for foreign investment. The state's developmental logic and intolerance of dissent stymied women's groups' ability to operate freely and led to coercive state interference in Rwandans' lives. Moreover, while government-backed "women's empowerment" efforts have made some progress toward gender equality, they have also created new forms of oppression for women, ranging from gender-based violence to a heightened dependence on men for accessing political rights (see Berry 2015b).

In Bosnia, a "political-business-criminal nexus" (Bassuener 2012) emerged to run the country, leading to widespread NGO corruption wherein leaders linked to political parties personally profited from humanitarian aid. Political elites, under pressure from women activists, worked to integrate women in formal political spaces, but many of these efforts have resulted in the promotion of women with close ties to party elites who have little interest in advocating on behalf of women's collective interests. Further, by dividing the country into two ethnically defined and increasingly homogenous entities, the political system inscribed at Dayton has encouraged the continued dominance of nationalists. This political system perpetuates the masculine, military culture associated with the war in the first place, constraining women's ability to advocate for gender-sensitive reforms. As I show in the examples that follow, there is little room for women in politics today.

In both cases, hierarchies and economies of victimhood emerged as different victim groups used their victim status as a commodity to be competed for or sold.[1] The state, with support from INGOs, encouraged "raped women" to come forward in order to receive aid. Community organizations competed in "oppression Olympics"[2] by claiming that the people they served were *more* victimized or *more* oppressed than others in order to receive funds. Groups who most effectively displayed their victimhood held all the moral capital.[3] Of course, giving the most help to those most victimized seems like a smart approach. Yet, rather than empowering these populations, the distribution of aid on the basis of victimhood served to further social divisions and to reduce women's experiences to a single, marginal, and disenfranchised identity.

The Rwandan State

Rwandan state efforts to modernize the country in the past two decades – in part, through the empowerment of women – have also paradoxically undermined women's ability to mobilize. In its ambitious Vision 2020 plan, the Rwandan government states its goal to transform Rwanda's economy into a middle-income country by the year 2020. To achieve this, the country must "transform from a subsistence agriculture economy to a knowledge-based society, with high levels of savings and private investment" (Republic of Rwanda 2000). This requires reengineering the rural agricultural sector: eliminating subsistence farming by professionalizing farming techniques and restructuring landholdings (Pottier 2006; Ansoms 2009). It also requires developing a modern workforce with advanced education and technical skills. Because of such "high-modernist" (Scott 1998) development goals, scholars have characterized Rwanda as a patrimonial developmental state (Booth and Golooba-Mutebi 2012; Kelsall 2013).

In order to achieve these ambitious plans, President Kagame and his small clique of Tutsi military officers centralized their control over the country. The government champions cleanliness and security as part of a plan to make Rwanda "the Singapore of East Africa." Authorities impose fines on the population for failing to wear shoes, use mosquito nets, or regularly bathe (Ingelaere 2011: 74) – in other words, for appearing "undeveloped." Plastic bags are outlawed in order to prevent urban clutter, and citizens are forbidden from walking on grass in many public places. Street hawkers and other informal laborers, common in many parts of the Global South, are criminalized in Rwanda without a proper permit. Those engaging in such work are often arrested and detained (Human Rights Watch 2015). In 2017, Human Rights Watch produced evidence that Rwandan security forces had even murdered dozens of citizens suspected of petty crimes.

The government of Rwanda also exerts tight control over civil society, limiting community organizations' ability to function without constant state interference. Freedom House ranks Rwanda as "not free," grading the country a 24 out of 100 in terms of political rights and civil liberties (with 100 being the "most free"). Legislation passed in 2001 gave the government the power to control the management, finances, and projects of national and international NGOs. As a result of this legislation, many civil society organizations have been taken over by government proxies, typically people with close ties to the RPF (Gready 2010). Under the guise of promoting security, these infiltrators aim to tame an organization's political agenda and to crush any latent political dissent. Government proxies have essentially taken over women's organizations like Avega-Agahozo, as well as survivor organizations like Ibuka; only regime-sanctioned individuals are permitted to hold leadership positions in both organizations. Independent, critical organizations like LIPRODHOR, the largest human rights organization, have been effectively shut down (Human Rights Watch 2013). This climate of fear and distrust results in those working within organizations to engage in self-sanctioning behavior (Hintjens 2008). Former RPF elites who defected from the party issued a report in 2010 stating, "There is less room for political participation [in Rwanda] than there was in 1994. Civil society is less free and effective. The media is less free. The Rwanda government is more repressive than the one that it overthrew" (Nyamwasa et al. 2010).

Hierarchies of Victimhood

In this repressive climate, the government of Rwanda has put forth an ambitious plan for development that relies heavily on social engineering. Part of the government's vision to modernize the country centers on the elimination of the ethnic categories that purportedly led to the violence in the first place. Under the theory that ethnicity promotes "divisionism" or a "genocide mentality," a 2003 law gives the police the authority to arrest anyone using ethnic language in public. Instead, the government has sanctioned new forms of social categorization based on one's experience during the genocide: minority Tutsi as survivors (or *rescapés*), majority Hutu as perpetrators or bystanders, and the Tutsi-dominated RPF as the country's liberators (Republic of Rwanda 2007). The regime has carefully constructed an official narrative of the events of 1994, blaming European colonialists for creating ethnic categories and Hutu extremists for initiating the atrocities aimed at eliminating Tutsi.[4]

According to this narrative, only Tutsi were targeted during the genocide. Any Tutsi in the country between October 1, 1990 (the date of the RPF invasion), and December 31, 1994, were deemed "survivors" (Gourevitch 1998; Jefremovas 2002). Little mention was made of Batwa victims or Hutu targets of the former genocidal regime – they were deemed victims of the war, not genocide.[5] Hutu women who had been raped by FAR soldiers or Hutu militias during the war could not access the same resources offered to Tutsi rape victims; their rape was not "genocidal" rape, but was rather relegated to less-political arena of interpersonal violence and domestic abuse (Buss 2009; Burnet 2012: 111).

Further, Hutu whose family members had been killed by the RPF were not entitled to any victim identity. While victims of genocide are buried in memorial sites during elaborate national commemorations, victims of RPF crimes are not spoken of – their bodies are passed off as genocide victims and buried without recognition (Burnet 2012). Andrea Purdeková describes how this distinction undermines the meaning of unity and reconciliation:

> The differential treatment of violent death – on one side ostentatiously displayed and thus affirmed, on the other side adamantly albeit shallowly buried and thus "nonexistent" – is one of the key forces a priori undermining any process of reconciliation. (2015: 66)

Burials – and *reburials* – of those killed during the violence have become forums for the RPF to reiterate and entrench its politicized narrative that portrayed Tutsi as victims, Hutu as perpetrators, and the RPF as the country's savior. *Gacaca* courts served a similar purpose (see Chakravarty 2015; Ingelaere 2016).

Making ethnicity coterminous with a category of behavior was particularly detrimental to Hutu, whom the regime collectively considered guilty. Mamdani cites one official's estimate that the number of "perpetrators" rose from 3–4 million in 1995 to 4–5 million in 1997 – far higher than the entire adult male Hutu population at the time (2001: 266; see also Eltringham 2004). Other government officials advanced similar numbers, globalizing the guilt of a few to the guilt of an entire ethnic group (Vidal 2001). Hutu who had fled to DR Congo were particularly likely to be considered perpetrators, and when these "new caseload" refugees returned to Rwanda they were treated with suspicion.

In essence, the RPF regime – through political speeches, state-controlled news outlets, radio and television announcements, and so on – fused victim categories and social categories, elevating the suffering of Tutsi victims and disregarding others. The foreign media and humanitarian aid industry picked up on these discursive categories, reifying and formalizing these new forms of social division. As a result, the experiences of Hutu and Twa victims were erased from public discourse, facilitating what Jennie Burnet has called an "amplified silence" (2012; see also Straus and Waldorf 2011; Thomson 2013).

Beyond creating divides between people from different ethnic backgrounds, these victimhood hierarchies have also deepened divides between members of the same ethnic group. Most notably, the divide between Tutsi "survivors" and "returnees" – those who grew up in exile and then returned to the country after 1994 – has been especially pronounced. "Returnees" often occupied a higher social and economic position than those who had lived through the violence. Moreover, because the RPF was a political movement built in exile, many who returned had strong connections to the government. In contrast to returnees who spoke Swahili or English, Rwandan-born Tutsi learned French in schools, in addition to Kinyarwanda. The RPF privileged English in government positions, generating what one leader of a women's organization referred to as "a kind of misunderstanding between the survivors and those coming from exile" (Interview #29, April 2012).

Intra-ethnic divides have inhibited the ability of women to mobilize across ethnic and social differences, and victimhood hierarchies – both between and within ethnic groups – have been particularly detrimental for women's groups. Prior to the RPF's consolidation of power in the mid-1990s, women's organizations were some of the only cross-ethnic entities in the country (Powley and Pearson 2011; Burnet 2012; Berry 2015a). Yet the hierarchies fractured women's organizing by creating suspicion and divisions between women, thereby undermining women's ability to sustain collective action around shared interests, such as access to financial capital or protection against gender-based violence. As international organizations distributed aid on the basis of these new victim identities, Tutsi "survivor" organizations were best positioned to receive funding. Funders treated other, non-Tutsi organizations with suspicion, fearing that any organization targeting Hutu would indirectly aid those complicit in atrocities. These divisions inhibited prospects for inclusive or intersectional collective action around shared gender interests.

Thus, while the civil war and genocide in Rwanda caused shifts in women's political engagement, the state has pursued its ambitious development goals by fracturing and repressing civil society. Such an approach echoes past "high modernist" efforts to make societies more organized and controllable in order to bring about development (Scott 1998). Human disasters in China, Tanzania, Russia, Mozambique, and Ethiopia have demonstrated that ambitious development projects can become lethal if states are willing to use coercive force to bring development to fruition, while civil society is too weak to resist. My interviews with Rwandan street vendors and other poor women suggest that the government is indeed prepared to use force to maintain control – President Kagame himself has repeatedly referenced the potential for violence, once stating, "We will continue to arrest more suspects and if possible shoot in broad daylight those who intend to destabilize our country."[6] Despite the advances in community organizations after the war, today Rwandan civil society is likely too weak to resist (see Mann and Berry 2016). These repressive government policies make ordinary women's advancement more difficult, giving pause to celebrations of Rwanda's success in promoting "women's empowerment."

The Bosnian State

While in Rwanda the state intervened in its citizens' lives with a brutal, authoritarian force, the political settlement in Bosnia was more dysfunctional; nevertheless, it similarly fractured women's organizing efforts and set back many prior gains by codifying divides between women with different war experiences. Part of this dysfunction stemmed from the lack of resolution of the war's aims in Bosnia. While the Rwandan state has sanitized and simplified the historical narrative of the war, suppressed ethnic identities, and curated a memorialization narrative that places blame on colonial outsiders in an attempt to move the country forward, in Bosnia the war is ever-present and still debated. Bosnia might be considered a postwar country, but it is not a post-conflict country. As I heard many times during my fieldwork, the Dayton Accords may have ended the violence, but a war of a different kind continues today. Seida, the director of a women's NGO described, "ten years ago, we had hope. But now, I think we're living the war" (Interview #87, May 2016).

The war's continued dominance over the political and social landscape is made possible, in part, due to the country's separation into two ethnically defined entities. Non-Serbs who have returned to homes and communities within Republika Srpska feel like second-class citizens: they struggle to rebuild their homes, face harassment from neighbors and local authorities, and lack recognition from Serb politicians for crimes committed against them. While watching a football match in a bar one night in a town near Prijedor in Republika Srpska, I met a young man who lamented that his (Bosniak) friends keep killing themselves because the situation is so dire – they cannot find jobs, and Serbs constantly harass them. At the same time, Serbs who memorialize their own dead from the war are demonized by their Bosniak neighbors who accuse them of starting the "aggression" and of committing genocide. The Serb women who were raped during the war have not been acknowledged by their own politicians, nor by the international community. Few cross-ethnic memorials to those lost in the war exist in Bosnia today, and different groups proffer different histories of the violence, with no single, dominant history emerging across the country. Politicians from all ethnic groups are the masterminds of this dysfunction, as they cling to power by appealing to extremists and thereby further entrench social divisions.

The divide between Republika Srpska and the Federation undermines the establishment (or reestablishment) of cross-ethnic solidarity on the basis of women's collective interests and complicates women's organizing efforts. For example, women's organizations and activists campaigned for the enactment of a 2006 federal law that classified women rape survivors as civilian victims of war. This classification entitles them to small, regular welfare payments, as well as medical assistance, legal aid, and priority in finding employment and housing (Cockburn 2013b). This classification is rooted in international law that grants all victims of sexual violence the right to remedy and reparation (e.g., restitution, compensation, and rehabilitation; Amnesty International 2009). But women who live within Republika Srpska (and the independent federal district of Brčko) are not entitled to these benefits unless a health commission deems them to have 60 percent "bodily damage" – in other words, permanent physical disfigurement or disability (Amnesty International 2009; de Vlaming and Clark 2014). Those suffering from PTSD or other psychological ailments are not entitled to benefits. In contrast, the Federation has declared that the 60 percent threshold does not apply to survivors of rape, opening the possibility that rape survivors may be deemed eligible.[7] As such, some Bosniak and Croat women in Republika Srpska maintain residences in the Federation just to be eligible for these payments, as they are unable to access sufficient support from Serb authorities. This places an undue financial burden on these women.

To make matters even worse for women survivors of rape living in Republika Srpska, some perpetrators of war crimes occupy high government positions. For example, in Prijedor, the director of the Social Welfare Center is the former commander of a territorial defense unit that was allegedly involved in the atrocities in the region. Further, the head of the Department for the Protection of War Veterans and Invalids was an interrogator at the Omarska concentration camp (Amnesty International 2009: 46). According to several women I interviewed, the presence of these suspected war criminals in high government positions discourages survivors of war crimes to seek assistance.

Even within the Federation, women struggle to acquire the designation of "civilian victim of war" due to government corruption and ineptitude.[8] Many survivors of sexualized violence I spoke with described how accessing support requires going from institution to institution, explaining over and over what happened to them and feeling humiliated in the process. One rape survivor, Sayira, complained how "it is so much more complicated for victims than criminals," since victims have to struggle for recognition and pay for their health care, medicine, lawyers, and so on, while criminals have all of these things provided by the state during their incarceration (Interview #48, May 2013). "The government doesn't support us," she continued, "they keep giving us different amounts of money each month so we can't plan, we can't work properly." Sayira's frustrations about government were nearly universal among the women I interviewed and paralleled the experiences of many women in Rwanda.

Hierarchies of Victimization

These bureaucratic and structural divisions formalized and amplified the hierarchies of victimization that emerged during the war. In May 1993, Bill Clinton declared that Bosnian Serbs' "savage and cynical ethnic cleansing offends the world's conscience and our standards of behavior," obscuring the fact that many Serbs suffered from the violence as well, or that Bosniak and Croat forces also committed atrocities.[9] This sentiment motivated Bosniak nationalist politicians to center raped women and widows as "pure victims" of Serb territorial aggression in order to rally international support. In the years since the violence, Bosniak nationalists have used "raped women" and "widows" as propaganda weapons, inflating or deflating estimates of the number of women in each group to serve political ends and to marshal nationalist support. For example, in 1993, Bosniak foreign minister Haris Silajdžić claimed that at least 30,000 women had been raped. This statement – while based on little evidence – rallied international attention to Bosnia; *Newsweek* published a story shortly thereafter citing estimates of 30,000 to 50,000 victims, unleashing global pity and horror.[10] Of course, tens of thousands of women did likely suffer tremendously from sexualized violence during the war. But by instrumentally using women's suffering to serve political ends, politicians doubly victimized women.

In the years since the war, Bosniak politicians have turned to women's groups like Mothers of Srebrenica and Women Victims of War to bolster their political campaigns. As a member of one of these organizations put it, "[Politicians] only call us before elections to get votes from us or take pictures with us during a burial, so it's only for political points" (Interview #69, June 2013). Conversely, Serb politicians claim that Bosniak women have invented claims of being raped and that Serbs must band together to avoid such accusations. Such framings again instrumentalize women's suffering to buttress political positions that are often detrimental for women's interests.

Foreigners bought into this almost voyeuristic obsession with "rape victims," as I discussed in Chapter 7, and embarked on a mission to find, speak to, and help so-called "raped women." The fact that most rape survivors were Muslim – even if they were agnostic or hardly considered themselves religious – inspired a particular kind of pity based on stereotypes of Muslim women as already victims of "patriarchal," "backward" Islam. Journalists could make headlines by interviewing them, and their pictures in global news outlets drew horror from people around the world. Humanitarian NGOs decided that this "epidemic of rape" warranted swift and immediate attention. They began constructing centers for "raped women," which offered psychological therapy, financial resources, and other types of social support.

These well-intentioned projects rested on several problematic assumptions. The first was that women survivors of sexualized violence would willingly assume the identity of "rape victim" and perform particular behaviors or scripts expected of them as a result of that experience. Bakira Hasečić, a rape survivor who has made her appeal for justice in public, said:

I come from a family of seventeen members, and I did not mention that I was raped, because that was a taboo subject. I was putting myself at risk if I said that ... Part of society considers that a disgrace for women ... a lot of marriages fell apart, because they could not cope with that. Their kids left them, as well, because they could not cope with it. (Interview #46, May 2013)

In the patriarchal local context, women who identified as rape victims were expected to be ashamed, guilty, and silent.[11] This victim identity diminished survivors who articulated their experience as one of survival and, moreover, stigmatized rape survivors as "soiled" and pitiful (Summerfield 1999; Mertus 2000: 28). Admitting to being raped was also seen as a dishonor to the victim's male relatives, as rape was often a tactic of emasculating men through the abuse of their "property" (i.e., wives and daughters) and the threat to their genealogical lineage. As a result, few women wished to identify publicly as having suffered sexual violence during war. Bakira was one of these women; several years after the war she joined with other rape survivors to speak out against their perpetrators. The backlash was tremendous; rape victims were not expected to be "loud." As she put it, "War criminals started contacting us, provoking us, humiliating us. They told us, 'Are you coming back so we can finish what we started?'." At the time of our interview in 2013, Bakira was regularly receiving harassing calls, texts, emails, and Facebook messages from anonymous people. In the middle of our conversation in her office she brought me and my research assistant over to her computer to show us a photograph that a Serb man had sent her that morning of his penis, along with a host of disparaging messages. She described this constant abuse as continued "psychological warfare."

Moreover, such programs for "raped women" assumed a narrow focus on rape over the many other forms of gender-based violence, and further assumed sexual violence harmed women more than other forms of victimization.[12] As I discussed in Chapter 6, women did not always articulate rape as the most traumatizing event they experienced, especially among those who had lost a child or spouse. Yet many recounted that when seeking counseling or aid for other war experiences, humanitarian NGOs told them to talk about their rape first and other sufferings later. Being a rape victim was a currency that women could cash in on for treatment; but, in doing so, they risked stigmatizing themselves for life. Tabiha, a survivor of the Omarska concentration camp, exemplifies this tension. Serb forces killed Tabiha's eldest son during the war. They also detained her at Omarska and raped her. In her mind, her own experiences pale in comparison to the pain she feels about her son's murder. As of 2017, Tabiha's son's body still had not been found, causing her tremendous anguish. And yet journalists and NGOs with whom she has interacted over the years have been primarily interested in her experiences at Omarska, imposing on her the identity of "rape victim" (Interview #52, May 2013).

By identifying "rape victims" as in need of particular forms of care, these efforts ignored women who did not fit into this victim category. According to psychologist Derek Summerfield, a leading expert in the field of postwar trauma, "trauma models, where the focus is on a particular event (rape) ... exaggerate the difference between some victims and others, [and] risk disconnecting them from others in their community" (1999: 1456). Such a narrow framing of victim categories compelled "rape survivor" groups to compete for foreign funds against groups of widows, concentration camp survivors, and returnees – without recognizing that some people were simultaneously situated in multiple categories.

Even further, these efforts also focused almost exclusively on Bosniak and Croat women, neglecting the thousands of Serb women – not to mention men of all ethnicities – who also experienced sexualized violence during war (see also Korac 1998). Like Hutu victims in Rwanda, Serb women who were subjected to sexualized torture during the war had their experiences relegated to the less-political arena of interpersonal violence and criminality, rather than genocide or ethnic conflict. This meant that the suffering of many Serbs was unrecognized by international actors and legal frameworks, and, moreover, they were unable to join organizations or claim benefits related to their war experience.

The elevation of these "special victims" over others who had also greatly suffered from war worked to fracture the women's movement. Whereas during the war women had come together to form small, informal self-help organizations (Cockburn, Stakic-Domuz, and Hubic 2001; Helms 2013), in the aftermath, many of these organizations became specialized – they were exclusively for rape victims, widows, survivors of concentration camps, and so forth. Not only did these specialized groups ignore women who were situated in multiple categories or who did not fit cleanly into a particular one, they also pitted "rape survivor" groups against widows, concentration camp survivors, and returnees in competition for donor funds, leading to infighting, a lack of trust, and limited opportunities for collaboration. Medina, a middle-aged woman who survived a concentration camp but escaped sexual torture, described how this prevented her from feeling welcome in one women's group:

[I was in an organization that had] knitting circles and they would pay us and give us a bus ticket, and most of the women who were coming there were victims of sexual violence. But I'm not, and we asked if we were going to get paid for anything they were producing and the woman said that I wouldn't because I wasn't a victim of sexual violence ... I was then excluded from the circle. (Interview #11, July 2016)

Hierarchies of victimhood in Bosnia also extended beyond individual experiences, and involved the elevation of the massacre at Srebrenica over all other crimes in the country. For those living in the region around Prijedor – the area with the second highest rate of civilian killing – the international community's disproportionate attention to Srebrenica's victims generated tremendous frustration. Srebrenica was the largest single massacre during the war and was eventually labeled "genocide" by the International Court of Justice and the ICTY. As I discussed in Chapter 1, this is one reason that I am cautious about using the term "genocide," as applying it in this case elevated the deaths of Srebrenica victims over the deaths of tens of thousands of others killed during the war. This hierarchy of victimhood continues today, as associations from Srebrenica continue to secure politicians' attention, international funding, and a global media platform. In contrast, organizations in the Krajina region that address missing people or engage in peacebuilding efforts struggle to access funds. According to Tabiha:

I am very angry because of that. I am really angry because we [in the Krajina region] do not get the attention we deserve. They do not care about us. I am angry at internationals and those in the Bosnian government, as well. What happened in Srebrenica – they got killed in a few days, but we were bleeding from the knee. We had camps, rapes, [Serbs] stole stuff. They set our houses on fire. They put bombs on our doors, so that when you open[ed] your door, you blew up ... All of the humanitarian aid that came to Bosnia went to Srebrenica, and they behaved like we do not exist. (Interview #52, May 2013)

These hierarchies of victimhood *between* and *within* different ethnic groups have fractured the momentum women generated after the war. Competition for resources either from the state or from international actors has led to infighting and a lack of trust. Fighting between different "victim" groups has limited opportunities for collaboration and caused groups to privilege the identities thought to bring about the most funding. Further, initiatives designed to support women created perverse incentives for women to claim they had been raped (whether they had or not) in order to receive aid. Such incentives were ultimately disempowering at an individual and a collective level, as they stripped women of agency in determining which identities were the most salient in their lives and presumed a greater understanding of what women needed than women themselves. Combined, these hierarchies limited the prospects for cross-entity, interethnic collaboration and peacebuilding in the long run.

INTERNATIONAL ACTORS IN "AIDLAND"

Humanitarian aid is essential for keeping people alive and healthy after episodes of mass violence, and development assistance is critical for a country's recovery. The humanitarian response in both Rwanda and Bosnia kept millions of people alive and did a great deal to mitigate suffering. But the arrival of a virtual army of foreign workers and aid programs also had unintended effects. Many INGOs partnered with grassroots organizations in order to implement programs, but, in doing so, they shaped the structure and mission of these organizations to align better with international funding priorities than with local needs. This ultimately undermined and stunted some women-led grassroots initiatives.

In the post–World War II era, INGOs, multinational agencies, and religious organizations have arrived in postwar contexts with a mandate to save lives through medical and humanitarian relief, reduce the pain of loss through social support programs, and build peace through programs focused on transitional justice or women's empowerment.[13] Since the 1980s, a host of humanitarian agencies and NGOs – including the UN Refugee Agency (UNHCR), World Vision, Doctors without Borders, the International Committee of the Red Cross and Red Crescent, the World Food Programme, and Caritas – have become essential for delivering emergency relief in the aftermath of violence (de Waal 1997).

Such efforts have at times echoed past colonial projects, as foreign actors have intervened with far-reaching aims to transform society from one capable of war to one in line with Western ideals of democracy and capitalism. As a result, a large scholarship critiquing the international humanitarian aid industry – dubbed "Aidland" – exists, and is growing.[14] As Severine Autesserre (2014) notes in reference to peacekeeping missions, foreign actors can do nothing, make some improvements, or make things worse after war. The same typology applies to humanitarian aid, and in my research in Rwanda and Bosnia I found countless examples of all three. I focus here on the ways in which humanitarian actors make things worse in order to shed light on why women's advances have been limited and even set back over time.

International actors can "make things worse" for many reasons. To begin, peacebuilders and humanitarian workers are typically part of a transnational elite that values technocratic knowledge over local wisdom. INGOs can thus implement programs that succeeded elsewhere, while paying little attention to local experiences or expertise. In the 1990s, most international actors encouraged giving aid to organizations engaged in "democracy promotion," and they pushed for elections and the privatization of industry after transitions from war or socialism.[15] In pushing neoliberal ideas and technocratic knowledge, foreign actors undermined and antagonized local actors, sweeping into an area and setting up initiatives that fell outside of local needs (Rieff 2003). Unequal power relations between these international actors and the local population bred resentment and even hostility, and ultimately structured new local inequalities as well.

"Hot topics" in aid also rapidly shifted from one month to the next – varying from psychosocial trauma to microcredit – which weakened the efforts of high-functioning grassroots organizations specializing in a single area. International experts displaced local experts; "Western" training was deemed more credible, even if practitioners had little knowledge of the cultural or social context. In both Rwanda and Bosnia, for example, teams of foreign psychiatrists deemed trauma counseling a top priority; however, many locals were more concerned about economic survival and establishing a daily routine, and thus may have been better served by various income-generating projects.

International actors also learned about both countries through global media coverage, which tends to depict the world as inherently anarchical and violent, and these narrow views informed their approaches to aid. Within this realist paradigm, the media portrayed women as suffering victims, morally pure "innocents" caught amid a war not of their making. As a result, "women" becomes coterminous with "victims." Men – who were also victims, including of sexualized assaults – were left out of this victim narrative, which allowed them to maintain their hegemonic masculinity (see also Žarkov 2001; Connell and Messerschmidt 2005; Helms 2007, 2013; Buss 2009). Women and others who did not fall into the categories of victimhood set out by humanitarian actors often found it difficult to obtain aid (Buss 2009; Moran 2010). For instance, when the Rwandan and Yugoslav Tribunals redefined rape as a "weapon of war" and as an "instrument of genocide," they only recognized women of a certain ethnicity as victims – the rape of Hutu women (not to mention men), was not prosecutable at the ICTR.[16] Scholars have not fully explored how this hierarchy of victimhood, impacted women's ability to mobilize. Further-more, global news coverage depicted "Muslim women" and "African women" as doubly victimized, both by their experiences during war and by the patriarchal cultures that purportedly perpetuate their oppression. Thus, programs designed to aid women were premised on this presumption of victimhood. Moreover, such interventions often presupposed the internal homogeneity of "women" as a group or as a series of ethnic groups, ignor-ing the regional, class, linguistic, and other categories of difference that divide women in each country (Mohanty 1988; Crenshaw 1991).[17]

As discussed in the introduction and elsewhere throughout this book, such depictions can have two outcomes. They can provide women activ-ists with some distance from the male-dominated political realms dis-credited by war, and thereby allow women space to mobilize; at the same time, however, such depictions can also essentialize and demobi-lize women. When INGOs implemented policies and programs to aid rape victims, widows, or refugees, they often cemented these identities for those seeking service. I propose here that such approaches to inter-national aid may undermine grassroots organizing efforts and reinforce patriarchal structures of inequality.

International Involvement in Rwanda

Most of the discussion about the international community's failings in Rwanda centers on its failure to intervene and stop the violence. In the United States, the Clinton administration was aware of the scale and extent of the killings as the violence began (Dallaire 2003; Power 2003). The administration delayed action, however, because there was little popular support for putting U.S. troops on the ground in the wake of American troop deaths in Somalia just months earlier. Debates about whether the killings constituted genocide stymied the UN's response and led to differing interpretations of what was occurring. While these debates have been the subject of extensive study in recent years (see discussions in Melvern 2000; Power 2003; Rieff 2003; Kuperman 2004; Stanton 2004; Barnett 2011), the humanitarian aid response, which I examine here, has received less attention.

The international community struggled to make sense of the violence in Rwanda as it was unfolding, yet even more uncertainty emerged in its aftermath. The confusion centered on whether the RPF-controlled "tran-sitional government" was making decisions in the interest of the country as a whole, or whether it was involved in a "Tutsification" of the state and a consolidation of power (Uvin 2010). Much of this debate centered on Paul Kagame, and whether he was a visionary leader or an emergent dictator. While Kagame technically served as vice president between 1994 and 2000 to Hutu President Pasteur Bizimungu, there was little doubt that Kagame and a small cadre of Tutsi elites were the most powerful political force in the country. As evidence of the RPF-orchestrated massacre at Kibeho and reports of other extrajudicial killings emerged, some in the international community worried that aid would be used to prop up a brutal, exclusionist regime.[18]

Foreign actors (e.g., INGOs, government agencies) were split in these debates. Some countries, including France, initially saw the RPF as the instigator of the atrocities and sent massive amounts of funding and humanitarian infrastructure (about $2 billion) to DR Congo to aid in the refugee crisis. This infuriated Kagame and the RPF, who wanted the aid to be spent on genocide survivors, rather than its perpetrators. It also led to confusion and a lack of coordination in the aid response (Ericksson 1996). Another set of donors, primarily from the United States and the United Kingdom, were enraptured by Kagame and gave him *carte blanche* to pursue his domestic agenda unfettered by foreign concerns over his human rights record. These donors believed that some extrajudicial violence was inevitable given the circumstances (Mann and Berry 2016). While promoting democratic reforms was initially at the top of the donor community's agenda, democracy soon took a backseat as Kagame cautioned that elections would be too dangerous. Most donors agreed, understanding that stability – even if achieved with political oppression and violence – was a higher priority than democracy.

The divergent interpretations of the violence among the humanitarian aid industry resulted in disagreements about who deserved aid. Initially, the disagreement focused on what to prioritize: the refugee crisis in DR Congo – where tens of thousands of people were dying of dysentery and cholera – or Rwanda itself. International aid organizations at first focused on saving lives by providing food, shelter, medical care, and sanitation facilities to the massive number of displaced. By the end of 1994, they redirected funds to the human and institutional devastation resulting from the genocide and civil war (Eriksson 1996). Much of this aid was earmarked for widows, survivors, orphans, and rape victims – all categories the RPF defined in conjunction with foreign donors.

As discussed earlier, the government of Rwanda promoted a simplified narrative of the violence that equated ethnic categories with broad categories of participation during the violence. Only Tutsi were survivors, and Hutu were collectively associated with guilt. This politicization of victimhood had acute implications for the distribution of aid and other resources in the aftermath. For example, the UK-based Survivor Fund supports initiatives for "survivors" of the Rwandan genocide – and takes the postwar government's definition of "survivor" seriously. It funds Rwandan organizations like Avega-Agahozo (for widows), AERG (student survivors), Uyisenga-N'Manzi (HIV-positive child-headed households), and Solace Ministries (Christian survivors).[19] "Survivors" are entitled to all of the resources that these various organizations provide – including cash payments, medical care, housing assistance, school fees, vocational training, and trauma counseling. Since only Tutsi victims of the genocide could be considered "survivors," all survivor organizations are essentially Tutsi organizations. Hutu victims of the war and genocide may not join these organizations, except under exceptional circumstances. As a result, Tutsi-led "widow" or "survivor" organizations were better positioned than Hutu-led organizations to access international funds, and they were more likely to formalize and develop a platform from which members could climb the economic ladder, enter public spaces, and fill new political vacancies. By distributing funds along these victim categories, the international aid community endorsed the government's erasure of Hutu experiences of survival from political discourse.[20]

Problems in Implementation

The international involvement in Rwanda also impeded women's ability to mobilize in other ways. Top-down technocratic knowledge about how to care for refugees and rebuild infrastructure, for example, replaced local knowledge or efforts about the same projects. International humanitarian personnel feared that if Rwandans – particularly Rwandan Hutu – organized, they could potentially undermine order (Pottier 1996). As such, they often viewed all Hutu as a security threat and as having nefarious political motives. This led to a serious neglect of bottom-up organizing efforts. For example, in a refugee camp in DR Congo, displaced women (likely mostly Hutu) developed a system to foster nearly 7,000 unaccompanied minors (Pottier 1996: 412–413). But representatives from Norwegian People's Aid lamented the lack of a proper orphanage and intervened to take charge of the children's relocation – despite that, in Rwandan tradition, orphaned children are typically cared for by extended family or neighbors. Small loans or microcredit schemes may have significantly bolstered these emerging groups and thereby local economies. Instead, expensive expatriate-led humanitarian relief programs created

cycles of dependence, which may have ultimately destabilized local economies (Pottier 1996), not to mention grassroots mobilization efforts.

Due to this top-down approach, humanitarian aid agencies often did
not provide funding, logistical support, or security to grassroots self-help
organizations in certain parts of the country, many of which were led by
women. Instead, foreign NGOs frequently shut down or supplanted local
organizing efforts. They sometimes did this directly, by preventing groups
(specifically, Hutu) from organizing in public spaces under the idea that
such groups posed a security risk. They also did this indirectly, by hiring
the most impressive emerging leaders from civil society, granting them
positions that could eventually lead to their promotion within the global
structure of these organizations. While such promotions were likely good
for the financial and social status of those hired, they deprived many local
women's organizations (and likely organizations more generally) of their
strongest members.

In the years that followed the initial humanitarian response, INGOs
did give funding to women's grassroots organizations within Rwanda.
However, little of this aid extended to women organizing in refugee
camps outside of the country (Joint Evaluation of Emergency Assistance
to Rwanda [3] 1996; Pottier 1996). This meant that INGOs gave Tutsi
women in survivors' associations funding and other technical assistance,
while often neglecting Hutu women. As described in Chapter 3, this support helped facilitate some Tutsi women's ascent in Rwandan politics,
while providing few channels for Hutu women to gain positions of economic or political power. It also entrenched social divisions in society and
limited chances for women to form cross-ethnic alliances.

International Involvement in Bosnia

Like in Rwanda, the problematic implementation strategies pursued by
the international community impeded grassroots organizing in Bosnia
after the war, for women and men alike. More researchers have explored
this rich topic in the Bosnian context than in Rwanda (see Smillie 1996;
Korać 1998; Walsh 1998; Summerfield 1999; Smillie and Everson 2003;
Bagić 2006; Helms 2013). Many of the people I interviewed expressed
frustration at the international community's response as a whole, and
especially at the Dayton Accords. Setting aside the myriad problems
that emerged from the governing structures put forth at Dayton (see critiques by Chandler 2000; Bose 2002; Bjorkdahl 2012), here I specifically
address the problems linked to humanitarian aid.

Bosnia was a unique setting for humanitarian aid because of its location in Europe. Unlike far-flung conflicts around the globe, Europeans could drive to Bosnia to participate in aid relief – as thousands did. In many respects, Bosnia became the paradigmatic example of humanitarian aid and state-building in the post–Cold War era. People from all parts of the globe got involved (Andreas 2004). In Rwanda, the RPF regime was suspicious of the international community, both because of its colonial history and also because of its failure to intervene in the genocide; as a result, it actively resisted much of the international involvement in the aftermath. In contrast, NATO stopped the war in Bosnia and the country became an international protectorate managed by foreign institutions like NATO, the UN, the Office of the High Representative, the OSCE, and the Peace Implementation Council. Bosnian politicians had little incentive to restrict the massive influx of INGOs and other foreigners after the violence.

The sheer number of humanitarian aid NGOs, trauma experts, development specialists, peacebuilders, and human rights activists that arrived in Bosnia after the war had a lasting impact on various social sectors. Like in Rwanda, most of these foreigners came from the United States and from Western Europe, while some also came from countries in the Middle East, including Saudi Arabia, Iran, the United Arab Emirates, and Kuwait, as well as from Japan (Mertus 2004: 24). Most of these foreign actors aimed to immediately assist Bosnia's reconstruction and eventual entry into global financial markets and the broader European community. These international actors offered a technical toolkit of short-term reconstruction and postwar reconciliation strategies derived from success in other places. But as they implemented various policies and programs, they frequently made decisions that suggested a staggering lack of knowledge about the lived realities of ordinary Bosnians (Walsh 1998; Jansen 2006; Helms 2013). Many came with Orientalist assumptions that Bosnia was a low-developed, "primitive" place fraught with religious strife, rather than a middle-income industrial economy in the heart of Europe (Žarkov 2014). They also assumed all Bosnian women were victims with few skills or little education. Studies of the postwar period in Bosnia suggest that the Bosnian public largely viewed "internationals" as arrogant, ignorant, and inept (Jansen 2006; Helms 2013).

Problems in Implementation

The humanitarian aid industry in Bosnia employed countless problematic strategies. Funding priorities were ephemeral and changed on a whim to accommodate donor demands. Humanitarian agencies would prioritize "peacebuilding" one day, but "democracy promotion" the next. While this strategy ostensibly aimed to provide flexible and responsive aid, in reality it added a level of uncertainty for recipients who depended on donor funds for their programs. According to Smillie and Everson (2003), the first "hot topic" was emergency psychological assistance. As a result, Bosnians founded social welfare organizations that could accommodate trauma projects. Funding agencies prioritized reconstruction next, and welfare organizations morphed into building and renovation organizations. Microcredit followed, and as Smillie and Everson put it, "welfare organizations scrambled to understand interest rates" (298). In 1998, this was replaced by a shift in focus to refugees' return. These erratic shifts meant that grassroots organizations that received external or international funding often had to change their programs to accommodate donor requirements – or at least had to tweak their programs to *appear* to adhere to donor requirements. This led to inconsistent implementation and constant uncertainty (see Walsh 1998), foregoing the responsibility many scholars and practitioners believe humanitarian NGOs hold "to provide local NGOs with the freedom and the ability to bring promising projects to a successful conclusion" (Evans-Kent and Bleiker 2003: 109).

Programs dedicated to "rape victims" further assumed that foreign programs had superior technocratic expertise to local agents. Bosnia was the first major international crisis in which humanitarian aid responders prioritized trauma healing as humanitarian intervention (Abramowitz 2009: 49), and this trauma-based aid privileged outsider knowledge over local understandings (Summerfield 1999). Interveners generally assumed that the entire population suffered from PTSD and therefore needed expert medical treatment, without considering that many Bosnians had developed ways of dealing with trauma that were rooted in their local understandings and social networks. For instance, many found comfort through their faith or through a heightened sense of national belonging. The emphasis on trauma-mediating projects incentivized NGOs to overestimate the number of their clients with PTSD, since the more diagnoses NGOs could make of clients with PTSD, the more funding they could receive. As such, NGOs encouraged women to come forward as "rape victims" in order to receive trauma support. This was incredibly problematic, as there is little in the medical literature to suggest that rape is a discrete cause of psychological vulnerability in conditions of war, nor that a specific therapy strategy could be sufficiently effective to justify the increased risk of exposing women's experiences to their communities (Summerfield 1999: 1456).

These ill-conceived funding priorities caused widespread resentment among Bosnians trying to work in their communities, particularly as local organizations competed over funds. Dr. Antić-Štauber described this constant re-funding of new initiatives as inhibiting her ability to make real progress in her organization – it was "just like a tornado," she said. "We're all just going in a circle, around and around, and nothing will be resolved" (Interview #23, July 2010). Organizations with staff who spoke English or had marketing skills were often better able to morph their organizations' programs to appeal to the latest donor trend. Ultimately, programs that were hastily constructed and poorly conceived received funding.

With little knowledge of the local context, INGOs also implemented programs that targeted women as a monolithic group, and thereby reinforced essential gender stereotypes. For instance, INGOs implemented programs aimed at creating income-generating projects for women. But, without conducting skills assessments of the women they were trying to serve, many assumed Bosnian women had little education or technical abilities. They therefore enlisted women in sewing, knitting, or housekeeping businesses that confined women to low-profit, gender-segregated work (Walsh 1998: 336). Highly educated women I interviewed found these projects insulting and a way of further undermining their dignity.

Such ill-conceived programs also generated tension between foreign NGO staffers and locals. Like in Rwanda, the arrival of more than 100,000 foreigners – most of whom were in a far superior financial position to average Bosnians – artificially inflated local economies. NGO salaries sustained restaurants, drivers, translators, sex workers, and security personnel; businesses sprang up to cater to foreigners' needs (Evans-Kent and Bleiker 2003: 110; Pugh and Cooper 2004). The demand for sex workers fueled by these international actors – particularly by UN troops – led to massive increases in human trafficking from Ukraine, Moldavia, and Romania throughout Bosnia and Southeast Europe as whole (Human Rights Watch 2002; Pugh and Cooper 2004; Kondracki 2010).[21] Beginning in 1995, the UN suspected that a quarter of the women and girls working in Bosnian nightclubs and bars were trafficked. These women were often held in debt bondage, forced to perform sexual acts for clients, and beaten by their "owners." Investigators found that international aid and military personnel – including private defense contractors working from U.S. military bases – were complicit in the trafficking and exploitation of these women (Human Rights Watch 2002). The UN's police monitoring force (IPTF), comprised entirely of foreigners, was repeatedly implicated for its involvement.

When aid began to dry up in 1999 with the escalation of the crisis in Kosovo, these inflated economies collapsed. INGOs abandoned local NGOs, as they no longer needed local implementing partners (Cockburn 2001). Unemployment and economic recession followed (Pugh and Cooper 2004: 161–162). Women I interviewed expressed resentment of these shortsighted international efforts.

International involvement in both Bosnia and Rwanda set back women's organizing in many ways. Competition for resources between community organizations led to infighting, a lack of trust, and the withholding of information. This created further divisions within society – *within* and *between* ethno-national groups. In Bosnia, fighting between different "victim" groups limited opportunities for collaboration and stalled projects aimed at erecting memorials to war victims.[22] In Rwanda, suspicion of certain groups and a preference for funding "survivor"-led initiatives led particular community organizations to thrive. Several of my respondents noted that after the war they were amazed at how united women were, but since then divisions between women's groups have polarized women in general. These divisions have also led many community-based organizations to be ethnically homogenous, limiting prospects for long-term inter-ethnic collaboration and peacebuilding.

REVITALIZATION OF PATRIARCHY

In both Rwanda and Bosnia, women's gains were further pushed back or undermined because of a third process: a revitalization of patriarchal norms, reflecting men's "perennial sense of entitlement to women's bodies" (Cockburn 2013b: 3). Patriarchal norms underscore women's day-to-day life around the globe, typically through disproportionate time use, as well as subtle forms of intimidation and violence that ensure women's subordinate status to men. This is nothing new. But while patriarchal values and systems can be suspended during war as women take on men's traditional roles and experience physical separation from their male family members, in the aftermath of war, such patriarchal norms can not only reemerge, but can experience a revitalization that is critical to unpack when examining women's power. The line between war violence and violence more broadly is not always clear; it instead operates more like a continuum, as the same systems of militarism and patriarchy that drive war violence also shape women's daily lives.

While much attention has been given to the violence inflicted on women during both periods of war, the rates and forms of violence in the years since are alarming. According to Cynthia Cockburn:

[Men] are brought up, even in the most peaceful of times, to identify manhood with a readiness to exercise authority over women and to wield force, against women and other men. In war-time they are further trained, and rewarded, for the practice of wounding, raping, killing. Often this experience traumatizes men as well as their victims. And it shapes their behaviour after war, for the disposition to violence is not readily put aside with demobilization. (2013b: 3)

I argue that this reflects a *patriarchal backlash* to the gains women make in their homes and communities during war, which threaten men's hegemonic control. Women's rights and progress – regardless of whether they are gained during periods of violence or stability – can mask "hidden cruelties," to borrow Wendy Brown's phrasing, and "unemancipatory relations of power ... in [their] sunny formulations of freedom and equality" (2000: 230). In other words, women's gains can often mask women's continued oppression.

This echoes an evolving field of literature that documents links between women's economic or educational gains and rates of domestic violence within the home (see Vyas and Watts 2009; Rahman, Hoque, and Makinoda 2011). Women's political gains can also instigate a backlash. Mona Lena Krook (2015), for example, draws on Blalock's (1967) concept of "intrusiveness" to demonstrate how growing numbers of women in politics can provoke hostile and even violent responses. Moreover, Sylvia Walby describes how women's advances are often met "with renewed determination by patriarchal forces to maintain and increase the subordination of women" (1993: 76). This tension, between simultaneous progress and slippage in the process of women's emancipation, must draw our attention to the limitations of inclusion as a means for promoting women's power without concurrent attention to dismantling the underlying systems that produce women's subordination.

Despite the impressive progress that women in both Rwanda and Bosnia have made in the postwar period, a study on masculinities in both countries found that men firmly view themselves as the power holders and decision makers within the household, while they view women as primarily responsible for children and the domestic sphere (Promundo IMAGES 2011). Of course, these gender roles were disrupted during the conflict, and, since the war, international and domestic actors have advanced norms, legal frameworks, and public awareness campaigns designed to challenge these beliefs. These efforts have clearly been insufficient; there is a "stickiness" to patriarchal power relations in both countries. More alarming, however, is evidence of a *backlash* against this progress. Women I interviewed identified violence against women – including physical violence, verbal assaults, accusations about sexual immorality, and so on – as a way of undermining women's ability to consolidate their postwar gains and continue mobilizing in their communities. As such, patriarchal violence reflects a profound limitation to women's gains after war.

Data on physical and sexual violence in postwar contexts are hard to come by. Scholars have debated whether rates of domestic violence increase in the aftermath of conflict, or simply whether awareness about domestic violence increases, leading to a higher rate of reporting. This is in part due to the lack of a reliable baseline from before the war. As I note in what follows, however, some studies have indicated an increase in domestic violence – at the minimum, they suggest that levels of violence against women are extremely high in both countries. This might be due to men's experience during war, but might also be a reaction to the gains women made in their homes and communities during the war (Rombouts 2006; Slegh et al. 2013).[23]

Rwanda

In Rwanda, a nationally representative survey in 2010 found that 57.2 percent of Rwandan women had experienced gender-based violence from a partner (Rwanda Men's Resource Center 2010). Thirty-two percent of women reported that their partners had forced them to have sex. The same study revealed that men who were directly affected by the war or genocide – nearly 80 percent of all men – had higher rates of violence against female partners than men who had not been directly exposed to violence. This suggests that exposure to violence has led to an uptick in intimate partner violence (Slegh et al. 2013).

But the association between war violence and violence against women in the aftermath is only part of the story. In my conversations with women across Rwanda, some reported that their husbands were most likely to beat them when they returned home from a women's group, such as the increasingly popular income and loan savings cooperatives. National surveys corroborate this, as men also indicated that they beat their wives with more frequency now that women are engaged in profit-making activities outside of the home (Slegh et al. 2013: 19). Literate, educated, and employed women experience the highest rates of community violence, suggesting that men use violence as a way of repressing women's increased status (Rombouts 2006: 206). Claire, a survivor of severe domestic violence in her early forties, outlined the problem:

The biggest challenge that women have right now, which is happening all around in the community, is home-based violence. Most of the husbands are not respecting the rights of their wives, so there are some husbands who think that, "If my wife joins a ladies' group, they may think about some activities which can generate money," and the wife might outperform the husband at his responsibility ... so the husband will say, "This lady is no longer my wife. She became a husband." (Interview #63, February 2013)

Claire rightly names how women's liberating, novel economic power threatens traditional, domineering masculinity. To avoid this violence, women often defer to men within the home regardless of the positions they have taken on in their communities. One study found that 75 percent of Rwandan women said that their husbands dominated all decision-making within the family unit (Slegh et al. 2013: 21).

Several of my respondents also suggested that men justified spousal abuse by saying that their wives were making the extra income as "prostitutes" – a socially devastating slur (Interviews #63, #64; see also Barker and Schulte 2010). This accusation – that women engage in sex work – was shockingly common among the women I interviewed in both countries. Men inside and outside women's families often accuse women, especially young, urban, single women, of being "prostitutes" (typically the word "whore" was used in Bosnia) and subject women to violence and harassment as a result.[24] In Rwanda, various types of abuse ranged from forced virginity tests, to public or police harassment for wearing revealing clothing, to intimidation from medical professionals when unmarried women seek to access birth control (see Berry 2015b). Human Rights Watch (2015) reported that women simply shopping at markets in Kigali were accused of being prostitutes and arrested. Accusing a woman of being a sex worker is a way of degrading her status among family, friends, and community. It reflects a process of abjection, in which women are positioned as repulsive and are cast out and down from society (see Kristeva 1982).

Countless examples of women's sexual and physical abuse after the war emerged during my fieldwork in Rwanda. I asked almost all of my interviewees what they thought the most significant challenge was facing women in Rwanda today. For political elites, the answer was almost always poverty. For ordinary women, however, the answer was almost always violence. When pressed further, my respondents described various ways that violence manifests in their lives long after the genocide and war have ceased. For example, Delphine, a twenty-seven-year-old woman from Bugesera, described how she was visiting her uncle and walking in his village when a young man attacked and raped her by the side of the road (Interview #83, January 2013). She said that she screamed for help, but even though people were around, nobody came to her aid. Despite an array of campaigns aimed at raising awareness about women's legal rights after gender-based violence, her family forced her to become her attacker's wife. She bore three children by him, one of whom died. This man regularly beat her, eventually causing her to leave the marriage. Now she suffers because she cannot afford to feed her children; since she never attended school, she is unable to find decent work. She survives by "digging" – offering her labor to larger landholders in exchange for about a dollar a day.

Naomi, a twenty-eight-year-old woman from the same region, described how a man got her pregnant and then refused to marry her (Interview #64, February 2013). She described how the hospital workers considered her a "prostitute," since she did not have a legal husband to claim paternity of the baby. Eventually the man agreed to marry her, but infected her with HIV and became extremely abusive, often locking her out of her house and forcing her to sleep in the banana fields nearby. These stories, and dozens of others that I heard during my fieldwork, hint at the extent of gender-based violence in Rwanda and remind us of the persistence of heightened patriarchy in a country often celebrated for its successful "empowerment" of women.

Bosnia

In Bosnia, women of all ethno-national backgrounds and classes face high rates of violence in the family (Agency for Gender Equality of BiH 2013). A 2013 nationally representative survey found that 44.9 percent of women had experienced violence from a male partner (Dušanić 2013). While violence against women certainly existed long before the war, this study showed a positive correlation between war experience and domestic abuse.

Women who were raped during the war have reportedly suffered some of the most extreme forms of violence in the aftermath (Amnesty

International 2009; Interview #73, June 2013). Lejia, now in her early sixties, was raped during the war and bore a child by her rapist (Interview #6, July 2016). It became an open secret in her marriage; her husband pretended that the child was his and they never spoke of it, but he tortured her – physically and emotionally – until his death from "trauma from the violence." Many knew what had happened to her during the war, and she described how her neighbors gossiped constantly about her sexual promiscuity.

The director of an NGO working with survivors of war noted that 90 percent of the women who approach her organization after suffering domestic violence are also survivors of wartime sexual assault (Interview #23, April 2013). Many of these women resist seeking help because they fear further stigmatization. During my fieldwork, I heard countless instances where men had casually and unfeelingly referred to women who survived sexual violence or forced detention as "whores" (Interviews #46, #54, May 2013). This degrading labeling maintains patriarchy by positioning men as entitled to women's bodies.

Many of my respondents explained these heightened rates of postwar violence by suggesting that men drank more alcohol after the war and that trauma persisted. According to Lana, a woman in her late twenties when I interviewed her in 2013, the war emotionally damaged both her and her husband, who now regularly beat her. She described how, "We still remember things. We wouldn't live like this if there wasn't war … because the war influenced anything everyone could remember from the age of seven to seventy-seven" (Interview #21, April 2013). With some compassion, she described how alcohol drove many of his fits.

Like in Rwanda, there is also evidence that some forms of violence may indicate a backlash to the gains women made that threatened men's masculinity. For example, Branka Rajner, the director of a human rights NGO in Bosnia described how after the war:

Women got offered to take bigger power. More power. Because foreigners tried to empower women through a lot of projects. But it wasn't very wise because of the mentality of Bosnia. Women got empowered, men came back from war, they're traumatized after war without work. And then the war in families start[ed]. Because men weren't in charge anymore. And war empowered women. And the balance in the marriage was disrupted. (Interview #72, June 2013)

This response suggests that the disruption in the gendered status quo as a result of the war triggered a *patriarchal backlash*, whereby women's gains and newfound freedoms were met with renewed resistance. The decline of men's social status – or the loss of men's hegemonic control over household and community power – is a fundamental cause of this backlash. This may have been particularly acute among former combatants, who experienced a decline in their material and symbolic status after the war. After participating in an armed conflict in which looting and black-market trade was common, most former combatants struggled to find employment. This financial insecurity, when combined with trauma and violence "know-how," likely amplified rates of violence (Bougarel 2006). As Vedrana, a woman from the region around Srebrenica, put it, "when husbands have no work they can't provide in the family needs ... they sometimes turn to alcohol, they go to the coffee bar, make a problem over there and get drunk, and women suffer in silence" (Interview #69, June 2013).

Like in Rwanda, the pervasiveness of gender-based violence in Bosnia suggests that men have increasingly used violence to curtail women who threaten their hegemonic control, limiting women's ability to exercise control over their postwar gains. Despite the fact that gender relations can be in flux during war, as society stabilizes, patriarchal power relations remain firmly entrenched. Some feminist scholars have rightly argued that thwarting the revitalization of patriarchy in the aftermath of war requires women to be included in the peace process. UNSCR 1325 later established this as well, urging states to include women in all peace and security efforts. Yet in Bosnia, women were strikingly absent at the Dayton Accords, which established a peace that was far from gender-just (Björkdahl 2012; Cockburn 2013b). In Rwanda, the military victory of the RPF and the establishment of a rebel army as the new governing power meant that there was never a formal peace process. While women held high ranks in the RPF, the core power structure of the regime is dominated by a small group of men with close ties to President Kagame. Still, as I discussed throughout this book, women's grassroots mobilization and international norms influenced the postwar governments of both Rwanda and Bosnia to establish legal provisions to promote women and to protect them from gender-based violence and other harms. While these legal protections have not eradicated patriarchal structures embedded in both societies, they are nevertheless a substantial improvement from the prewar era – and, hopefully, reflect lasting moral, political, and legal gains.

CONCLUSION

Despite the shifts war precipitated in women's lives in Rwanda and Bosnia, the political settlement, international actors, and the persistence of patriarchy complicated and restricted women's gains. In future interventions after mass violence, policymakers should consider whether the international community could alter its programming in order to amplify women's mobilization at the grassroots and harness women's political engagement for peacebuilding and transitional justice – rather than inadvertently fracture and undermine it. One simple way to do this would be to give greater attention to how victimhood is a status that is produced within systems of power. Whose victimhood is made visible – and whose is rendered invisible – shapes the prospects for community healing, reconciliation, and peace after war. Further, victimhood, like gender, ethnicity, race, ability, class, and so forth, can serve as a regime of difference after war, affording some individuals greater or lesser power in the postwar political context (see Berry 2017). Women's ability to participate in various postwar initiatives is thus not uniform; women with particular identities are privileged and granted opportunities to organize, receive aid, and grieve, while those with marginalized identities are seen as suspicious, less deserving of aid, and unfit to suffer. Humanitarian interventions that provide incentives to collaborate, rather than compete, across these various regimes of difference may be more effective in cultivating and sustaining women's mobilization after war.

In addition, policymakers might consider how to effectively design platforms for local actors to determine the most urgent issues facing their communities without outside pressure, and to distribute aid accordingly. Aid models that put funding decisions into the communities' hands are likely to be most effective in developing dynamic women's initiatives. As we have seen, voices from the local community reflect both the most politically vital and morally important expertise for designing postwar humanitarian interventions. These voices – not seemingly benevolent, technocratic experts – can best realize just settlements and begin to build equitable, durable peace within local communities. International conceptions of rights may cascade into these local arrangements (see Sikkink 2011), but they should only do so through the voices and will of local participants. Such an approach honors the concept of democracy.[25]

Underlying any efforts to mitigate harm after atrocities, however, will be the continued persistence of patriarchy. While patriarchal norms were in flux during the wars in Rwanda and Bosnia, they reemerged, with renewed strength, in the aftermath. As a result, women in both countries face high levels of violence from spouses and family members. This violence limits women's ability to take advantage of many of the legal rights afforded to them since the war, and positions some women as undeserving subjects perpetually subordinate to men. These experiences of quotidian violence highlight the importance of not just establishing peace after mass violence, but of establishing a "gender-just peace" (Björkdahl 2012) that mitigates the brutalities of patriarchy and false masculinities, recognizes women's agency, and secures *all* women's full autonomy and control over their bodies, rights, and lives.

9

Conclusion

In 2013, I visited an exhibit commemorating the Srebrenica massacre in downtown Sarajevo. Walking into the dimly lit exhibit hall, I was confronted by large photos of victims before the slaughter and of daily life shattered – an abandoned doll, a woman's hands, some discarded clothing. A soft heartbeat sound hauntingly filled the room. On the far wall of the rectangular exhibit room a slideshow of war images flickered and played in a loop. They appeared to be from the Siege of Sarajevo – snipers, mortar explosions on modern city sidewalks, civilians shot down in the streets, children running for cover. Before leaving the exhibit, I watched the scrolling images with more attention and realized they were not from Sarajevo. Instead, they were from Syria, and had been taken in the past twelve months.

War, at its most fundamental level, is an accelerated period of social change. It destroys lives, fractures social structures, dismantles institutions, and alters power relations. In this book, I examined war as a period of liminality – a critical juncture when institutions, social structures, and gender relations are in flux, but are also constrained by the social and historical structures that predate the violence. Such periods of flux can loosen the hold of traditional gendered power relations, restructure the institutional and structural layout of society, and ultimately facilitate women's participation in new social roles.

If one thing became clear to me throughout the course of this research, it is that *violence begets violence* – it never fully ends in the lives of those who live through it, and it shifts form, reemerging with different logics and dynamics. For the people who live through war, memories of the violence, the loss of loved ones, constant fear and instability all leave their marks, which may fade but rarely disappear. This is an extremely depressing way to end a book. Yet it draws our attention to a moral imperative for social scientists in the twenty-first century: violence is and will continue to be a central feature of our social world. It thus requires our attention; better understanding war's transformative potential will be critical if we are to develop ways to prevent violence in the future.

If we are to successfully prevent violence, mitigate its effects, and thwart its reoccurrence, women will – and *must* – play an integral role. Women survive war as complex, resilient human beings; their deep knowledge and power to create social change must be recognized as tremendous, untapped potential to build more gender-equitable, inclusive, and peaceful societies in the aftermath. Scholars, activists, and policymakers should thus look for unexpected opportunities for gender emancipation amid such periods of destruction, and the structural shifts I illustrated throughout this book provide a framework for beginning to do so.

REVISITING THE ARGUMENT

In Rwanda and Bosnia, war precipitated three major intersecting and overlapping shifts that facilitated the increased mobilization of women in public, political life. The first shift was in the demographic composition of society due to the disproportionate death, conscription, and imprisonment of men, and the massive displacement of people from their homes. This demographic shift led women – and particularly those in women-headed households – to assume new roles in their households and families. It also facilitated the creation of new social networks, as displacement forced people into new routines and modes of social interaction.

The second shift was economic, triggered by macroeconomic collapse during war and exasperated by the corresponding destruction of infrastructure and agricultural capacity. This shift led to urgent material needs among the population for food, water, shelter, and medical care. Whereas before the violence women performed traditional caregiving roles within the domestic sphere (e.g., caring for children), afterward women became active in public spaces and sought aid from international humanitarian NGOs, government institutions, and neighbors. Women formed thousands of informal self-help groups to help them meet these urgent material and emotional needs. These emergent organizations institutionalized a system of women's leadership at the grassroots level, helped women develop self-reliance, encouraged profit-making activities, and facilitated a shift in how women controlled surplus income.

A third shift was cultural. As women's participation in grassroots organizations and public spaces became increasingly common, the cultural understanding of who constituted a legitimate public actor shifted. Individual women and women's organizations advocated for their increased presence in public spaces by pointing to the fact that they were not responsible for the war. Women strategically juxtaposed their "more peaceful" nature with men's propensity for violence. As a result, citizens became increasingly accustomed to the idea of women as legitimate community leaders or political actors.

These three shifts facilitated women's mobilization in informal political capacities. Women took on work that was previously considered men's work, interacted with government institutions and INGOs as the representatives of their households, and went outside of the home to find basic goods to keep their families alive – all activities constituting what Asef Bayat has termed a "politics of practice." Activities involved with daily survival became part of a larger political project to establish normalcy within conditions of widespread upheaval. And these activities began to accumulate, as hundreds of thousands of women found themselves in similar situations. This led to a mushrooming of women's organizations, through which women could meet the needs of daily life, undertake collective projects, and build new social networks. These organizations did not aim to challenge women's oppressed status, but rather to help women survive the circumstances at hand. They also institutionalized women's leadership at the community level and provided a platform for some women to launch further political careers. With exposure to feminist activism and an open civic space, many women in Bosnia had the additional opportunity to engage in public protest activities. After the installation of an entirely new, gender-sensitive regime seeking to establish popular legitimacy, some women in Rwanda found opportunities to engage in formal political roles within the national government. Other countries with similar postwar political settlements may also find an increased opening for women to enter the formal political realm.

EXTENDING THE ARGUMENT

Rwanda and Bosnia had very different histories, experiences during war, and aftermaths. Yet despite these differences, the cases showed many similarities in how women organize, suggesting a more universal pattern in women's experiences after war. Might we expect to see similar mobilization in other contexts? History provides some clues. From the rise of the international women's movement in the wake of World War I, to American women's increased employment in traditionally male-dominated jobs during World War II, wars throughout history have pushed women into new social roles. Evidence from Northern Ireland and Israel shows that even low-level violence catalyzed women's political mobilization and created an atmosphere in which women expanded the number of legitimate political roles they could assume (Aretxaga 1997; Sharoni 2001; Donahoe 2017). Further, evidence of women mobilizing for greater political rights during war is present in El Salvador, Sri Lanka, East Timor, and many other places. Of course, the aftermath of war often sets back women's wartime gains.

When considering possible extensions of this book's main arguments, two key parameters are worthy of mention. First, a crucial part of the process of women's grassroots mobilization in both Rwanda and Bosnia was the arrival of a mass of humanitarian aid agencies that incentivized women's organizations to form and formalize in the wake of war. The massive involvement of international humanitarian NGOs is a relatively recent development, dating from the 1980s – although the involvement of international actors in foreign conflicts has been on a steady incline since the formation of the United Nations in the aftermath of World War II (Rieff 2003; Uvin 2004). Thus, we would expect to see similar processes of women's grassroots mobilization through informal self-help organizations in other cases of mass violence that experienced an influx of international humanitarian organizations after war. While the emergence of women's organizations preceded the arrival of these INGOs, these foreign actors cultivated and nourished emergent women's organizations, allowing them to develop and formalize. In closed societies without humanitarian INGOs, we may not see a similar process of grassroots organizational formation. Further, mass violence in previous historical periods would likely not be followed by a similar process of women's grassroots organizational formation and formalization.

The second parameter of the argument is the scale of the conflict, and more specifically, the corresponding demographic impact of violence on the population. Around one-half of the populations of both Rwanda and Bosnia was displaced from their homes during and after violence. As I explain throughout this book, this displacement resulted in the fragmentation of social networks and the destruction of previous patterns of life. To survive – and indeed to move forward after such pervasive violence – displaced women in both countries developed new social networks, searched for essential goods, and sought help from others in new locations. Such massive disruption, then, was key for such a large number of women to engage in forms of everyday politics, which led to the formation of self-help organizations. That said, a review of other cases of violence in the past few decades, and studies by scholars like Sharoni (1995) and Viterna (2013), suggests that even in lower-intensity or regionally contained wars, women often take on new roles in their households and communities during the upheaval. But the extent of women's mobilization in such cases would likely be more limited, affecting fewer changes in women's overall status. This is substantiated by Hughes and Tripp (2015), who found that higher deaths in civil wars in Sub-Saharan Africa are correlated with higher rates of female legislative representation.

LIMITATIONS

Like any research project, this study has limitations. The biggest limitation of this project is that in both countries a significant amount of time has now passed since the violence. Since I relied most heavily on interview data, women's recollections of their experiences immediately after the violence may be fuzzy, or may be intermingled with narratives produced by the state, media, or other women. Moreover, my sample of women respondents was biased in several ways, including that it privileged women from the capital cities in both countries. It was primarily for this reason that I supplemented the interview data with organizational reports and government documents. While I have made attempts to triangulate the available information, I possess no comprehensive data about precisely how many grassroots organizations formed as a result of the violence in each country, who the founders were on average, and who participated in the immediate aftermath of the violence.

Another limitation of this study was that I do not fluently speak the local languages in either case. While I took private and group lessons in both languages, I still needed to use research assistants during all interviews conducted in the local languages. Unexpectedly, I found that having a research assistant was, in many ways, advantageous. At times, I was able to establish a sense of women's solidarity during the interviews, particularly in my interviews with poorer women or women who had survived tremendous trauma during the wars in both countries. In these interviews, I encouraged my research assistants to cultivate a sense that we were all on a team – they were encouraged to ask appropriate follow-up questions within the context of the interviews, and they occasionally shared bits of information about their own lives and experiences.

I believe it would be valuable for researchers to observe, in real time, the process of women's mobilization during and after mass violence. This, of course, would most likely involve living and conducting ethnography in a war zone. If it could be done safely and ethically, it would mean further specifying the way that women often take on new social roles during war that push them into new public spaces and mobilize them to work toward creating normalcy during conditions of chaos. Future research might also aim to observe shifts in women's roles at different intervals after war – for instance, five, ten, fifteen, or even fifty years after war has ended. Such a longitudinal perspective would help isolate and identify the various actors involved in both facilitating and inhibiting women's mobilization after atrocity. The findings would have much to offer not only sociological theory, but more critically, humanitarian aid policy and international policy efforts to mitigate the suffering caused by war.

THEORETICAL CONTRIBUTIONS

With these parameters and limitations in mind, this book makes a number of contributions. For scholars of war and historical institutionalism, this study continues in the tradition of Weber, Skocpol, Mann, Tilly, and others who explore the transformative impact of war, while giving particular attention to how such transformations play out differently for men and women from the bottom up. This focus allows for a more comprehensive understanding of the gendered dynamics of violence that shape social structures and institutions. This study, moreover, uses a historical institutionalist approach to examine institutional transformation over a mid-range period of time. In contrast, much research in historical sociology is concerned with large invisible social trends that stretch over centuries – such as the rise of capitalism, the advent of the labor movement, or the emergence of revolutions.

My approach in this project has thus been to look over a shorter timeframe – approximately twenty years – and to examine more bottom-up processes of societal transformation. To do so, I embraced William Sewell's (1996) call for an "eventful history" in which events are understood as turning points, or "concentrated moments of political and cultural creativity where by the logic of historical development is reconfigured by human action but by no means abolished" (McAdam and Sewell 2001: 102). Here I seek not to explain why an event occurred, but rather what a major event (war) produced. This endeavor flips Tilly's inquiry into how mobilization led to revolution, asking instead how violence might lead to mobilization. Further research could use a similar approach to look at the impact of war on ethnic identities, institutional policy, legal rights, gender-based violence, or other institutional variables.

This study makes another contribution to scholarship on gender by examining both the destructive and transformative effects of war for women. This approach illuminates several ways that women in postwar countries have challenged the feminist truism from the 1970s that gender sameness is the route to gender equality (Lorber 1994; Epstein 1997; Walby 2005). In the aftermath of war, women in Rwanda and Bosnia drew upon their "intrinsic nature" as "peaceful" or as "mothers" to justify their increased presence in political activities. While essentializing, such framings allowed women the ability to organize political projects under the guise of being apolitical, and in doing so, allowed women to work across ethnic divides to undermine patriarchy. This reminds us that "gender difference" might be an alternative route to women's emancipation under certain conditions./However, it also requires us to consider whether such framings can ever produce movements that can fundamentally transform the social institutions producing intersectional oppressions in the first place.

This study makes an additional contribution to the study of social movements, as I demonstrate how a Western understanding of politics obscures more diffuse and less formal spaces of political mobilization. Focusing on everyday politics – and not only on formal politics – allows for a more nuanced and rich understanding of how war transforms women's lives and political power. Most critically, concentrating on more informal, diffuse, and emergent forms of mobilization reveals ways that political action and resistance may be occurring in contexts where a traditional social movement approach would not see mobilization. Looking from the grassroots up, then, suggests that even in periods of widespread upheaval and destruction, people may engage in collective political action.

This book also offers important insights for policymakers and scholars embracing the Women, Peace, and Security agenda.[1] While I argued throughout that war can transform gendered power relations, I explained in the previous chapter how any gains women make after war must be safeguarded. Ironically, the various institutions designed to safeguard women's rights – including INGOs, multinational organizations like the United Nations, and foreign powers like the United States – often inadvertently stifle and suppress women's organizing and mobilization after war. This is because they arrive on scene with a set of funding priorities established not in the local context, but at the international nation-state level. Misdirected international humanitarian efforts can create new forms of inequality and entrench hierarchies of victimhood, which can fracture women's organizing around collective interests and at times even undo progress women made during and after the war. As such, it is essential for women's empowerment efforts after war to center the voices of local women, account for the multiple and intersecting identities and oppressions women have, and design policy interventions that account for dynamic and multifaceted systems of power that are particular to a given context.

Peacebuilding efforts should similarly take note. Attempts to impose formulaic prescriptions based on success in other contexts risk establishing a "negative peace" (Galtung 1969), in which war has stopped but the dynamics of violence rage on in other forms. For instance, gender-based violence, a lack of justice, and structural inequality continue to pervade Bosnian and Rwandan women's lives. As I suggested in Chapter 8, international interveners, however well intentioned, must value local expertise and experiences on par with international priorities or technocratic knowledge. This contribution cautions against assuming that all efforts to mitigate suffering and rebuild societies after violence are positive – or, at worst, neutral.

Finally, this book intervenes in debates over genocide and human rights more broadly by emphasizing that violence is always more complex than good versus evil. In many ways, the emergence of human rights as a dominant frame since World War II has drawn divisions between certain types of legitimate and illegitimate violence. Genocides are illegitimate, as they are understood as immoral, barbaric, and even irrational. Wars, conversely, are simply part of a state's normal repertoire of behavior. But the distinctions between genocide and war are blurred in practice.

The contemporary discourse surrounding genocide has problematically identified three archetypal actors during conflict. Perpetrators are the ruthless savages; victims are the helpless innocents; and saviors are generally members of the international community that have the power to intervene.[2] This discourse is rooted in the human rights framework, initially formulated so the oppressed could resist power. But as Mahmood Mamdani (2010) has rightly noted, today the language of rights has, in many contexts, become *the* language of power. This means that as external actors debate whether "genocide" occurs, they simplify the conflict's complexity to situate the violence within a framework of good and evil.

This schema of classification is powerful; it establishes Hutu and Serbs as perpetrators, Tutsi and Bosniaks as innocent. It determines that only Tutsi and Bosniak women were raped during genocide – assigning blame for the rape of Hutu or Serb women to separate processes of violence that were somehow less abhorrent, more associated with "normal" criminality. This has resulted in framings of the violence that reduce individual identities to simplified ones: victim, survivor, perpetrator, and so on.

I reject this simplified characterization of the violence because it creates hierarchies of victimhood that determine a group's ability to gain power or access aid in the aftermath and, moreover, lets certain actors off the hook for their involvement in the violence. This was the case with the Rwandan Patriotic Front in Rwanda, which was given free rein to consolidate power after killing tens of thousands of civilians with impunity. It also allowed the international community to escape much serious blame in Bosnia, despite overseeing a massacre in Srebrenica, orchestrating a dysfunctional political settlement that rewarded nationalist aggressors, and fostering a culture of humanitarian relief that allowed foreigners to engage in human trafficking and sexual violence. Future researchers should pay attention to the complexity of violence and strive to deconstruct categories of victim and perpetrator that are too often accepted without question.

AN ABSENCE OF WAR, STILL FAR FROM PEACE

Looking at both Rwanda and Bosnia today illuminates how "the relationship between war and peace is that of a continuum, not a dichotomy" (Autessere 2009: 276). More than twenty years after the end of the wars in Rwanda and Bosnia, peace is still a long way off, and violence pervades ordinary citizens' lives in many ways. In Rwanda, there has been no resurgence of ethnic violence since the end of the genocide and war, and the postwar regime should be commended for this accomplishment. This security, however, has largely been possible because the state's coercive apparatus (i.e., the police and military) is deeply embedded in citizens' daily lives, suppressing free expression and creating a climate of fear. In Kigali, armed guards are stationed at regular intervals on the streets. State representatives wear guns and batons at community meetings. Police at regular checkpoints ensure every vehicle is registered and obeys traffic laws – but also detain civilians at will. During the country's annual holiday commemorating the end of the genocide and the "liberation" of the country by the RPF, enormous trucks of soldiers armed with automatic weapons and bazookas blanket the streets of Kigali, while military helicopters run exercises overhead. This reminds citizens that the state monopolizes the use of violence and will not hesitate to use that violence against its citizens, who alter their behavior in order to avoid punishment (see Thomson 2013; Mann and Berry 2016). This climate of fear has also led many independent-thinking Rwandans – like the four young men I mentioned at the outset of Chapter 2 – to flee the country. And, despite the high percentage of women in Rwanda's national government, women who have dared to challenge President Kagame's grip on power – like Victoire Ingabire and Diane Rwigara – are in prison.[3]

In Bosnia, violence is less material, but is structurally embedded in the dysfunctional political system that bifurcated communities into ethnic enclaves and rewarded war criminals with a state within a state. In the years since the war, children from different ethnic groups have grown up increasingly separated: the infamous "two schools, one roof" policy created discrete schools in the same building, ensuring that Serb or Croat students were taught a completely distinct curriculum from Bosniak students. Towns and cities in the country are increasingly mono-ethnic. Survivors of the war feel threatened when nationalist Serb politicians, such as Republika Srpska President Dodik, publicly deny that genocide or war crimes were committed and threaten Republika Srpska's secession. In 2015, I received an email from a young Bosnian friend lamenting the ongoing crisis in his country. He asked me to imagine how people in the United States would feel if they were surrounded all the time by Ku Klux Klan members. "This is how I feel when surrounded by nationalists," he said, "and they are everywhere." Such structural violence – and fear of overt violence – pervades everyday life in Bosnia.

The end of violence in Rwanda and Bosnia did not bring about a "positive" peace, nor a "gender just" one. While the war precipitated women's increased participation in political life, and formal laws protecting women's rights have secured women's legal gains, significant barriers to all women's equality persist. In both countries, the specter of future violence is always on the horizon, and the struggle for gender emancipation endures.

Notes

1 War, Women, and Power

1 See extensive scholarship in this area by Elshtain (1987), Enloe (1989, 1993), Mertus(1994), Cockburn (1998, 2007), Tripp (2000), Bauer and Britton (2006), Meintjes, Pillay, and Turshen (2001).

2 See additional literature on this topic in Latin American cases by Chinchilla (1983), Luciak (2001), and Kampwirth (2004).

3 The Popular Organization of East Timorese Women.

4 See other scholarship on how war created opportunities to build more inclusive institutions for racial minorities in the United States, such as African American men during the Civil War (Gilbert 2012).

5 UCDP/PRIO Armed Conflict Dataset: Main Conflict Table: www.prio.org/ Data/Armed-Conflict/UCDP-PRIO/Armed-Conflicts-Version-X-2009/.

6 See U.S. Supreme Court cases *Pittsburgh Press Co.* v. *Pittsburgh Commission on Human Relations* (1973), *Cleveland Board of Education* v. *LaFleur* (1974), *Meritor Savings Bank* v. *Vinson* (1986), and others.

7 Although in the aftermath of World War II, as these scholars and others show, women's gains in the labor force were set back as men returned from military duty and women's roles were once again conceived of as being within the home.

8 For further discussion, see Landes (1988, 1998), Pateman (1988), Habermas (1989), Gal and Kligman (2000, chapter 3), and Gal (2002).

9 See an extended debate in the feminist literature on the difference between "practical gender interests" and "strategic gendered interests" (Molyneux 1985; Chinchilla 1992; Lorber 1994; Agarwal 1992; Hale 1993).

10 While I refer to "women" throughout this project, I in no way aim to suggest that women are a monolithic group, or that women respond to and feel the same way about various social changes. In this study, I aim to recognize the range of individual women and groups of women involved in the processes under study, and aspire to give voice to each. Certainly, I will fall short, and thus feel it is important to state that I acknowledge a study that looks at

"women" cannot capture all of the complexity that exists within this heterogeneous category.

11   I thank Susan Watkins for this term.

12   Although an Office of the High Commissioner, established at Dayton, continues to serve as the ultimate authority in the country.

13   The only NGO executives that I considered part of this initial category were from government-run NGOs. This was more relevant in Rwanda than in Bosnia. For example, the Rwandan National Women's Council is technically an NGO, but the government appoints its directors and heavily regulates its activities.

14   Put another way, I aimed to interview women from different class backgrounds – NGO founders and leaders tended to be from middle-class backgrounds, while women who were the beneficiaries of these organizations tended to be poorer women from rural or lower-class backgrounds.

15   While I was careful not to ask respondents in Rwanda direct questions about their ethnic identity, it was often possible to have a "best guess" about a respondent's ethnicity based on references to their place of birth, history of movement inside and outside of Rwanda, time spent abroad, linguistic ability, victim status, or experience during the genocide and war.

16   In 2016, I returned to Bosnia to conduct additional interviews with women outside of Sarajevo. In this last period of fieldwork, I collaborated with Jessica M. Smith (George Mason University) to run a series of traditional interviews alongside Photovoice workshops in an effort to more safely and thoughtfully broach topics related to their wartime experience and the difficulties they faced in the aftermath. As part of this collaboration, I conducted traditional focus groups and one-on-one interviews with twenty-two women; Jessica led corresponding Photovoice workshops with the focus group participants. As a result, some of the responses from these women occur in both of our data sets.

17   Tuzla is not directly situated in the Drina Valley, but many refugees from the Drina Valley region fled to Tuzla during the war, and many remain there today. Therefore, it is an important location for finding survivors of the massacres in Srebrenica and the surrounding area.

18   Only about ten interviewees were not comfortable with the audio recording. All of these were in Rwanda; none of my interviewees in Bosnia indicated any hesitation about being audio recorded.

19   Some interviews were not transcribed because of poor sound quality, or because of the limited utility of the interview responses. In these cases, I analyzed the handwritten notes I took during each interview.

20   In general, when I refer to individuals by only their first names, these are pseudonyms. Many more participants granted me permission to use their names than I ultimately used, largely because of the increasingly volatile political situation in Rwanda. As a result, I ended up anonymizing many women officials who had originally granted me permission to use their names because I feared what might happen to them (now, or in the future) if they were linked to a foreign academic perceived as critical of the regime.

21 Technically, the United Nations Convention on the Prevention and Punishment of the Crime of Genocide.

22 Many other categories of people were of course also targeted, including Roma, Catholics, homosexuals, the handicapped, and communists. Raphael Lemkin coined the term in response to the massacres of Armenians during World War I. See a rich field of genocide scholarship by Kuper (1981), Chalk and Jonassohn (1990), Fein (1993), Charney (1994), Totten, Parsons, and Charny (1997), Harff and Gurr (1988), Weitz (2003), Mann (2005), and Kiernan (2007), and many others. There are many other problems with the UN's definition of genocide, including the political context in which the definition was codified (see Kuper 1981; Power 2003; Weitz 2003). Most notable is the omission of "political groups" from the definition adopted by the UN because of resistance from the Soviet Union's delegation.

23 Of course, statistics on civilian deaths in ongoing conflicts are hard to come by and debated. In particular, it is not always straightforward to determine who counts as a combatant. Sources for this claim include the Iraq Body Count (December 10, 2015, from www.iraqbodycount.org), the Syrian Observatory for Human Rights, the International Rescue Committee, and the Human Security Report Project.

24 Of course there were many rallies and protests against the Iraq war as well. The protests against the genocide in Darfur also catalyzed NGOs that lasted far longer than the protests themselves (e.g., STAND, Save Darfur, ENOUGH Project).

25 M. Rosenberg, March 17, 2016. "Citing Atrocities, John Kerry Calls ISIS Actions Genocide." *The New York Times.* www.nytimes.com/2016/03/18/world/middleeast/citing-atrocities-john-kerry-calls-isis-actions-genocide.html.

26 Or, as the Government of Rwanda would prefer, the "1994 Genocide against the Tutsi." See E. Kagire, E., 2014. "Genocide against the Tutsi: It's Now Official." *The East African,* www.theeastafrican.co.ke/news/UN-decides-it-is-officially-genocide-against-Tutsi/2558-2169334-x8cirxz/index.html.

27 In Rwanda today, Hutu killed during the violence are deemed lesser victims than Tutsi, and the families of Hutu victims are not afforded the same opportunities to mourn their dead as a result. As I discuss in Chapter 8, only Tutsi are deemed genocide "survivors," and as such are the only ones eligible to receive financial benefits from their losses (see Hintjens 2008; the Straus and Waldorf 2011 edited volume; Reyntjens's work in general). This politicized hierarchy of victimhood has profound repercussions for ordinary Rwandans' lives, and is largely made possible by the narrow framing of the entire episode of violence as "the 1994 Genocide against the Tutsi."

2 Historical Roots of Mass Violence in Rwanda

1 See the World Bank, "Doing Business." www.doingbusiness.org/data/exploreeconomies/rwanda.

2 My friend's identity card marked him as a Tutsi, although his father was a well-known Hutu. Since my friend's mother was not his legal wife, he had officially assumed her ethnic identity, although many assumed he was Hutu because of his father.

3 See an account of one journalist here: http://africanarguments.org/2014/05/06/taking-sides-in-rwanda-by-steve-terrill/. The government-run newspaper, the *New Times*, and a series of government-backed blogs also regularly attack foreign researchers, journalists, and human rights workers, discrediting them publicly in order to scare them away from covering Rwanda. See www.newsofrwanda.com/forum/21853/french-broadcaster-rfi-fabricates-kagames-quotes/ or http://theremakingrwanda.blogspot.com.

4 For more information on these cases, as well as for more information about the research context in Rwanda, see Human Rights Watch (2009), Straus and Waldorf (2011), and Reyntjens (2013). See also the GenoDynamics webpage (http://genodynamics.weebly.com/), which hosts information about the data project conducted by Christian Davenport and Allan Stam, which led to significant controversy.

5 This section draws heavily from Codere (1973).

6 Women averaged approximately eight births up until the genocide. In 1978, women averaged 8.6 births each (Republic of Rwanda 2014).

7 The time period when this occurred is unclear. Codere uses the term "early days" – probably in reference to the precolonial era or to the early days of the colonial era. It is unknown how common this was, or if it was widespread.

8 *Uburetwa* was a labor system that required poor Hutu to regularly sell their labor to their "patrons" – often two days out of every five – which undermined their ability to provide for themselves and made survival a challenge (Pottier 2002: 13).

9 *Umuheto* required that clients give cattle on a regular basis to their "patrons" in exchange for protection (Mamdani 2001: 65).

10 Some of the programs targeting women included the creation of social centers (*foyers sociaux*) for women that focused on women's literacy and health and provided leadership opportunities for the women who came to head them (Burnet 2012: 50).

11 Banyarwanda refers to Kinyarwanda speakers in the Great Lakes region of Central Africa.

12 This appears to be a revised number from Prunier 1995, which cites a much higher figure (p. 70). Estimates of many statistics in Rwandan history vary, given the poor measures used to calculate the figures and the lack of access to unbiased reporting.

13 Throughout this book I refer to both the military and political wings of the movement as the RPF.

14 There is no consensus on how Rwigyema was killed, although some sources suggest that he was killed during a dispute with his own officers. Prunier suggests that his death was accidental (1995: 95).

15 Kagame was in the United States training at Fort Leavenworth, Kansas, at the time of the initial RPF attack on October 1, 1990.

16 Experts debate how much truth there was in these rumors. Certainly, the RPF committed some atrocities against civilians during this period, but the rumors of its ruthlessness likely far outsized the reality.

17 The peace negotiations experienced a setback in February 1993, when the RPF launched an aggressive military attack that brought it within thirty kilometers of Kigali. The FAR was unable to withstand the assault and called on French troops for support.

18 There is, however, a growing debate about whether this group was indeed responsible for the genocide, or whether the RPF constructed the group after its victory to clearly trace the "intent" for genocide back to an identifiable set of actors.

19 In hindsight, it is tempting to see the escalation of violence as a deliberate, orchestrated process; indeed, as established by the 1948 UN Genocide Convention, identifying clear "intent" is necessary to determine "genocide" was committed. Like others (e.g., Mamdani 2001; Mann 2005), however, I view the genocide as more emergent and contingent. Hutu radicalization was a response to real RPF threats against the northern Hutu stronghold on the state (Mann 2005: 443).

20 It is worth noting that Agate was likely appointed prime minister because she was widely seen as politically weak. Her own MDR political party immediately kicked her out of the party upon her appointment, and Habyarimana formally fired her from the post eighteen days later. She stayed on in a caretaker capacity until her death during the first days of the genocide.

21 For these figures, Prunier (1995) cites the *Commission Internationale d'Enquete sur Les Violations des Droits de l'Homme au Burundi despuis le 21 Octobre 1993*, Rapport final, Brussles, July 1994. That report estimated that roughly 60 percent of the dead were Tutsi, while 40 percent were Hutu.

22 In February 1994, Hutu extremists assassinated Félicien Gatabazi, the executive secretary of the PSD opposition party, triggering massive outrage among Hutu moderates. In response, angry mobs killed the CDR chairman – who happened to be traveling in Gatabazi's hometown of Butare that day (Prunier 1995: 206). These killings led to further unrest in Kigali: dozens were killed and hundreds injured (Dallaire 2003: 189).

23 See discussions in Prunier (1995: 213); Des Forges (1999: 181); Mann (2005: 450); and Straus (2006: 44). A French magistrate inquiry concluded that the RPF was likely responsible, before reversing its decision and attributing the missiles to Habyarimana's troops (see http://blogs.voanews.com/breaking-news/2012/01/10/french-inquiry-clears-rwandan-president-aides-in-94-plane-attack/). An inquiry conducted by the Rwanda government perhaps unsurprisingly found that Hutu troops were to blame (see www.theguardian.com/world/2010/jan/12/rwanda-hutu-president-plane-inquiry).

24 Des Forges (1999) and Straus (2006) also cite these numbers. Prunier (2009) cites the Gersony report estimates of 25,000 to 45,000.

25 Many accounts of the genocide overplay the use of dehumanizing speech in motivating violence. Straus (2006) shows how terms like "*inyenzi*" or "cockroach" were historically rooted terms used to refer to Tutsi rebels who attacked at night (as discussed previously). Such a cautioned perspective is

important, as it rejects the "ancient tribal hatreds" explanation of violence and instead attributes people's actions to fear of a militarized enemy.

26 Weapons were readily available; several reports indicate that one could buy a hand grenade at any market in Kigali for about $3 USD immediately before the violence began (Prunier 1995; Dallaire 2003: 166).

27 Field notes 2013, Kigali.

28 I use the term "sexualized violence" to denote violence that does not result merely out of sexual desire but rather out of contestations over power, militarization, violence, aggression, humiliation, and masculinity more generally (see Enloe 2000; Connell and Messerschmidt 2005; Baaz and Stern 2009).

29 Few concrete sources back up this figure, however. Like other statistics about Rwanda, numbers often get reported by a single agency or report, and then are picked up and re-reported by other sources without validating the methods used to calculate the figures. In this case, the estimate of 250,000 raped women stems from the number of babies born from rape after the genocide – a questionable way of calculating rape statistics, especially given the many other factors that could have influenced pregnancy during the genocide. Straus (2006: 52) aptly points out that, according to the 1991 census, there were only 163,738 Tutsi women over the age of fourteen in the country (although certainly girls younger than fourteen were also raped). But, given that the majority of rape victims were of childbearing age, this census figure suggests that either the figure of 250,000 is inflated, or that sexualized violence extended beyond Tutsi and included Hutu and Batwa women as well. In 2003, the World Health Organization issued a revised figure of 15,700 rape victims between the ages of thirteen and sixty-five (see Turshen 2001: 58).

30 See www.icc-cpi.int/nr/rdonlyres/ea9aeff7-5752-4f84-be94-0a655eb30e16/0/rome_statute_english.pdf.

31 The Government of Rwanda redrew the administrative districts in the country in 2006 in order to change the names of some of the areas most associated with the genocide. While the country was formerly comprised of twelve districts, it has now been redrawn into four provinces in addition to Kigali City. The new levels of administration are national, province, district, sector, and cellule.

32 Lorch, D. (April 14, 1994). "Anarchy Rules Rwanda's Capital and Drunken Soldiers Roam City." *New York Times*.

33 *New York Times* (no author). July 24, 1994. "The Rwanda Disaster: The Capital; in Kigali, More People Have Gone than Have Stayed Behind." www.nytimes.com/1994/07/24/world/rwanda-disaster-capital-kigali-more-people-have-gone-than-have-stayed-behind.html (accessed May 2017).

34 Many scholars believe that Tutsi were undercounted in the 1991 census, as the Habyarimana regime wanted to minimize the level of Tutsi in the population.

35 Field notes 2009, Nyamata Memorial.

36 These numbers refer to Kigali Ngali, as the name of the district was not changed until 2006 (after the earlier population and housing survey).

37 This debate is ongoing. Marijke Verpoorten, whose careful analysis of multiple censuses and a single province is perhaps the most methodologically

sound study, argues that 512,000 to 662,000 Tutsi were likely killed in the violence. If the death toll is higher – which it likely is – the additional deaths are Hutu (see http://africanarguments.org/2014/10/27/rwanda-why-davenport-and-stams-calculation-that-200000-tutsi-died-in-the-genocide-is-wrong-by-marijke-verpoorten/).

3 War and Structural Shifts in Rwanda

1 *New York Times* (July 14, 1994). "Rwandans Flee in Panic to Zaire."
2 Bonner, R. (July 16, 1994). "Trail of Suffering as Rwandan Exodus Continues." *New York Times.*
3 Bonner, R. (July 27, 1994). "Rwandan Refugees Caught 'between Two Deaths.'" *New York Times.*
4 Lorch, D. (May 1, 1994). "Refugees Flee into Tanzania from Rwanda." *New York Times.*
5 For more on the refugee crisis and the new crises it initiated, see Pottier (2002), Lemarchand (2009), and Prunier (2009).
6 This emphasis on villagization was eventually relaxed. See subsequent studies of the *imidugudu* policy by Van Leeuwen (2001), Hilhorst and Van Leeuwen (2000), Pottier (2006), and Ansoms (2009).
7 According to the International Committee of the Red Cross, more than 2,300 prisoners died between July 1994 and January 1996 as a consequence of the overcrowding and unsanitary conditions in prisons across the country (Amnesty International 1996b: 15). The ICRC began providing one meal a day for prisoners in 1998 in an effort to improve conditions (Bouka 2013: 226).
8 Other women became *de facto* widows because their husbands were sent to reeducation camps, where they were taught the "truth" about Rwandan history and instructed on how to confess genocide crimes. These centers, known as *ingando* (reeducation) camps, lasted an average of three months, and continue in Rwanda today (see Thomson 2011).
9 Moreover, approximately one-third of the aid that was disbursed was used to pay arrears on the former government's debt (Prunier 2009: 37).
10 Jennie Burnet (2012) discusses a Rwandan proverb, "*Abagore ntibafite ubwoko,*" translated as "Wives have no ethnicity" (page 43). This suggests that because of Rwanda's patrilineality, whereby women entered their husbands' families upon marriage, ethnic identity was "softer" for women.
11 See Chapter 2: Kanjogera killed the king to make way for her own biological son's rule, and also killed many political opponents. Because of her prominent role in the genocide, Agathe Kanziga Habyarimana, the president's wife, was dubbed "a Kanjogera."
12 These attacks were common and lethal. Amnesty International (1996a, 1996b) has documented many of the attacks, which frequently occurred around Gisenyi and Ruhengeri (near the border with DR Congo).
13 Perhaps (but unlikely) a coincidence, I discovered this exact same sentence in Jeanne Vickers's book *Women and War* (1993: 151).

4 Women's Political Mobilization in Rwanda

1 See also the Women's Commission for Refugee Women and Children (1997: 8).
2 Portions of this analysis were previously published in Berry 2015a.
3 The new RPF regime eliminated groups suspected of allying with the former regime or of opposing RPF rule. This meant that agents of the state tightly controlled political space – and civil society more broadly – and quickly arrested (or worse) anyone they deemed suspicious. This tightly controlled political and civic space continues to this day.
4 See the 1995 Beijing Platform of Action: www.un.org/womenwatch/daw/beijing/platform/plat1.htm#statement. Several Rwandan women attended the 1995 UN Women's Conference in Beijing.
5 See also Newbury and Baldwin (2000: 4) and Gervais (2003: 544).
6 Organic Law No. 08/2005 of 14/07/2005 Determining the Use and Management of Land in Rwanda, and Law No. 22/99 of 12/11/1999 to Supplement Book I of the Civil Code and to Institute Part Five Regarding Matrimonial Regimes, Liberalities and Successions, O.G. No. 22 of 15/11/1999.
7 While outside the scope of this chapter, it is important to note that the inheritance law only permitted women in formal (legally recognized) marriages to claim access to their husbands' land, and yet many marriages in Rwanda are not officially documented. Moreover, the law could not be retrospectively applied, so women whose husbands or fathers died in the genocide were not given access to their land (Pottier 2006: 519–520). It also codified the importance of the "family council" in determining whether a woman inherits (Republic of Rwanda 1999, Article 51). This stipulation allows for greater nuance in the application of the law, ultimately denying women's inheritance if the head of the "family council" objects (Human Rights Watch 2004; Pottier 2006: 520).
8 INGOs weakened some of these burgeoning civil society organizations by poaching their leaders (USAID 2000: 15).
9 Assassinations of heads of survivors' associations mentioned by Human Rights Watch include Assiel Kabera (2000) and Landuardi Bayijire (2007).

5 Historical Roots of Mass Violence in Bosnia-Herzegovina

1 Susan Woodward (1995) emphasized the critical role international economic policies and political pressures played, as well as the breakdown of political and civil order during the collapse of the Yugoslavian state. V. P. Gagnon (2006) highlighted the role the nationalist political parties played within Yugoslavia as they attempted to concentrate their political power. Lenard Cohen (1993) suggested that Serbs have utilized a victim mentality to foster a culture of violence fomented by elites, while Viktor Meier (2005) underlined the role of Slobodan Milošević as a charismatic leader

driving the violence. Warren Zimmermann (1995), the last U.S. ambassador to Yugoslavia before its collapse, blamed Slovenia for instigating the violence by leaving the Yugoslavia Federation at a volatile time, and villainized nationalist political leaders. Other scholars, like Burg and Shoup (1999), noted that Germany's diplomatic recognition of Croatia and Slovenia played a crucial role in igniting violence. Michael Pugh and Neil Cooper (2004) emphasized the preceding economic crisis and struggles for economic control. Norman Cigar (1995), Laura Silber and Allan Little (1997), Michael Mann (2005), and Sabrina Ramet (1992; 2006) placed the majority of blame on the historical unworkability of the Yugoslav state, economic decline, and Serb territorial ambitions.

2 This differed from forced conversions elsewhere, such as in Bulgaria.

3 It is worth noting that both Macedonia and Serbia have a rich tradition of women's involvement in revolutionary movements and war. In Macedonia, peasant women were active in the Internal Macedonian Revolutionary Organization (IMRO) around the turn of the twentieth century. Female guerrilla fighters during World War I were active in the Macedonian underground (Jancar-Webster 1990: 30). Serbia also had a tradition of female combatants, dating back to the Serbian defeat in the Battle of Kosovo in 1389. During World War I, hundreds of Serb women in Belgrade participated in fighting, as they helped defend the city and were active participants in street fights and firefighting, as well as the more traditionally female roles of caring for the sick and burying the dead (Jancar-Webster 1990: 31). Bosnia had less of a tradition of female combatants, and yet during World War I, peasant women fought to protect their food supplies against Austrian troops (Jancar-Webster 1990: 31).

4 By the end of the war, between 750,000 and 800,000 Serbians and Montenegrins had died out of a population of around 4.5 million (Newman 2011: 47). This was in addition to the 300,000 Bosnians who were either killed or fled to Turkey during the war (Malcolm 1996: 163).

5 While initially *zadruga* simply referred to a living arrangement involving more than two generations, it eventually became known as a unit of collective property during the latter socialist period (Bringa 1995: 42).

6 Here Jancar-Webster cites work in Serbo-Croatian by Dunja Rihtman-Augustin (1984).

7 In this section, particularly in the discussion of women's involvement with Tito's Partisans, I heavily draw from Jancar-Webster (1990), which represents the first and most substantial English-language text on women in Tito's National Liberation Movement.

8 There were no women participants among the Četniks, who believed it immoral for women to give up their daily activities to fight alongside men (Jancar-Webster 1990: 47). However, many women supported the movement.

9 Proclamation of the KPJ Central Committee to the People of Yugoslavia, July 25, 1941.

10 Ultimately, ninety-two women were designated "national heroes" by the Yugoslav government as a result of their courage and bravery during the Partisan struggle. Of these women, twenty-one were from Serbia, seventeen

were from Croatia, eleven were Muslims, twenty-one were Slovenian, and the rest were from other parts of the region.

11 Cominform was the Soviet-dominated organization of communist parties founded after World War II. The nonaligned movement refers to states that did not wish to align themselves with either of the Cold War superpowers: the Soviet Union or the United States.

12 This is a measure of the Total Period Fertility Rate (TPFR), a cross-section of women between fourteen and forty-nine in a given calendar year. By 1990, the total births per woman was 1.7, and then after the war this dropped to between 1.6 and 1.7 in 1996 to around 1.3–1.4 in 2000 (Sardon and Confession 2004: 214).

13 In 1994, the female replacement rate was +17.38 among Albanians, compared to -2.93 among Serbians (Cockburn 1998: 161).

14 In 1389, the Ottoman Empire defeated the medieval Serbian kingdom at the Battle of Kosovo. Nationalist Serb politicians frequently referenced the defeat in the build-up to the war in the 1990s.

15 Ramet (2005: 10) notes reports that indicated some Serbs may have been kept from the polls by Karadžić's Serbian Democratic Party.

16 While some reports of the time indicated that women were very involved with the peace protests in Sarajevo, my own examination of photos by Ron Haviv on display at the Sarajevo History Museum in March 2013 suggested that men outnumbered women ten to one at these rallies.

17 Ustaše fascists had used the word *čišćenje*, or cleansing, during World War II to describe the expulsion of Serbs from certain areas under their control (Shaw 2007: 49). To "cleanse" the land, Serb paramilitaries created panic and terror and destroyed markers of Muslim culture. See further discussion of the origins of this term in Petrović (1994) and Silber and Little (1997: 244).

18 Croatia quickly turned into a massive refugee camp – it hosted almost one million refugees during the war in a population of just 4.7 million people (Silber and Little 1997: 247).

19 Other estimates suggest this number is high. According to Gjelten (1995: 10), the Bosnian Institute for Statistics reports that 34.1 percent of marriages in 1991 were of mixed nationality.

20 Field notes, April 2013. Krajina region.

21 Five other areas across the country were eventually declared UN Safe Zones as well.

22 There were also reports that Dutch peacekeepers were guilty of raping women seeking their protection (Amnesty International 2009).

23 Attempting to hide evidence of the atrocities, Serb forces buried and then reburied many of the bodies, often moving mass graves with bulldozers and other heavy machinery. As a result, many dead bodies were decapitated or otherwise severed into multiple pieces after the initial burial (field notes 2013; meetings with ICMP officials). During my fieldwork, I visited the ICMP identification facility in Tuzla, which contains the partial remains of dozens of those killed in massacres in the region. Some bodies have just a single bone; others are missing a skull or other parts. The postmortem decapitation of bodies posed significant challenges for identifying the dead and seeking justice in the aftermath.

24 More than 200 men are now members of the Association of Women War Victims, a group that has assumed the duty of officially deeming individuals rape survivors (Interview, Bakira Hasečić, May, 2013).

25 There is an interesting parallel here to women "victims" of human trafficking. See work by Jennifer Musto (2009), Gail Kligman and Stephanie Limoncelli (2005), and Elena Shih (2015).

26 The Bosnian Book of the Dead registered 57,584 combatant deaths and 38,012 civilian deaths between 1992 and 1995.

27 Technically, the accords were called the General Framework Agreement for Peace in Bosnia and Herzegovina. The agreement was entered into force as a treaty in Paris two weeks later.

28 Of course, the irony of this was that the international community lauded Bosnia's multiculturalism prior to the war, and yet proposed a solution that threatens to erase it.

6 War and Structural Shifts in Bosnia-Herzegovina

1 Kinzer, S. (October 31, 1992). "Croats Send Back Bosnian Refugees." *New York Times*.

2 Williams, C. (November 12, 1992). "Borders Are Barrier for Bosnian Refugees: Fleeing the War, Most Find that Inundated Croatia Has Closed the Door." *Los Angeles Times*.

3 There were, however, several typhoid outbreaks in Bosnia (see *Los Angeles Times*, November 12, 1992).

4 Field notes 2013, Sarajevo.

5 The war also caused other demographic shifts, including a "delay effect" in age at first marriage in Bosnia, and fertility rates decreased from 1.9 children per woman to a rate of 1.2 after the war (Staveteig 2011: 148).

6 However, as I discuss in Chapter 8, NGOs may have had incentives to overestimate this figure.

7 Staveteig (2011) reports similar findings.

8 By 1997, only 40,000 of these houses had been repaired.

9 This forced some humanitarian missions to use air drops to get urgent supplies to besieged cities (Cigar 1995: 58).

10 The organizations that did exist were often linked to political parties, especially during the socialist era when many social clubs and cultural organizations were popular.

11 Note that this is not representative of the entire country – since I aimed to interview women involved in organizations, I often interviewed the organizations' founders.

12 Elissa Helms provided similar examples. For instance, while living in divided Mostar after the war, Helms recounts how it was common for women to cross to the side of the city where they no longer "belonged" to run basic errands (2013: 144). If they were not wearing a visible marker of their religion (e.g., an Islamic *hidžab*), strangers could not easily recognize a women's ethnic identity.

7 Women's Political Mobilization in Bosnia-Herzegovina

1 See www.un.org/womenwatch/osagi/wps/.

2 This phrase was also uttered before the war, and is the title of a song by Dubioza Kolektiv, a popular anti-nationalist Bosnian rock band.

3 ICTY. www.icty.org/sections/AbouttheICTY.

4 Field notes, May 2013, Tuzla.

5 See, for example, Rule 96 of the ICTY's Rules of Procedure and Evidence. www.icty.org/sections/LegalLibrary/RulesofProcedureandEvidence.

6 *Prosecutor* v. *Dusko Tadic* (Opinion and Judgment), IT-94-1-T, International Criminal Tribunal for the Former Yugoslavia, May 7, 1997. While protections against gender-based crimes were espoused in early legal commissions (see the Fourth Geneva Convention of 1949 and Additional Protocols), wartime rape was generally addressed in a monolithic manner and gender-based crimes were not seen as genocide, crimes against humanity, or war crimes until the work of the ICTY and the ICTR (Oosterveld 2005: 69–70). The first case at the ICTY, *Prosecutor* v. *Tadic*, produced the first conviction for sexual violence since World War II for crimes committed against men. In the subsequent *Čelebići* case, the ICTY found that rape constituted torture, and further established that the doctrine of command responsibility applied to those who did not directly commit rape. The *Kunarac* case that followed addressed issues of sexual slavery (Oosterveld 2005: 72–79).

7 Jobs with international humanitarian agencies also gave some locals access to supply routes and transportation that allowed them to engage in part-smuggling operations, as described by Peter Andreas's research on Sarajevo (2008). I also discuss some of the negative repercussions of this employment in Chapter 8.

8 Not her real name.

9 Field notes, May 2013. Kozarac.

10 During my fieldwork, I heard many examples of discrimination against non-Serbs. For example, one bar owner described how R.S. authorities frequently inspect his bar and find some minor violation to threaten him with. Another woman described how she tried to get her child signed up for tennis lessons, but the Serb instructor quoted her a price double what she knew other people paid.

11 Field notes, May 2013. Kozarac.

12 Note: I interviewed Dr. Antić-Štauber twice for this project (in 2010 and 2013).

13 The organization was initially called the Center for Women Returnees.

14 See Svetlana Slapšak, 1000 Peace Nobel (2005). http://word.world-citizenship.org/wp-archive/1530.

15 Note: Two of my interviewees indicated that these protests began in 1995 (Nura #68, and Vedrana #69, June 2013).

16 This commemoration occurs in Potočari each year on July 11. In recent years, hundreds of people have participated in a "Peace March," a religious

and reflective experience in which they walk for days from different parts of the country to Srebrenica in memory of those killed.

17 See coverage here: Associated Press (April 11, 2013). "US, Canada, Jordan boycott UN meeting on global criminal justice that excluded war victims." Accessed June 13, 2017: www.foxnews.com/world/2013/04/11/us-canada-jordan-boycott-un-meeting-on-global-criminal-justice-that-excluded/.

18 BBC News. (April 25, 2013). "Serbian president apologises for Srebrenica 'crime.'" Accessed June 12, 2017: www.bbc.com/news/world-europe-22297089.

19 Biljana Plavšić was elected President of the newly-created Republika Srpska. As a key counter-example to the idea that women are biologically predisposed to peace, Plavšić become well known for her belief in the biological superiority of Serbs. However, gender stereotypes also likely prevented her from being seen as threatening to peace as her male counterparts (Aganović, Miftari, and Veličković 2015).

20 There was also a short-lived Women's Party (Stranka Žena), formed by Amila Omersoftić in 1996. The OSCE was an integral supporter of these and others initiatives. See Aganović, Miftari, and Veličković (2015) for further discussion.

21 Eurovision is a long-running international song contest. It is one of the most popular non-sporting events in the world.

8 Limits of Mobilization

1 See a master's thesis by Julia Dowling (2013) for further discussion of these concepts in the Bosnian case.

2 This term emerged several times in my fieldwork during conversations with self-reflective INGO employees.

3 I am grateful to Bill Roy for this phrasing and insight.

4 See scholarship on this topic by Vidal (2001), Hintjens (2008), Burnet (2012), and Thomson (2013).

5 Batwa were largely omitted from "survivor" categories despite the fact that perhaps one-third of their total population was killed during the violence (Lewis 2000; Beswick 2011). In some communities, up to 80 percent of the Batwa population was killed (Overeem 1995).

6 U.S. Department of State (2015). 2014 Country Report on Human Rights Practices: Rwanda. Accessed June 15, 2017: www.state.gov/j/drl/rls/hrrpt/2014/af/236394.htm.

7 Moreover, if rape survivors in Republika Srpska do manage to qualify for the social benefits, they are only entitled to 100 KM ($55 USD) per month, which is far short of what most need to live. In the Federation, the benefit is 563 KM ($210 USD) per month (Amnesty International 2009: 43).

8 Moreover, the law precludes people from acquiring this status if they lived outside of the country for more than three months; this automatically excludes women who sought refuge abroad during or after the war (Cockburn 2013a).

9 See Elaine Sciolino (May 9, 1993), "Bosnia's Serbs Smirk, Keep Shooting," *New York Times* (accessed via ProQuest).

10 Newsweek, January 3, 1993. "A Pattern of Rape." www.newsweek.com/pattern-rape-192142.

11 This process of externally determining that women are victims, as mentioned earlier, echoes the literature on women "victims" of human trafficking (see Musto 2009; Shih 2015). Often called "slaves" by well-intentioned anti-trafficking activists, such externally imposed identities can be demobilizing and disempowering to individual women, who often do not choose such identities.

12 Moreover, such programs focused exclusively on "war rape," rather than addressing the various forms of gender-based violence that exist along a continuum of violence both in and out of the war context.

13 This legacy began before the UN Charter with the United Nations Relief and Rehabilitation Administration, which was founded in 1943 and subsequently replaced by the UN International Refugee Organization and the World Health Organization.

14 See De Waal (1997), Anderson (1999), Easterly (2001), El-Bushra (2008), Apthorpe (2011), Barnett (2011), Mosse (2011), Fechter and Hindman (2011).

15 See two important documents for this period: 1997 OECD Guidelines on Peace, Conflict and Development Cooperation, and the 1998 UN Secretary General's report on Priorities for Post-conflict Peace-Building.

16 Not to mention that rape was an extremely narrow conception of gender-based violence, which should more broadly include all forms of gender-based harm, from forced recruitment to sex-selective massacres (see Carpenter 2006).

17 In addition, the category of "women" is, in itself, part of a colonial construction. In many African cultures, gender has not existed the same way or with the same importance as in Western societies. See Oyewumi (1997).

18 See the discussion of Kibeho in Chapter 2, in addition to reports by Amnesty International (1995a, 1996a), Human Rights Watch (1995), and Alison Des Forges's comprehensive work (1999).

19 Survivor funds led by the government similarly exclude non-Tutsi victims from the distribution of aid. See, for example, the Assistance Fund for Genocide Survivors (FARG).

20 See Hintjens 2008; Gready 2010; Ingelaere 2010; Burnet 2012; Thomson 2013 for further discussion.

21 See the film *The Whistleblower* (2010), directed by Larysa Kondracki, which documents the appalling complicity of a UN contractor in facilitating and then covering up the human trafficking crime syndicates operating out of Bosnia during and after the war. Ed Vulliamy describes the film's origins in detail in his 2012 book (pp. 117–122). He quotes Madeleine Rees, the leading UN officer for gender issues, as saying, "I went to work with large numbers of women who had been the victims of rape during the war, but I ended up working as much with women who were being trafficked and raped by soldiers and police officers sent to keep the peace" (p. 122).

22 The lack of a memorial at the Omarska concentration camp, for example, ultimately had more to do with infighting between camp survivor groups than opposition from Serb political leaders (even if politicians, like Prijedor Mayor Marko Pavić, did not make it easy).

23 La Mattina (2012) suggests it might be due to a decline in the availability of desirable male partners.

24 Field notes 2010–2013. Kigali.

25 I am grateful to Alan Gilbert for thinking through the moral imperative of this approach with me.

9 Conclusion

1 The Women, Peace, and Security agenda refers to the programming and advocacy around women's engagement in peace and security efforts, as outlined by UN Women, UNSCR 1325 and subsequent resolutions, the Beijing Platform for Action, and the Convention on the Elimination of All Forms of Discrimination against Women.

2 In Rwanda's case, the RPF was positioned as the country's savior.

3 Victoire Ingabire was sentenced to fifteen years in prison in 2012. As of writing in November 2017, Diane Rwigara has been arrested and charged with offences against state security, insurrection, and forgery. She is facing a minimum of twenty years in prison if convicted.

Glossary

Akazu: "The little house," used to refer to the inner core of Habyarimana's regime, including his wife, Agate Kanziga, and her clan.

Bosniak: Term that came into widespread use in 1993 to describe an ethnic Bosnian Muslim, but without asserting a specific religious affiliation. Not to be confused with "Bosnian," which is a citizen of Bosnia of any ethnicity (Serb, Croat, Bosniak, or other). The term "Bosnian Muslims" was used to refer to the same group prior to 1993.

Croat: Bosnian citizen of Catholic heritage. Not to be confused with Croatian, which indicates a citizen of Croatia.

Federation: One of two semi-autonomous political entities in Bosnia, sometimes referred to as the Muslim-Croat Federation. It comprises 51 percent of the territory of Bosnia as established through the Dayton Accords. It shares a loose federal government with Republika Srpska, but also maintains its own government institutions.

Gacaca: A court system resurrected from precolonial Rwanda, which the post-genocide government implemented to try the millions of cases related to genocide crimes.

Génocidaires [Derived from French but incorporated into Kinyarwanda lexicon]: Term used to refer to anyone who committed the genocide. Has taken on new political meaning, as it is used to accuse people in Rwanda who challenge or oppose the new RPF regime in any capacity.

Interahamwe: "Those who fight together"/"Those who work together." The name of the militias who conducted much of the killing during the genocide. Many were former MRND political party members, especially from the youth wings. Technically a civilian militia.

Inyenzi: "Cockroaches" in Kinyarwanda. Derogatory term used to refer to Tutsi. Often used during the genocide against the RPF, as well as against ordinary Tutsi.

Kinyarwanda: The language of Rwanda. (As Prunier (1995) smartly points out, it is spoken *exactly* the same by Hutu and Tutsi.)

Mwami (plural: *Abami*):   King in Kinyarwanda.

Republika Srpska: One of two semi-autonomous political entities in Bosnia, known as the Serbian entity as established through the Dayton Accords. It comprises 49 percent of the territory of Bosnia-Herzegovina, and shares a loose federal government with the Federation of Bosnia-Herzegovina, but also maintains its own government institutions.

Serb: Bosnian citizen of Serbian Orthodox heritage. Not to be confused with Serbian, which indicates a citizen of Serbia.

Ubuhake: A form of personal contract in traditional Rwandan society, in which an individual was bound as a producer to their "patron" or "chief" and was required to give their labor in that service.

Bibliography

Abramowitz, S. A. (2009). *Psychosocial Liberia: Managing suffering in post-conflict life*. Dissertation, Department of Anthropology. Harvard University, Cambridge, MA.

Abu-Lughod, L. (1990). The romance of resistance: Tracing transformations of power through Bedouin women. *American Ethnologist, 17*(1), 41–55.

African Rights. (1995a). *Rwanda: Death, despair and defiance*. London: African Rights.

(1995b). *Rwanda: Not So Innocent: When women become killers*. London: African Rights.

(2004). *Broken Bodies, Torn Spirits: Living with genocide, rape and HIV/AIDS*. Kigali, Rwanda: African Rights.

Aganović, A., E. Miftari, and M. Veličković. (2015). *Women and Political Life in Post-Dayton Bosnia and Herzegovina: 1995-2015*. Sarajevo: Sarajevo Open Center.

Agarwal, B. (1992). The gender and environment debate: Lessons from India. *Feminist Studies, 18*(1), 119–158.

Agency for Gender Equality of BiH. (2013). *Prevalence and Characteristics of Violence against Women in BiH 2013*. Gender Equality Agency of Bosnia and Herzegovina. Edited by Samra Filipović – Hadžiabdić. Ministry for Human Rights and Refugees of BiH. Sarajevo, BiH.

Ali, Daniel Ayalew, Klaus Deininger, and Markus Goldstein (2014). Environmental and gender impacts of land tenure regularization in Africa: Pilot evidence from Rwanda. *Journal of Development Economics, 110*, 262–275.

Amnesty International. (1993). *Bosnia-Herzegovina: Rape and sexual abuse by armed forces* (No. 63). London: Amnesty International.

(1994). *Rwanda: Reports of killings and abductions by the Rwandese Patriotic Army, April–August 1994* (No. 47). London: Amnesty International.

(1995a). *Burundi and Rwanda Crisis Response: Army killings in Kibeho Camp, Rwanda*. London: Amnesty International.

(1995b). *Rwanda: Arming the perpetrators of genocide* (No. 2). London: Amnesty International.

(1995c). *Rwanda: Crying out for justice* (No. 47). London: Amnesty International.

(1996a). *Rwanda: Alarming resurgence of killings* (No. 47). London: Amnesty International.

(1996b). *Rwanda and Burundi: The return home – rumors and realities* (No. 2). London: Amnesty International.

(1997). *"Who's Living in My House?" Obstacles to the safe return of refugees and internally displaced people* (No. EUR 63/01/97). London: Amnesty International.

(2004). *Rwanda: The enduring legacy of the genocide and war* (No. 47). London: Amnesty International.

(2009). *"Whose Justice?" The women of Bosnia and Herzegovina are still waiting.* London: Amnesty International.

Anderson, K. (1981). *Wartime Women: Sex roles, family relations, and the status of women during World War II.* Westport, CT: Greenwood Press.

Anderson, M. B. (1999). *Do No Harm: How aid can support peace – or war.* Boulder, CO: Lynne Rienner Publishers.

Andjelkovic, B. (1998). Reflections on nationalism and its impact on women in Serbia. In M. Rueschemeyer (Ed.), *Women in the Politics of Postcommunist Eastern Europe* (pp. 235–248). Armonk, NY: M.E. Sharpe.

André, C. and J. Platteau. (1998). Land relations under unbearable stress: Rwanda caught in the Malthusian trap. *Journal of Economic Behavior & Organization*, 34(1), 1–47.

Andreas, P. (2004). The clandestine political economy of war and peace in Bosnia. *International Studies Quarterly*, 48(1), 29–52.

(2008). *Blue Helmets and Black Markets: The business of survival in the siege of Sarajevo.* Ithaca, NY: Cornell University Press.

Annan, J., C. Blattman, D. Mazurana, and K. Carlson. (2011). Civil war, reintegration and gender in northern Uganda. *Journal of Conflict Resolution*, 55(6), 877–908.

Ansoms, A. (2008). Striving for growth, bypassing the poor? A critical review of Rwanda's rural sector policies. *Journal of Modern African Studies*, 46(1), 1–32.

(2009). Re-engineering rural society: The visions and ambitions of the Rwandan elite. *African Affairs*, 108(431), 289–309.

Apthorpe, R. (2011). With Alice in Aidland: A seriously satirical allegory. In D. Mosse (Ed.), *Adventures in Aidland: The anthropology of professionals in international development* (pp. 199–219). New York; Oxford: Berghahn Books.

Aretxaga, B. (1997). *Shattering Silence: Women, nationalism, and political subjectivity in Northern Ireland.* Princeton, NJ: Princeton University Press.

Athanasiou, A. (2013). The poetics of dissent and the political courage of Women in Black. In S. Zajović, S. Stojanović, and M. Urošević (Ed.), *Women in Black* (pp. 47–66). Belgrade, Serbia.

Autesserre, S. (2009). Hobbes and the Congo: Frames, local violence, and international intervention. *International Organization, 63*(2), 249–280.

(2014). *Peaceland: Conflict resolution and the everyday politics of international intervention.* Cambridge: Cambridge University Press.

Baaz, M. E. and M. Stern. (2009). Why do soldiers rape? Masculinity, violence, and sexuality in the armed forces in the Congo (DRC). *International Studies Quarterly, 53*(2), 495–518.

Bagić, A. (2004). Talking about donors. Ethnographies of aid – exploring development texts and encounters. Roskilde University Occasional Paper in International Development Studies, 24, 222.

(2006). Women's organizing in post-Yugoslav countries: Talking about "donors." In M. M. Ferree and A. M. Tripp (Eds.), *Global Feminism: Transnational women's activism, organizing, and human rights* (pp. 141–165). New York: New York University Press.

Balcells, L. (2012). The consequences of victimization on political identities: Evidence from Spain. *Politics & Society, 40*(3), 311–347.

Barker, G. and J. Schulte. (2010). *Engaging Men as Allies in Women's Economic Empowerment: Strategies and recommendations for CARE country offices.* Edited by C. Norway. Oslo: International Center for Research on Women.

Barnett, M. (2011). *Empire of Humanity: A history of humanitarianism.* Ithaca, NY: Cornell University Press.

Bassuener, K. (2012). *Statement for the Oireachtas,* Joint Committee on EU Affairs. Edited by D. P. Council. Sarajevo, BiH: Democratization Policy Council.

Bauer, G. and H. E. Britton. (2006). *Women in African Parliaments.* Boulder, CO: Lynne Rienner Publishers.

Baumel, J. T. (1999). Women's agency and survival strategies during the Holocaust. *Women's Studies International Forum, 22*(3), 329–347.

Bayat, A. (1997). *Street Politics: Poor people's movements in Iran.* New York: Columbia University Press.

(2007). *Making Islam Democratic: Social movements and the post-Islamist turn.* Redwood City, CA: Stanford University Press.

(2010). *Life as Politics: How ordinary people change the Middle East.* Redwood City, CA: Stanford University Press.

Bećirević, E. (2014). *Genocide on the Drina River.* New Haven, CT: Yale University Press.

Bellows, J. and E. Miguel. (2009). War and local collective action in Sierra Leone. *Journal of Public Economics, 93*(11–12), 1144–1157.

Benderly, J. (1997). Women's movements in Yugoslavia, 1978–1992. In M. K. Bokovoy, J. A. Irvine, and C. S. Lilly (Eds.), *State–Society Relations in Yugoslavia 1945–1992* (pp. 183–209). New York: St. Martin's Press.

Benford, R. D. and D. A. Snow. (2000). Framing processes and social movements: An overview and assessment. *Annual Review of Sociology, 26,* 611–639.

Berry, M. E. (2015a). From violence to mobilization: War, women, and threat in Rwanda. *Mobilization: An International Quarterly, 20*(2), 135–156.

(2015b). When "bright futures" fade: Paradoxes of women's empowerment in Rwanda. *Signs: Journal of Women in Culture and Society*, 41(1), 1–27.

(2017). Barriers to Women's Progress After Atrocity: Evidence from Rwanda and Bosnia-Herzegovina. *Gender & Society*, 31(6): 830–853.

Berry, M. E. and M. Lake. (2017). Thematic review: Gender politics after war: Mobilizing opportunity in post-conflict Africa. *Politics & Gender*, 13(2), 336–349.

Beswick, D. (2011). Democracy, identity and the politics of exclusion in post-genocide Rwanda: The case of the Batwa. *Democratization*, 18(2), 490–511.

Bijleveld, C., A. Morssinkhof, and A. Smeulers. (2009). Counting the countless rape victimization during the Rwandan genocide. *International Criminal Justice Review*, 19.

Björkdahl, A. (2012). A gender-just peace? Exploring the post-Dayton peace process in Bosnia. *Peace & Change*, 37(2), 286–317.

Blalock, H. M. (1967). *Toward a Theory of Minority–Group Relations*. New York: John Wiley & Sons.

Blattman, C. (2009). From violence to voting: War and political participation in Uganda. *American Political Science Review*, 103(2), 231–247.

Booth, D. and F. Golooba-Mutebi. (2012). Developmental patrimonialism? The case of Rwanda. *African Affairs*, 111(444), 379–403.

Bop, C. (2001). Women in conflict: Their gains and their losses. In S. Meintjes, M. Turshen, and A. Pillay (Eds.), *The Aftermath: Women in post-conflict transformation*. London: Zed Books.

Bose, S. (2002). *Bosnia after Dayton: Nationalist partition and international intervention*. Oxford: Oxford University Press.

Bougarel, X. (2006). The shadow of heroes: Former combatants in post-war Bosnia Herzegovina. *International Social Science Journal*, 58(189), 479–490.

Bougarel, X., E. Helms, and G. Duijzings. (2007). *The New Bosnian Mosaic: Identities, memories and moral claims in a post-war society*. Aldershot, England; Burlington, VT: Ashgate Press.

Bouka, Y. A. F. (2013). In the shadow of prison: Power, identity, and transitional justice in post-genocide Rwanda. PhD Dissertation, American University, Washington, DC.

Bradol, J. and M. Le Pape. (2017). *Humanitarian Aid, Genocide and Mass Killings: The Rwandan experience*. Manchester: Manchester University Press.

Bringa, T. (1995). *Being Muslim the Bosnian Way: Identity and community in a central Bosnian village*. Princeton, NJ: Princeton University Press.

Brown, S. E. (2014). Female perpetrators of the Rwandan genocide. *International Feminist Journal of Politics*, 16(3), 448–469.

Brown, W. (2000). Suffering rights as paradoxes. *Constellations*, 7, 208–229.

Brownmiller, S. (1994). Making female bodies the battlefield. In A. Stiglmayer (Ed.), *Mass Rape: The war against women in Bosnia-Herzegovina* (pp. 180–182). Lincoln; London: University of Nebraska Press.

Burg, S. L. and P. Shoup. (1999). *The War in Bosnia-Herzegovina: Ethnic conflict and international intervention*. Armonk, NY: M. E. Sharpe.

Burnet, J. E. (2008). Gender balance and the meanings of women in governance in post-genocide Rwanda. *African Affairs*, 107(428), 361–386.

(2012). *Genocide Lives in Us: Women, memory, and silence in Rwanda.* Madison: University of Wisconsin Press.

(2017). Sorting and suffering: Social classification in post-genocide Rwanda. In Jan Shetler (Ed.) *Gendering Ethnicity in African Women's Lives* (pp. 206–230). Madison: University of Wisconsin Press.

Buss, D. E. (2007). The curious visibility of wartime rape: Gender and ethnicity in international criminal law. *Windsor Yearbook of Access to Justice,* 25(1), 3.

(2009). Rethinking "rape as a weapon of war." *Feminist Legal Studies, 17,* 145–163.

Capoccia, G. and R. D. Kelemen. (2007). The study of critical junctures: Theory, narrative, and counterfactuals in historical institutionalism. *World Politics,* 59(3), 341–369.

Carnegie Commission. (1997). *Preventing Deadly Conflict: Final Report.* New York: Carnegie Corporation.

Carpenter, R. C. (2006). Recognizing gender-based violence against civilian men and boys in conflict situations. *Security Dialogue,* 37(1), 83–103.

Celestino, M. R. and K. S. Gleditsch. (2013). Fresh carnations or all thorn, no rose? Nonviolent campaigns and transitions in autocracies. *Journal of Peace Research,* 50(3), 385–400.

Census Bureau of Bosnia-Herzegovina (2013). Preliminary Census Report. www.bhas.ba/obavjestenja/Preliminarni_rezultati_bos.pdf.

Chakravarty, A. (2015). *Investing in Authoritarian Rule: Punishment and patronage in Rwanda's gacaca courts for genocide crimes.* New York: Cambridge University Press.

Chalk, F. R. and K. Jonassohn. (1990). *The History and Sociology of Genocide: Analyses and case studies.* New Haven, CT: Yale University Press.

Chandler, D. (2000). *Bosnia: Faking democracy after Dayton.* London; Sterling, VA: Pluto Press.

Charney, I. W. (1994). *The Widening Circle of Genocide, Vol. 3.* New Brunswick, NJ; London: Transaction Publishers.

Chinchilla, N. S. (1983). *Women in Revolutionary Movements: The case of Nicaragua.* East Lansing: Michigan State University.

(1992). Marxism, feminism, and the struggle for democracy in Latin America. In A. Escobar and S. E. Alvarez (Eds.) *The Making of Contemporary Social Movements in Latin America* (pp. 37–51). Boulder, CO: Westview Press.

Cigar, N. L. (1995). *Genocide in Bosnia: The policy of "ethnic cleansing."* College Station: Texas A&M University Press.

Clark, J. N. (2010). Bosnia's success story? Brčko district and the "view from below." *International Peacekeeping,* 17(1), 67–79.

Clemens, E. S. (1993). Organizational repertoires and institutional change: Women's groups and the transformation of U.S. politics, 1890–1920. *American Journal of Sociology,* 98(4), 755–798.

(1996). Organizational form as frame: Collective identity and political strategy in the American labor movement, 1880–1920. In D. McAdam, et al. (Eds.) *Comparative Perspectives on Social Movements* (pp. 205–226). Cambridge: Cambridge University Press.

(1999). Securing political returns to social capital: Women's associations in the United States, 1880s–1920s. *Journal of Interdisciplinary History*, 29(4), 613–638.

Cockburn, C. (1998). *The Space between Us: Negotiating gender and national identities in conflict*. London; New York: Zed Books.

(2007). *From Where We Stand: War, women's activism and feminist analysis*. Zed Books.

(2013a). Against the odds: Sustaining feminist momentum in post-war Bosnia-Herzegovina. *Women's Studies International Forum*, 37(1), 26–35.

(2013b). Sexual violence in Bosnia: How war lives on in everyday life. *50.50 Inclusive Democracy, Open Democracy*. www.opendemocracy.net/5050/cynthia-cockburn/sexual-violence-in-bosnia-how-war-lives-on-in-everyday-life. Accessed March 2015.

Cockburn, C., with R. Stakic-Domuz and M. Hubic. (2001). *Women Organizing for Change: A study of women's local integrative organizations and the pursuit of democracy in Bosnia-Herzegovina*. Zenica, BiH: Medica Women's Association.

Codere, H. (1973). *The Biography of an African Society: Rwanda 1900–1960: Based on forty-eight Rwandan autobiographies*. Tervuren: Musée royal de l'Afrique centrale.

Cohen, L. J. (1993). *Broken Bonds: The disintegration of Yugoslavia*. Boulder, CO: Westview Press.

Cohen, M. H., A. d'Adesky, and K. Anastos. (2005). Women in Rwanda: Another world is possible. *Journal of the American Medical Association*, 294(5), 613–615.

Cole, A. (2010). International criminal law and sexual violence: An overview. In C. McGlynn and V. Munro (Eds.), *Rethinking Rape Law: International and comparative perspectives* (pp. 47–60). London: Routledge.

Collier, P. and A. Hoeffler. (2004). Greed and grievance in civil war. *Oxford Economic Papers*, 56(4), 563–595.

Collier, R. B. and D. Collier. (1991). *Shaping the Political Arena*. Princeton, NJ: Princeton University Press.

Connell, R. W. and J. W. Messerschmidt. (2005). Hegemonic masculinity: Rethinking the concept. *Gender & Society*, 19(6), 829–859.

Cramer, C. (2006). *Civil War Is Not a Stupid Thing: Accounting for violence in developing countries*. London: Hurst & Co.

Crenshaw, K. (1991). Mapping the margins: Intersectionality, identity politics, and violence against women of color. *Stanford Law Review*, 43(6), 1241–1299.

Crisafulli, P. and A. Redmond. (2012). *Rwanda, Inc.: How a devastated nation became an economic model for the developing world*. London: Macmillan.

Dallaire, R. (2003). *Shake Hands with the Devil: The failure of humanity in Rwanda*. New York: Carroll & Graf.

Davenport, C. and A. Stam. (2007). Rwandan Political Violence in Space and Time. Unpublished manuscript, available online: https://bc.sas.upenn.edu/system/files/Stam_03.26.09.pdf.

De Alwis, M. (1998). Women's political participation in contemporary Sri Lanka. In P. Jeffery and A. Basu (Eds.), *Appropriating Gender: Women's activism and politicized religion in South Asia* (pp. 185–202). New York; London: Routledge.

De Luca, G. and M. Verpoorten. (2015). Civil war and political participation: Evidence from Uganda. *Economic Development and Cultural Change*, 64(1), 113–141.

De Vlaming, F. and K. Clark. (2014). War reparations in Bosnia and Herzegovina: Individual stories and collective interests. In D. Žarkov and M. Glasius (Eds.), *Narratives of Justice In and Out of the Courtroom: Former Yugoslavia and beyond* (pp. 172–194). London: Springer.

De Waal, A. (1997). *Famine Crimes: Politics & the disaster relief industry in Africa.* Bloomington: Indiana University Press.

De Walque, D. and P. Verwimp. (2010). The demographic and socio-economic distribution of excess mortality during the 1994 genocide in Rwanda. *Journal of African Economies*, 19(2), 141–162.

Del Zotto, A. C. (2002). Weeping women, wringing hands: How the mainstream media stereotyped women's experiences in Kosovo. *Journal of Gender Studies*, 11(2), 141–150.

Des Forges, A. (1999). *"Leave None to Tell the Story": Genocide in Rwanda.* New York; Paris: Human Rights Watch.

(2011). *Defeat Is the Only Bad News: Rwanda under Musinga, 1896–1931.* Madison: University of Wisconsin Press.

Di John, J. and J. Putzel. (2009). Political settlements: Issues paper. Discussion Paper. University of Birmingham, Birmingham, UK.

Dickemann, M. (1997).The Balkan sworn virgin: A cross-gendered female role. *Islamic Homosexualities: Culture, History, and Literature*, 197–203.

DiMaggio, P. J. and W. W. Powell. (1983). The iron cage revisited: Institutional isomorphism and collective rationality in organizational fields. *American Sociological Review*, 48(2), 147–160.

Dizdarevic, Z. (1993). *Sarajevo: A war journal.* New York: Fromm International.

Djokic, D. (2007). *Elusive Compromise: A history of interwar Yugoslavia.* New York: Columbia University Press.

Donahoe, A. (2017). *Peacebuilding through Women's Community Development: Wee women's work in Northern Ireland.* New York: Palgrave.

Dowling, J. (2013). Facing the past in Prijedor: A case study of local transitional justice initiatives. Master's Thesis: University of Sarajevo–University of Bologna, Sarajevo.

Dušanić, S. (2013). *Man and Gender Relations in Bosnia and Herzegovina: Results of "IMAGES" Research.* In collaboration with Promundo. Banja Luka, Bosnia.

Easterly, W. (2001). Can institutions resolve ethnic conflict? *Economic Development and Cultural Change*, 49(4), 687–706.

Eastmond, M. (2006). Transnational returns and reconstruction in post-war Bosnia and Herzegovina. *International Migration*, 44(23), 141–166.

Einhorn, B. (1993). *Cinderella Goes to Market: Citizenship, gender, and women's movements in East Central Europe.* London; New York: Verso Press.

El-Bushra, J. (2000). Transforming conflict: Some thoughts on a gendered understanding of conflict processes. In S. Jacobs, R. Jacobson, and J. Marchban

(Eds.), *States of Conflict: Gender, violence and resistance* (pp. 66–86). London: Zed Books.

(2008). The culture of peace or the culture of the sound-bite? Development practice and the "tyranny of policy." In D. Žarkov (Ed.), *Gender, Violent Conflict, and Development*. New Delhi: Zubaan.

El-Bushra, J. and C. Mukarubuga. (1995). Women, war and transition. *Gender & Development,* 3(3), 16–22.

Elshtain, J. B. (1981). *Public Man, Private Woman: Women in social and political thought.* Princeton, NJ: Princeton University Press.

(1987). *Women and War.* Chicago, IL: University of Chicago Press.

Eltringham, N. (2004). *Accounting for Horror: Post-genocide debates in Rwanda.* London: Pluto Press.

Engle, K. (2005). Feminism and its (dis)contents: Criminalizing wartime rape in Bosnia and Herzegovina. *The American Journal of International Law,* 99(4), 778–816.

Enloe, C. (1989). *Bananas, Beaches and Bases: Making feminist sense of international politics.* Los Angeles; Berkeley: University of California Press.

(1993). *The Morning After: Sexual politics at the end of the Cold War.* Berkeley: University of California Press.

(2000). *Maneuvers: The international politics of militarizing women's lives.* Oakland: University of California Press.

Epstein, C. F. (1997). The multiple realities of sameness and difference: Ideology and practice. *Journal of Social Issues,* 53(2), 259–277.

(2007). Great divides: The cultural, cognitive, and social bases of the global subordination of women. *American Sociological Review,* 72(1), 1.

Eriksson, J. (1996). The international response to conflict and genocide: Lessons from the Rwanda experience. In N. Dabelstein (Ed.) *Joint Evaluation of Emergency Assistance to Rwanda.* (pp. 1–205). London: Overseas Development Institute.

Evans-Kent, B. and R. Bleiker. (2003). NGOs and reconstructing civil society in Bosnia and Herzegovina. *International Peacekeeping,* 10(1), 103–119.

Fearon, J. and D. Laitin. (2003). Ethnicity, insurgency, and civil war. *American Political Science Review (APSR),* 97(1), 75–90.

Fechter, A. and H. Hindman. (2011). *Inside the Everyday Lives of Development Workers: The challenges and futures of Aidland.* Sterling, VA: Kumarian Press.

Fein, H. (1993). Accounting for genocide after 1945: Theories and some findings. *International Journal on Minority and Group Rights,* 1(2), 79–106.

Femenía, N. A. (1987). Argentina's Mothers of Plaza de Mayo: The mourning process from junta to democracy. *Feminist Studies,* 13(1), 9–18.

Finnof, C. R. (2010). Gendered vulnerabilities after genocide: Three essays on post-conflict Rwanda. PhD Dissertation, University of Massachusetts, Amherst, Amherst, MA.

Foucault, M. (1980). *Power/Knowledge: Selected interviews and other writings, 1972–1977.* New York: Pantheon.

Fox, N. (2011). "Oh, did the women suffer, they suffered so much": Impacts of gendered based violence on kinship networks in Rwanda. *International Journal of Sociology of the Family,* 37(2), 279–305.

Frank Chalk, K. J. (1990). *The History and Sociology of Genocide*. New Haven, CT: Yale University Press.

Franks, E. (1996). Women and resistance in East Timor: The centre, as they say, knows itself by the margins. *Women's Studies International Forum*, 19(1–2), 155–168.

Fuest, V. (2008). "This is the time to get in front": Changing roles and opportunities for women in Liberia. *African Affairs*, 107(427), 201–224.

Fujii, L. A. (2009). *Killing Neighbors: Webs of violence in Rwanda*. Ithaca, NY: Cornell University Press.

Funk, J. (2015). Sowing trust in minefields: Women's peace activism in post-war BiH. Paper presented at the Women in Peace and Conflict Conference, Archbishop Desmond Tutu Center for War and Peace Studies.

Gagnon, V. P. (2006). *The Myth of Ethnic War: Serbia and Croatia in the 1990s* (2nd edn.). Ithaca, NY: Cornell University Press.

Gal, S. (2002). A semiotics of the public/private distinction. *Differences: A Journal of Feminist Cultural Studies*, 13(1), 77–95.

Gal, S. and G. Kligman. (2000). *The Politics of Gender after Socialism: A comparative-historical essay*. Princeton, NJ: Princeton University Press.

Galtung, J. (1969). Violence, peace, and peace research. *Journal of Peace Research*, 6(3), 167–191.

Geisler, G. (1995). Troubled sisterhood: Women and politics in southern Africa: Case studies from Zambia, Zimbabwe and Botswana. *African Affairs*, 94(377), 545–578.

George, A. and A. Bennett. (2005). *Case Studies and Theory Development in the Social Sciences*. Cambridge, MA: Belfer Center, Harvard University.

George, P. (2004). *Hotel Rwanda*. Lionsgate.

Gerring, J. (2007). Is there a (viable) crucial-case method? *Comparative Political Studies*, 40(3), 231–253.

Gervais, M. (2003). Human security and reconstruction efforts in Rwanda: Impact on the lives of women. *Development in Practice*, 13(5), 542–551.

Gibbs, D. (2015). The Srebrenica precedent. *Jacobin Magazine*. www.jacobinmag.com/2015/07/bosnian-war-nato-bombing-dayton-accords/. Accessed May 2016.

Gilbert, A. (2012). *Black Patriots and Loyalists: Fighting for emancipation in the war for independence*. Chicago: University of Chicago Press.

Gjelten, T. (1995). *Sarajevo Daily: A city and its newspaper under siege*. New York: HarperCollins.

Goffman, E. (1974). *Frame Analysis: An essay on the organization of experience*. Cambridge, MA: Harvard University Press.

Goldstein, J. (2001). *War and Gender: How gender shapes the war system and vice versa*. New York: Cambridge University Press.

Goldstone, J. A. (1991). *Revolution and Rebellion in the Early Modern World*. Berkeley: University of California Press.

Goluboff, R. L. (2007). *The Lost Promise of Civil Rights*. Cambridge, MA: Harvard University Press.

Goodfellow, T. and A. Smith. From urban catastrophe to "model" city? Politics, security and development in post-conflict Kigali. *Urban Studies*, 50(15) (2013), 3185–3202.

Gourevitch, P. (1998). *We Wish to Inform You That Tomorrow We Will Be Killed with Our Families: Stories from Rwanda.* New York: Farrar, Straus, and Giroux.

Gramsci, A. (1971). *Selections from the Prison Notebooks of Antonio Gramsci.* New York: International Publishers.

Gready, P. (2010). "You're either with us or against us": Civil society and policy making in post-genocide Rwanda. *African Affairs, 109*(437), 637–657.

Guichaoua, A. (2010). *Rwanda, de la guerre au genocide: Les politiques criminelles au Rwanda (1990–1994).* Paris: La D'couverte.

Gutman, R. (1993). *A Witness to Genocide: The 1993 Pulitzer Prize–winning dispatches on the "ethnic cleansing" of Bosnia.* New York: Macmillan.

Habermas, J. (1989). *The Structural Transformation of the Public Sphere: An inquiry into a category of bourgeois society.* Boston, MA: MIT Press.

Hale, S. (1993). Gender, religious identity, and political mobilization in Sudan. In V. M. Moghadam (Ed.), *Identity Politics and Women: Cultural reassertions and feminisms in international perspectives* (pp. 125–146). Boulder, CO: Westview Press.

Hansen, L. (2000). Gender, nation, rape: Bosnia and the construction of security. *Feminist Journal of Politics, 3*(1), 55–75.

Harff, B. an T. R. Gurr (1988). Toward empirical theory of genocides and politicides: Identification and measurement of cases since 1945. *International Studies Quarterly, 32*(3), 359–371.

Hartmann, S. M. (1982). *The Home Front and Beyond: American women in the 1940s.* Boston, MA: Twayne Publishers.

Heath, R. M., L. A. Schwindt-Bayer, and M. M. Taylor-Robinson. (2005). Women on the sidelines: Women's representation on committees in Latin American legislatures. *American Journal of Political Science, 49*(2), 420–436.

Helman, S. and T. Rapoport. (1997). Women in Black: Challenging Israel's gender and socio-political orders. *British Journal of Sociology, 48*(4), 681–700.

Helms, E. (2002). Women as agents of ethnic reconciliation? Women's NGOs and international intervention in postwar Bosnia-Herzegovina. *Women's Studies International Forum, 26*(1), 15–33.

  (2007). "Politics is a whore": Women, morality, and victimhood in post-war Bosnia-Herzegovina. In X. Bougarel, E. Helms, and G. Duijzings (Eds.), *The New Bosnian Mosaic* (pp. 235–254). Hampshire, UK, and Burlington, VT: Ashgate Publishing.

  (2013). *Innocence and Victimhood: Gender, nation, and women's activism in postwar Bosnia-Herzegovina.* Madison: University of Wisconsin Press.

Hilhorst, D. and M. Van Leeuwen. (2000). Emergency and development: The case of *imidugudu*, villagization in Rwanda. *Journal of Refugee Studies, 13*(3), 264–280.

Hintjens, H. (2008). Post-genocide identity politics in Rwanda. *Ethnicities, 8*(1), 5–41.

Hughes, M. (2009). Armed conflict, international linkages, and women's parliamentary representation in developing nations. *Social Problems, 56*(1), 174–204.

Hughes, M. and A. M. Tripp. (2015). Civil war and trajectories of change in women's political representation in Africa, 1985–2010. *Social Forces*, 93(4), 1513–1540.

Human Rights Watch. (1992). *War Crimes in Bosnia-Hercegovina*. New York: Human Rights Watch.

(1994a). *Bosnia-Hercegovina: "Ethnic cleansing" continues in northern Bosnia*. (No. 6). New York: Human Rights Watch.

(1994b). *Bosnia-Herzegovina: Sarajevo*. (No. 6). New York: Human Rights Watch.

(1994c). *War Crimes in Bosnia-Hercegovina: Bosanski Samac*. (No. 6). New York: Human Rights Watch.

(1994d). Bosnia-Hercegovina "Ethnic Cleansing" Continues in Northern Bosnia. 6(16). New York: Human Rights Watch.

(1995). *The Fall of Srebrenica and the Failure of UN Peacekeeping*. (No. 7(13)). New York: Human Rights Watch.

(2000). *Rwanda: The search for security and human rights abuses*. (No. 12). New York: Human Rights Watch.

(2002). *Hopes Betrayed: Trafficking of women and girls to post-conflict Bosnia and Herzegovina for forced prostitution*. (No. 14). New York: Human Rights Watch.

(2004). *Struggling to Survive: Barriers to justice for rape victims in Rwanda*. (No. 16). New York: Human Rights Watch.

(2005). *Liberia at a Crossroads: Human rights challenges for the new government*. New York: Human Rights Watch.

(2007). *Killings in Eastern Rwanda*. New York: Human Rights Watch.

(2009). *Human Rights Watch Mourns Loss of Alison Des Forges*. New York: Human Rights Watch. www.hrw.org/news/2009/02/13/human-rights-watch-mourns-loss-alison-des-forges. Accessed October 2017.

(2013). *Rwanda: Takeover of rights groups*. New York: Human Rights Watch.

(2015). *Iraq: ISIS escapees describe systematic rape*. New York: Human Rights Watch.

(2017). *All thieves must be killed: Extrajudicial executions in western Rwanda*. New York: Human Rights Watch.

Hunt, S. (2004). *This Was Not Our War: Bosnian women reclaiming the peace*. Durham, NC: Duke University Press.

Hunt, S. and C. Posa. (2001). Women waging peace. *Foreign Policy*, (124), 38–47.

Hunter, K. (2017). Taking women to war: Understanding variation in women's integration into democratic militaries. Paper presented at Southern Political Science Association Annual Conference, New Orleans, LA.

IDEA. (2017). Gender quotas database. Bosnia and Herzegovina. www.idea.int/data-tools/data/gender-quotas/country-view/57/35. Accessed November 2017.

Independent Bureau for Humanitarian Issues (IBHI). (1998). *The Local NGO Sector within Bosnia-Herzegovina: Problems, analysis and recommendations*. Sarajevo, BiH: IBHI.

Ingelaere, B. (2010). Peasants, power and ethnicity: A bottom-up perspective on Rwanda's political transition. *African Affairs*, 109(435), 273–292.

(2011). The ruler's drum and the people's shout: Accountability and representation on Rwanda's hills. In S. Straus and L. Waldorf (Eds.), *Remaking Rwanda: State building and human rights after mass violence* (pp. 67–78). Madison: University of Wisconsin Press.

(2016). *Inside Rwanda's Gacaca Courts: Seeking justice after genocide.* Madison: University of Wisconsin Press.

International Crisis Group. (1997). *Going Nowhere Fast: Refugees and internally displaced persons in Bosnia and Herzegovina.* Washington, DC: International Crisis Group.

(1998). *Whither Bosnia?* Washington, DC: International Crisis Group.

(2000). *Bosnia's Municipal Elections 2000: Winners and losers.* Sarajevo, BiH/Washington, DC/Brussels: International Crisis Group.

International Labor Organization. (1991). ILOSTAT: Unemployment, general level. www.ilo.org/ilostat.

(1998). *Gender Guidelines for Employment and Skills Training in Conflict-Affected Countries.* Geneva, Switzerland: International Labor Organization.

Inter-Parliamentary Union. (2008, 2009, 2014, 2017). Women in parliaments: World and regional averages, online database. www.ipu.org/parline/: Inter-Parliamentary Union.

Iraq Body Count. (2015). www.iraqbodycount.org/.

Isaksson, A. (2013). Manipulating the rural landscape: Villagisation and income generation in Rwanda. *Journal of African Economies, 22*(3), 394–436.

Jancar-Webster, B. (1990). *Women & Revolution in Yugoslavia, 1941–1945.* Denver, CO: Arden Press.

Jansen, S. (2006). The privatisation of home and hope: Return, reforms and the foreign intervention in Bosnia-Herzegovina. *Dialectical Anthropology, 30*(3–4), 177–199.

Jefremovas, V. (1991). Loose women, virtuous wives, and timid virgins: Gender and the control of resources in Rwanda. *Canadian Journal of African Studies / Revue Canadienne des Études Africaines, 25*(3), 378–395.

(2002). *Brickyards to Graveyards: From production to genocide in Rwanda.* Albany: State University of New York Press.

Jessee, E. (2012). Conducting fieldwork in Rwanda. *Canadian Journal of Development Studies/Revue canadienne d'études du développement, 33*(2), 266–274.

(2017). *Negotiating Genocide in Rwanda: The politics of history.* Palgrave Macmillan.

Jessee, E. and S. E. Watkins. (2014). Good kings, bloody tyrants, and everything in between: Representations of the monarchy in post-genocide Rwanda. *History in Africa, 41,* 35–62.

Joint Evaluation of Emergency Assistance to Rwanda. (1996). *Study 3: Humanitarian aid and effects.* London: Overseas Development Institute.

Jones, W. (2012). Between Pyongyang and Singapore: The Rwandan state, its rulers, and the military. In M. Campioni and P. Noack (Eds.), *Rwanda Fast Forward: Social, economic, military and reconciliation prospects.* New York: Palgrave Macmillan.

(2014). Murder and create: State reconstruction in Rwanda since 1994. PhD dissertation, Oxford University.

Justino, P. and P. Verwimp. (2008). Poverty dynamics, violent conflict and convergence in Rwanda. MICROCON Research Working Paper No. 4.

Kagame, P. (2014). *Keynote Address by President Paul Kagame at the Women in Parliaments Global Forum – Joint session with MDG advocacy group.* Kigali, Rwanda: Office of the President.

Kaldor, M. (2013). *New and Old Wars: Organised violence in a global era.* Hoboken, NJ: John Wiley & Sons.

Kalyvas, S. N. and N. Sambanis. (2005). Bosnia's civil war: Origins and violence dynamics. In P. Collier and N. Sambanis (Eds.), *Understanding Civil War: Europe, Central Asia, and other regions* (pp. 191–230). Washington, DC: The World Bank.

Kampwirth, K. (2004). *Feminism and the Legacy of Revolution: Nicaragua, El Salvador, Chiapas.* Athens: Ohio University Press.

Kangura. (1990). Appeal to the Bahutu conscience. No. 6, December. www.rwandafile.com/Kangura/ko6a.html. Accessed May 2017.

Kapiteni, A. (1996). *La premiere estimation du nombre des victimes du genocide des Batutsi du Rwanda de 1994, commune par commume.* www.rwasta.net/uploads/media/1996-estimation-nombre-victimes-genocide-.

Kaplan, T. (1982). Female consciousness and collective action: The case of Barcelona, 1910–1918. *Signs: Journal of Women in Culture and Society,* 7(3), 545–566.

Kelsall, T. (2013). *Business, Politics, and the State in Africa: Challenging the orthodoxies on growth and transformation.* London; New York: Zed Books.

Keenan, T. (2002). Publicity and indifference (Sarajevo on television). *Publications of the Modern Language Association of America,* 104–116.

Kenworthy, L. and M. Malami. (1999). Gender inequality in political representation: A worldwide comparative analysis. *Social Forces,* 78(1), 235–268.

Kestnbaum, M. (2002). Citizen-soldiers, national service and the mass army: The birth of conscription in revolutionary Europe and North America. *Comparative Social Research,* 20, 117–144.

Key, E. (1909). *The Century of the Child.* Bingley, West Yorkshire: G. P Putnam's Sons.

Kiernan, B. (2007). *Blood and Soil: A world history of genocide and extermination from Sparta to Darfur.* New Haven, CT: Yale University Press.

Kinzer, S. (2008). *A Thousand Hills: Rwanda's rebirth and the man who dreamed it.* Hoboken, NJ: John Wiley & Sons.

Kleiman, M. (2007). *Challenges of Activism and Feminism in Creation of Women's Space: Work of Žene Ženama in local, national and regional context.* Sarajevo, BiH: Žene Ženama.

Kligman, G. and S. Limoncelli. (2005). Trafficking women after socialism: From, to, and through Eastern Europe. *Social Politics: International Studies in Gender, State and Society,* 12(1), 118–140.

Kondracki, L., R. Weisz, D. Strathairn, N. Kaas, A. Anissimova, R. Condurache, … and M. Bellucci (2010). *The Whistleblower* (Film). Impulse Home Entertainment.

Koomen, J. (2014). "Without these women, the tribunal cannot do anything": The politics of witness testimony on sexual violence at the International Criminal Tribunal for Rwanda. *Signs: Journal of Women in Culture and Society*, 38(2), 253–277.

Korac, M. (1998). Ethnic-nationalism, wars and the patterns of social, political and sexual violence against women: The case of post-Yugoslav countries. *Identities: Global Studies in Culture and Power*, 5(2), 153–181.

Kristeva, J. (1982). *Powers of Horror: An essay on abjection*. New York: Columbia University Press.

Krook, M. L. (2015). Empowerment versus backlash: Gender quotas and critical mass theory. *Politics, Groups, and Identities*, 3(1), 184–188.

Kubai, A. (2007). Walking a tightrope: Christians and Muslims in post-genocide Rwanda. *Islam–Christian Muslim Relations*, 18(2), 219–235.

Kumar, Krishna, ed. (2001). *Women and civil war: Impact, organizations, and action*. Boulder, CO: Lynne Rienner Publishers.

Kuper, L. (1981). *Genocide: Its political use in the twentieth century*. New Haven, CT: Yale University Press.

Kuperman, A. J. (2004). *The Limits of Humanitarian Intervention: Genocide in Rwanda*. Washington, DC, Brookings Institution Press.

La Mattina, G. (2012). When all the good men are gone: Sex ratio and domestic violence in post-genocide Rwanda. Boston, MA: Institute for Economic Development DP223, Boston University.

Lampe, J. R. (2000). *Yugoslavia as History: Twice there was a country*. London; New York: Cambridge University Press.

Lake, M., I. Muthaka, and G. Walker. (2016). Gendering justice in humanitarian spaces: Opportunity and (dis) empowerment through gender-based legal development outreach in the eastern Democratic Republic of Congo. *Law & Society Review*, 50(3), 539–574.

Landes, J. B. (1988). *Women and the Public Sphere in the Age of the French Revolution*. Ithaca, NY: Cornell University Press.

(1998). *Feminism, the Public and the Private*. New York: Oxford University Press.

Leed, E. J. (1981). *No Man's Land: Combat and identity in World War I*. Cambridge: Cambridge University Press.

Leitenberg, M. (2006). *Death in Wars and Conflicts in the 20th Century* (3rd edn.). Ithaca, NY: Cornell University Peace Studies Program.

Lemarchand, R. (1970). *Rwanda and Burundi*. New York: Praeger Publishers.

(2009). *The Dynamics of Violence in Central Africa*. Philadelphia: University of Pennsylvania Press.

Lewis, J. (2000). *The Batwa Pygmies of the Great Lakes Region*. London: Minority Rights Group International.

Lohani-Chase, R. S. (2014). Protesting women in the people's war movement in Nepal. *Signs: Journal of Women in Culture and Society*, 40(1), 29–36.

Longman, T. (2005). Rwanda's paradox: Gender equality or emerging authoritarianism? In G. Bauer and H. Britton (Eds.), *Women in African Parliaments* (pp. 210–233). Boulder, CO: Lynne Reinner Publishers.

(2006). Rwanda: Achieving equality or serving an authoritarian state? In G. Bauer and H. Britton (Eds.), *Women in African Parliaments* (pp. 133–150). Boulder, CO: Lynne Rienner Publishers.

(2011). Limitations to political reform: The undemocratic nature of transition in Rwanda. In S. Straus and L. Waldorf (Eds.), *Remaking Rwanda: State building and human rights after mass violence* (pp. 25–47), Madison: University of Wisconsin Press.

Lorber, J. (1994). *Paradoxes of Gender*. New Haven, CT: Yale University Press.

Lorentzen, L. A. and J. E. Turpin. (1998). *The Women and War Reader*. New York: New York University Press.

Lovenduski, J. and P. Norris. (1993). *Gender and Party Politics*. Thousand Oaks, CA: Sage Publications.

Luciak, I. A. (2001). *After the Revolution: Gender and democracy in El Salvador, Nicaragua, and Guatemala*. Baltimore, MD: Johns Hopkins University Press.

Luft, A. Toward a dynamic theory of action at the micro-level of genocide: Killing, desistance, and saving in 1994 Rwanda. *Sociological Theory, 33*(2): 148–172.

Maček, I. (2009). *Sarajevo under Siege: Anthropology in wartime*. Philadelphia: University of Pennsylvania Press.

Mageza-Barthel, R. (2015). *Mobilizing Transnational Gender Politics in Post-Genocide Rwanda*. Surrey: Ashgate Publishing Company.

Mahoney, J. (2000). Path dependence in historical sociology. *Theory and Society, 29*(4), 507–548.

Mahoney, J. and D. Rueschemeyer (Eds.). (2003). *Comparative Historical Analysis in the Social Sciences*. Cambridge: Cambridge University Press.

Malcolm, N. (1996). *Bosnia: A short history*. New York: New York University Press.

Mamdani, M. (2001). *When Victims Become Killers: Colonialism, nativism, and the genocide in Rwanda*. Princeton, NJ: Princeton University Press.

(2010). Responsibility to protect or right to punish? *Journal of Intervention and Statebuilding, 4*(1), 53–67.

Mann, L. and M. Berry. (2016). Understanding the political motivations that shape Rwanda's emergent developmental state. *New Political Economy, 21*(1), 119–144.

Mann, M. (1986). *The Sources of Social Power, Vol. 1*. New York: Cambridge University Press.

(1993). *The Sources of Social Power: The rise of the classes and nation-states, 1760–1914, Vol. 2*. New York: Cambridge University Press.

(2005). *The Dark Side of Democracy: Explaining ethnic cleansing*. New York: Cambridge University Press.

(2012). *The Sources of Social Power: Global empires and revolution, 1890–1945, Vol. 3*. New York: Cambridge University Press.

(2013). *The Sources of Social Power: Globalizations, 1945–2011, Vol. 4*. New York: Cambridge University Press.

Markoff, J. (1996). *Waves of Democracy: Social movements and political change.* Thousand Oaks, CA: Sage Publications.

Marx Ferree, M. (1992). The political context of rationality: Rational choice theory and resource mobilization. In A. D. A. Morris and C. M. Mueller (Eds.), *Frontiers in Social Movement Theory* (pp. 29–52). New Haven, CT: Yale University Press.

Massey, G., K. Hahn, and D. Sekulić. (1995). Women, men, and the "second shift" in socialist Yugoslavia. *Gender & Society,* 9(3), 359–379.

Matland, R. E. (1998). Women's representation in national legislatures: Developed and developing countries. *Legislative Studies Quarterly,* 23(1), 109–125.

McAdam, D. and W. H. Sewell Jr. (2001). It's about time: Temporality in the study of social movements and revolutions. In R. Aminzade (Ed.), *Silence and Voice in the Study of Contentious Politics* (pp. 89–125). New York: Cambridge University Press.

McAdam, D., S. G. Tarrow, and C. Tilly. (2001). *Dynamics of Contention.* New York: Cambridge University Press.

McMahon, P. C. (2004). Rebuilding Bosnia: A model to emulate or to avoid? *Political Science Quarterly,* 119(4), 569–593.

Meier, V. (2005). *Yugoslavia: A history of its demise* (2nd edn.). London: Routledge.

Meintjes, S., A. Pillay, and M. Turshen. (2001). *The Aftermath: Women in post-conflict transformation.* New York: Zed Books.

Melvern, L. (2000). *A People Betrayed: The role of the West in Rwanda's genocide.* New York: Zed Books.

(2006). *Conspiracy to Murder: The Rwandan genocide.* Brooklyn, NY: Verso Press.

Mertus, J. (1994). Woman in the service of national identity. *Hastings Women's Law Journal,* 5(5).

(2000). *War's Offensive on Women: Humanitarian action in Bosnia, Kosovo and Afghanistan.* San Francisco, CA: Kumarian Press.

(2004). *Women's participation in the International Criminal Tribunal for the Former Yugoslavia (ICTY): Transitional justice for Bosnia and Herzegovina.* In S. N. Anderlini (Ed.), *Women Waging Peace* (pp. 1–48). Washington, DC: Hunt Alternatives Fund.

Meznaric, S. and J. Zlatkovic Winter. (1992). Forced migration and refugee flows in Croatia, Slovenia and Bosnia-Herzegovina: Early warning, beginning and current state of flows. *Refuge,* 12(7), 3–5.

Miles, A. R. (1996). *Integrative Feminisms: Building global visions, 1960s–1990s.* New York: Routledge.

Milićević, A. S. (2006). Joining the war: Masculinity, nationalism and war participation in the Balkans war of secession, 1991–1995. *Nationalities Papers,* 34(3), 265–287.

Milkman, R. (1987). *Gender at Work: The dynamics of job segregation by sex during World War II.* Urbana: University of Illinois Press.

Mohanty, C. T. (1988). Under Western eyes: Feminist scholarship and colonial discourses. *Feminist Review,* 30, 61–88.

Moll, N. (2015). *Sarajevo's Best Known Public Secret*. Sarajevo, BiH. Available online: www.fes.ba/files/fes/pdf/publikationen/2014/2015/Moll_Final_Web_Version.pdf.

Molyneux, M. (1985). Mobilization without emancipation? Women's interests, the state, and revolution in Nicaragua. *Feminist Studies*, *11*(2), 227–254.

Moore, A. (2013). *Peacebuilding in Practice: Local experiences in two Bosnian towns*. Ithaca, NY; London: Cornell University Press.

Moore, B. (1966). *Social Origins of Dictatorship and Democracy: Lord and peasant in the making of the modern world*. Boston, MA: Beacon Press.

Moran, M. (2012). "Our mothers have spoken": Synthesizing old and new forms of women's political authority in Liberia. *Journal of International Women's Studies*, *13*(4), 51–66.

Moran, M. H. (2010). Gender, militarism, and peace-building: Projects of the postconflict moment. *Annual Review of Anthropology*, *39*, 261–274.

Morokvasic, M. (1986). Being a woman in Yugoslavia: Past, present and institutional equality. In M. Gadant (Ed.), *Women of the Mediterranean* (pp. 120–138). London: Zed Books.

Mosse, D. (2011). *Adventures in Aidland: The anthropology of professionals in international development*. New York: Berghahn Books.

Mostov, J. (1995). "Our womens"/"their womens" symbolic boundaries, territorial markers, and violence in the Balkans. *Peace & Change*, *20*(4), 515–529.

Mrvic-Petrovic, N. and I. Stevanovic. (2000). *Life in Refuge – changes in socio-economic and familial status. Women, Violence and War: Wartime victimization of refugees in the Balkans*. Budapest: Central European Press.

Mueller, J. (2000). The banality of "ethnic war." *International Security*, *25*(1), 42–70.

Mukamana, D. and P. Brysiewicz. (2008). The lived experience of genocide rape survivors in Rwanda. *Journal of Nursing Scholarship*, *40*(4), 379–384.

Mulinda, C. K. (2010). A space for genocide: Local authorities, local population and local histories in Gishamvu and Kibayi (Rwanda). PhD Dissertation, University of the Western Cape, South Africa.

Musto, J. L. (2009). What's in a name? Conflations and contradictions in contemporary U.S. discourses of human trafficking. *Women's Studies International Forum*, *32*(4), 281–287.

Nelson, B. S. (2003). Post-war trauma and reconciliation in Bosnia-Herzegovina: Observations, experiences, and implications for marriage and family therapy. *The American Journal of Family Therapy*, *31*(4), 305–316.

Newbury, C. (1980). Ubureetwa and Thangata: Catalysts to peasant political consciousness in Rwanda and Malawi. *Canadian Journal of African Studies*, *14*(1), 97–111.

(1988). *The Cohesion of Oppression: Clientship and ethnicity in Rwanda, 1860–1960*. New York: Columbia University Press.

(1995). Background to genocide: Rwanda. *Issue: A Journal of Opinion*, *23*(2), 12–17.

(1998). Ethnicity and the politics of history in Rwanda. *Africa Today* (no vol.), 7–24.

Newbury, C. and H. Baldwin. (2000). Aftermath: Women in postgenocide Rwanda. Working Paper No. 303, USAID Center for Development Information and Evaluation.

(2001). Profile: Rwanda. In K. Kumar (Ed.) *Women & Civil War* (pp. 27–38). Boulder, CO: Lynn Rienner Publishers.

Newbury, C. and D. Newbury. (1999). A Catholic mass in Kigali: Contested views of the genocide and ethnicity in Rwanda. *Canadian Journal of African Studies*, 33(2–3), 292–328.

Newman, J. P. (2011). Forging a united kingdom of Serbs, Croats, and Slovenes: The legacy of the First World War and the "invalid question." In D. Djokić and J. Ker-Lindsay (Eds.), *New Perspectives on Yugoslavia* (pp. 46–61). Abington: Routledge.

Nikolić-Ristanović, V. (1998). War, nationalism, and mothers in the former Yugoslavia. In L. A. Lorentzen and J. Turpin (Eds.), *The Women and War Reader* (pp. 234–239). New York: New York University Press.

Noonan, R. (1995). Women against the state: Political opportunities and collective action frames in Chile's transition to democracy. *Sociological Forum*, 10(1), 81–111.

Nowrojee, B. (1996). *Shattered Lives: Sexual violence during the Rwandan genocide and its aftermath*. Human Rights Watch Africa, Women's Rights Project, NY; Washington, DC; London: Human Rights Watch.

Nyamwasa, K., P. Karegeya, T. Rudasingwa, and G. Gahima. (2010). Rwanda briefing. http://rwandinfo.com/documents/Rwanda_Briefing_August2010_nyamwasa-et-al.pdf.

Nyseth Brehm, H. (2014). Conditions and courses of genocide. PhD dissertation, University of Minnesota, Minneapolis, MN.

(2017). Subnational determinants of killing in Rwanda. *Criminology*, 55(1), 5–31.

Nyseth Brehm, H., C. A. Uggen, and J. Gasanabo. (2017). Age, sex, and the crime of crimes: Toward a life-course theory of genocide participation. *Criminology*, 54(4), 713–743.

Oosterveld, V. (2005). Prosecution of gender-based crimes in international law. In D. Mazurana, A. Raven-Roberts, and J. L. Parpart (Eds.), *Gender, Conflict, and Peacekeeping* (pp. 67–82). Lanham, MD: Rowman & Littlefield Publishers, Inc.

Organization for Security and Cooperation in Europe (OSCE). (2007). High-level meeting on victims of terrorism: Background paper. Vienna: OSCE.

Otunnu, O. (1999). Rwandese refugees and immigrants in Uganda. In H. Adelman and A. Suhrke (Eds.), *The Path of a Genocide: The Rwanda crisis from Uganda to Zaire* (pp. 3–30). New Brunswick, NJ; London: Transaction Publishers.

Overeem, P. (1995). *Investigating the Situation of the Batwa People of Rwanda*. La Haye: Rapport de Mission, UNPO.

Oyewumi, O. (1997). *The Invention of Women: Making an African sense of Western gender discourses*. Minneapolis: University of Minnesota Press.

Pateman, C. (1988). *The Sexual Contract*. Redwood City, CA: Stanford University Press.

Paxton, P. (1997). Women in national legislatures: A cross-national analysis. *Social Science Research*, 26(4), 442–464.

Petrovic, D. (1994). Ethnic cleansing: An attempt at methodology. *European Journal of International Law*, 5, 342–359.

Phillips, A. (1995). *The Politics of Presence*. New York: Oxford University Press.

Pierson, P. (2003). Big, slow-moving, and ... invisible: Macrosocial processes in the study of comparative politics. In J. Mahoney and D. Rueschemeyer (Eds.), *Comparative Historical Analysis in the Social Sciences* (pp. 177–207). New York: Cambridge University Press.

(2004). *Politics in Time: History, institutions, and social analysis*. Princeton, NJ: Princeton University Press.

Pierson, P. and T. Skocpol. (2002). Historical institutionalism in contemporary political science. In I. Katznelson and H. V. Milner (Eds.), *Political Science: The State of the Discipline*, New York: W.W. Norton 3, 693–721.

Pottier, J. (1993). Taking stock: Food marketing reform in Rwanda, 1982–89. *African Affairs*, 92(366), 5–30.

(1996). Why aid agencies need better understanding of the communities they assist: The experience of food aid in Rwandan refugee camps. *Disasters*, 20(4), 324–337.

(2002). *Re-imagining Rwanda: Conflict, survival and disinformation in the late twentieth century*. Cambridge; New York: Cambridge University Press.

(2006). Land reform for peace? Rwanda's 2005 land law in context. *Journal of Agrarian Change*, 6(4), 509–537.

Power, S. (2003). *A Problem from Hell: American in the age of genocide* (2nd edn.). New York: HarperCollins.

Powley, E. (2003). *Rwanda: Women hold up half the parliament*. IDEA *Women in Parliament: Beyond Numbers*. www.idea.int/publications/wip2/upload/Rwanda.pdf.

(2004). Strengthening governance: The role of women in Rwanda's transition. In S. N. Anderlini (Ed.), *Women Waging Peace*. Washington, DC: Hunt Alternatives Fund.

(2006). Rwanda: The impact of women legislators on policy outcomes affecting children and families. In UNICEF (Ed.), *State of the World's Children Background Paper*.

Powley, E. and E. Pearson. (2007). "Gender is society": Inclusive lawmaking in Rwanda's parliament. *Critical Half* (Winter 2007). Women for Women International.

Promundo (G. Barker, J. M. Contreras, B. Heilman, A. K. Singh, R. K. Verma, and M. Nascimento, Eds). 2011. *Evolving Men: Initial results from the International Men and Gender Equality Survey (IMAGES)*. Washington, DC: International Center for Research on Women (ICRW) and Rio de Janeiro: Instituto Promundo.

Prpa-Jovanović, B. (1997). The making of Yugoslavia: 1830–1945. In J. Udovički and J. Ridgeway (Eds.), *Burn this House: The making and unmaking of Yugoslavia* (pp. 43–63). Durham, NC: Duke University Press.

Prunier, G. (1995). *The Rwanda Crisis, 1959–1994: History of a genocide*. London: Hurst.

(2009). *Africa's World War: Congo, the Rwandan genocide, and the making of a continental catastrophe*. Oxford: Oxford University Press.

Pugh, M. (2002). Postwar political economy in Bosnia and Herzegovina: The spoils of peace. *Global Governance*, 8(4), 467–482.

Pugh, M. C., N. Cooper, and J. Goodhand. (2004). *War Economies in a Regional Context: Challenges of transformation*. Boulder, CO: Lynne Rienner Publishers.

Purdeková, A. (2015). *Making Ubumwe: Power, state and camps in Rwanda's unity-building project*. Vol. 34. Berghahn Books.

Ragin, C. C. (1999). The distinctiveness of case-oriented research. *Health Services Research*, 34(5 pt. 2), 1137–1151.

Ragin, C. C. and H. S. Becker. (1992). *What Is a Case? Exploring the foundations of social inquiry*. Cambridge; New York: Cambridge University Press.

Rahman, M., M. A. Hoque, and S. Makinoda. (2011). Intimate partner violence against women: Is women empowerment a reducing factor? A study from a national Bangladeshi sample. *Journal of Family Violence*, 26(5), 411–420.

Ramet, S. P. (1992). *Balkan Babel: Politics, culture and religion in Yugoslavia*. Boulder, CO: Westview Press.

(1999). *Balkan Babel: The disintegration of Yugoslavia from the death of Tito to the war for Kosovo*. Boulder, CO: Westview Press.

(2005). *Thinking about Yugoslavia: Scholarly debates about the Yugoslav breakup and the wars in Bosnia and Kosovo*. Cambridge; New York: Cambridge University Press.

(2006). *The Three Yugoslavias: State-building and legitimation, 1918–2005*. Bloomington: Indiana University Press.

Ray, R. and A. Korteweg. (1999). Women's movements in the Third World: Identity, mobilization, and autonomy. *Annual Review of Sociology*, 25, 47–71.

Republic of Rwanda. (1984). *National Agricultural Survey*. Kigali, Rwanda: National Institute of Statistics of Rwanda.

(1984, 1989, 1991). *National Agricultural Survey*. Kigali, Rwanda: National Institute of Statistics of Rwanda.

(1999). *Country Progress Report on Implementation of Women's World Regional and National Action Platforms*. Kigali, Rwanda: Ministry of Gender & Women Development.

(2000). *Rwanda Vision 2020*. Kigali, Rwanda: Ministry of Finance and Economic Planning.

(2003). *General Census of Population and Housing*. Kigali, Rwanda: National Census Service.

(2004a). *Survey of Genocide Deaths*. Kigali, Rwanda: Ministry of Local Administration and Community.

(2004b). *Violence against Women*. Kigali, Rwanda: Ministry of Gender and Family Promotion (MIGEPROF).

(2005a). *National Unity and Reconciliation Report*. Kigali, Rwanda: National Unity and Reconciliation Commission.

(2005b). *The Role of Women in Reconciliation and Peace Building in Rwanda: Ten years after genocide 1994–2004.* Kigali, Rwanda: National Unity and Reconciliation Commission.

(2006). *Preliminary Poverty Update Report: Integrated Living Conditions Survey 2005/6 (EICV2).* Kigali, Rwanda: National Institute of Statistics of Rwanda.

(2007). *National Unity and Reconciliation Report.* Kigali, Rwanda: National Unity and Reconciliation Commission.

(2011). *The Third Integrated Household Living Conditions Survey (EICV3): Main Indicators Report.* Kigali, Rwanda: National Institute of Statistics of Rwanda.

(2012). *Fourth Population and Housing Census.* Kigali, Rwanda: National Institute of Statistics of Rwanda.

(2014). *Thematic Report: Fertility. Fourth Population and Housing Census.* Kigali, Rwanda: National Institute of Statistics of Rwanda.

Research and Documentation Center. (2007, 2013). *Bosnian Book of the Dead.* Sarajevo, BiH: Research and Documentation Center.

Reynolds, A. (1999). Women in the legislatures and executives of the world: Knocking at the highest glass ceiling. *World Politics, 51*(4), 547–572.

Reyntjens, F. (2004). Rwanda, ten years on: From genocide to dictatorship. *African Affairs, 103*(411), 177–210.

(2009). *The Great African War: Congo and regional geopolitics, 1996–2006.* New York; Cambridge: Cambridge University Press.

(2011). Constructing the truth, dealing with dissent, domesticating the world: Governance in post-genocide Rwanda. *African Affairs, 110*(438), 1–34.

(2013). *Political Governance in Post-Genocide Rwanda.* New York: Cambridge University Press.

(2014). *Political Governance in Post-genocide Rwanda.* Cambridge: Cambridge University Press.

Rieff, D. (2003). *A Bed for the Night: Humanitarianism in crisis.* New York: Simon and Schuster.

Roberts, A. (2010). Lives and statistics: Are 90% of war victims civilians? *Survival, 52*(3), 115–136.

Rombouts, H. (2006). Women and reparations in Rwanda: A long path to travel. In R. Rubio-Marin (Ed.), *What Happened to the Women?: Gender and reparations for human rights violations* (pp. 194–245). New York: Social Science Research Council.

Ruddick, S. (1989). *Maternal Thinking: Towards a politics of peace.* Boston, MA: Beacon Press.

Rwanda Men's Resource Centre. (2010). *Masculinity and Gender Based Violence in Rwanda: Experiences and perceptions of men and women.* Kigali, Rwanda: Commissioned by Rwanda Men Engage Network.

Saguy, A. C. (2013). *What's Wrong with Fat?* New York: Oxford University Press.

Sambanis, N. (2004). Using case studies to expand economic models of civil war. *Perspectives on Politics, 2*(2), 259–279.

Sarajevo Open Center (2014). *Women Documented: Women and public life in Bosnia and Herzegovina in the 20th century.* Sarajevo: Nacionalna i univerzitetska biblioteka Bosne i Hercegovine.

Sarajevo Survival Guide (No author) (1993). Sarajevo Survival Guide. www.sur vivalmonkey.com/threads/sarajevo-survival-guide.19312/. Accessed January 14, 2015.

Sardon, J. and A. Confesson (2004). *Childbearing Trends and Prospects in Low-Fertility Countries: A cohort analysis, Vol. 13*. New York: European Studies of Population, Springer.

Scott, J. C. (1985). *Weapons of the Weak: Everyday forms of peasant resistance.* New Haven, CT: Yale University Press.

(1990). *Domination and the Arts of Resistance: Hidden Transcripts.* New Haven, CT; London: Yale University Press.

Segal, M. W. (1995). Women's military roles cross nationally: Past, present, and future. *Gender & Society*, 9(6), 757–775.

Sewell, W. H., Jr. (1992). A theory of structure: Duality, agency, and transformation. *American Journal of Sociology*, 98(1), 1–29.

(1996). Three temporalities: Toward an eventful sociology. In T. J. McDonald (Ed.), *The Historic Turn in the Human Sciences* (pp. 245–280). Ann Arbor: University of Michigan Press.

Sharlach, L. (1999). Gender and genocide in Rwanda: Women as agents and objects of genocide. *Journal of Genocide Research*, 1(3), 387–399.

Sharoni, S. (1995). *Gender and the Israeli–Palestinian Conflict: The politics of women's resistance.* Syracuse, NY: Syracuse University Press.

(2001). Rethinking women's struggles in Israel-Palestine and in the north of Ireland. In C. M. A. F. Clark (Ed.), *Victims, Perpetrators or Actors: Gender, armed conflict and political violence* (pp. 85–98). London: Zed Books.

Shaw, M. (2007). *What Is Genocide?* Cambridge: Polity Press.

Shih, E. (2015). The Price of Freedom: Moral and political economies of the global anti-trafficking movement. PhD Dissertation, Sociology. University of California, Los Angeles.

Sikkink, K. (2011). *The Justice Cascade: How human rights prosecutions are changing world politics.* The Norton Series in World Politics. New York: W. W. Norton & Company.

Silber, L. and A. Little. (1997). *Yugoslavia: Death of a nation.* New York: Penguin Books.

Šiljak, Z. S. (2014). *Shining Humanity: Life stories of women in Bosnia and Herzegovina* Cambridge, MA: Cambridge Scholars Publishing.

Simić, O. (2009). What remains of Srebrenica? Motherhood, transitional justice and yearning for the truth. *Journal of International Women's Studies*, 10(4), 220–236.

Simmons, C. (2007). Women's work and the growth of civil society in post-war Bosnia. *Nationalities Papers*, 35(1), 171–186.

Sivac-Bryant, S. (2008). Kozarac school: A window on transitional justice for returnees. *International Journal of Transitional Justice*, 2(1), 106–115.

(2016). *Re-making Kozarac: Agency, reconciliation, and contested return in post-war Bosnia.* London: Palgrave Macmillan.

Sjoberg, L. and C. E. Gentry. (2007). *Mothers, Monsters, Whores: Women's violence in global politics.* London and New York: Zed Books.

Skjelsbæk, I. (2006). Victim and survivor: Narrated social identities of women who experienced rape during the war in Bosnia-Herzegovina. *Feminism & Psychology*, 16(4), 373–403.

Skocpol, T. (1979). *States and Social Revolutions: A comparative analysis of France, Russia, and China.* Cambridge; New York: Cambridge University Press.

(1992). *Protecting Soldiers and Mothers: The political origins of social policy in the United States.* Cambridge, MA: Harvard University Press.

Skocpol, T., Z. Munson, A. Karch, and B. Camp. (2002). Patriotic partnerships: Why great wars nourished American civic voluntarism. In I. Katznelson (Ed.), *Shaped by War and Trade: International influences on American political development* (pp. 134–80). Princeton, NJ: Princeton University Press.

Slapšak, S. (2001). The use of women and the role of women in the Yugoslav war. In I. Skjelsbæk and D. Smith (Eds.), *Gender, Peace and Conflict* (pp. 161–183). Oslo, Norway: International Peace Research Institute (PRIO).

Slegh, H., G. Barker, A. Kimonyo, P. Ndolimana, and M. Bannerman. (2013). "I can do women's work": Reflections on engaging men as allies in women's economic empowerment in Rwanda. *Gender & Development*, 21(1), 15–30.

Small, M. and J. D. Singer. (1982). *Resort to Arms: International and civil wars, 1816–1980.* Thousand Oaks, CA: Sage Publications.

Smillie, I. (1996). Service delivery or civil society? Nongovernmental organizations in Bosnia and Herzegovina. A report for CARE Zagreb (original report).

Smillie, I. and K. Evenson. (2003). Sustainable civil society or service delivery agencies? The evolution of non-governmental organizations in Bosnia and Herzegovina. In D. Dijkzeul and Y. Beigbeder (Eds.), *Rethinking International Organizations: Pathology and promise* (pp. 287–308). New York: Berghahn Books.

Smith, S. (2010). Performativity and civil society. PhD dissertation, Chapter 5. Department of Sociology and Criminology: University of California-Irvine, Irvine, CA.

Socialist Republic of Bosnia and Herzegovina. (1991). *Census, Zavod za statistiku Bosne i Hercegovine – Bilten no.234.* Sarajevo, BiH.

Solnit, R. (2016). *Hope in the Dark* (3rd edn.). Chicago, IL: Haymarket Books.

Sommers, M. (2012). *Stuck: Rwandan youth and the struggle for adulthood.* Athens; Washington, DC: University of Georgia Press, in association with the United States Institute of Peace.

Spivak, G. C. (1993). *Outside in the Teaching Machine.* New York: Routledge.

Stanley, L. and S. Wise. (1983). *Breaking Out: Feminist consciousness and feminist research.* London: Routledge & K. Paul.

Stanton, G. H. (2004). Could the Rwandan genocide have been prevented? *Journal of Genocide Research*, 6(2), 211–228.

Staveteig, S. E. (2011). Genocide, nuptiality, and fertility in Rwanda and Bosnia-Herzegovina. PhD Dissertation, University of California, Berkeley, CA.

Stephen, L. (1997). *Women and Social Movements in Latin America: Power from below.* Austin: University of Texas Press.

Stiglmayer, A. (1994). The rapes in Bosnia-Herzegovina. In A. Stiglmayer (Ed.), *Mass Rape: The war against women in Bosnia-Herzegovina* (pp. 82–169). Lincoln; London: University of Nebraska Press.

Straus, S. (2006). *The Order of Genocide: Race, power, and war in Rwanda.* Ithaca, NY: Cornell University Press.

Straus, S. and L. Waldorf. (2011). *Remaking Rwanda: State building and human rights after mass violence.* Madison: University of Wisconsin Press.

Summerfield, D. (1999). A critique of seven assumptions behind psychological trauma programmes in war-affected areas. *Social Science & Medicine,* 48(10), 1449–1462.

Swidler, A. (1986). Culture in action: Symbols and strategies. *American Sociological Review,* 51(2), 273–286.

Tamale, S. (1999). *When Hens Begin to Crow: Gender and parliamentary politics in Uganda.* Boulder, CO: Westview Press.

Tarrow, S. G. (2011). *Power in Movement: Social movements, collective action, and politics* (2nd edn.). Cambridge; New York: Cambridge University Press.

Taylor, C. C. (1999). *Sacrifice as Terror: The Rwandan genocide of 1994.* New York: Oxford University Press.

Taylor, V. (1999). Gender and social movements: Gender processes in women's self-help movements. *Gender & Society,* 13(1), 8–33.

Taylor, V. and L. J. Rupp. (1993). Women's culture and lesbian feminist activism: A reconsideration of cultural feminism. *Signs: Journal of Women in Culture and Society,* 19(1), 32–61.

    (2002). Loving internationalism: The emotion culture of transnational women's organizations, 1888–1945. *Mobilization: An International Journal,* 7(2), 141–158.

Thelen, K. (1999). Historical institutionalism in Comparative Politics. *Annual Review of Political Science,* 2, 369–404.

Thomas, J. L. and K. D. Bond. (2015). Women's participation in violent political organizations. *American Political Science Review,* 109(3), 488–506.

Thomson, S. M. (2011). Reeducation for reconciliation: Participant observations on Ingando. In S. Straus and L. Waldorf (Eds.) *Remaking Rwanda: State building and human rights after mass violence* (pp. 331–342). Madison: University of Wisconsin Press.

    (2013). *Whispering Truth to Power: Everyday resistance to reconciliation in post-genocide Rwanda.* Madison: University of Wisconsin Press.

Tickner, J. A. (1992). *Gender in International Relations: Feminist perspectives on achieving global security.* New York: Columbia University Press.

Tilly, C. (1984). *Big Structures, Large Processes, Huge Comparisons.* New York: Russell Sage Foundation.

    (1978). *From Mobilization to Revolution.* Reading, MA: Addison-Wesley Publishing Company.

    (1986). *The Contentious French.* Cambridge, MA; London: Belknap Press of Harvard University Press.

Tilly, L. A. (1981). Paths of proletarianization: Organization of production, sexual division of labor, and women's collective action. *Signs: Journal of Women in Culture and Society,* 7(2), 400–417.

Tito, J. (1941). *Proclamation of the KPJ Central Committee to the People of Yugoslavia*. Belgrade, Serbia.

Tomšič, V. (1980). *Woman in the Development of Socialist Self-Managing Yugoslavia*. Jugoslovenska stvarnost, Newspaper and Publishing House.

Totten, S., W. Parsons, and I. W. Charny. (1997). *Century of Genocide: Eyewitness accounts and critical views*. New York: Garland Publishing.

Tripp, A. M. (2000). *Women & Politics in Uganda*. Madison: University of Wisconsin Press.

(2015). *Women and Power in Post-conflict Africa*. New York: Cambridge University Press.

(2016). Comparative perspectives on concept of gender, ethnicity, and race. *Politics, Groups, and Identities*, 4(2), 307–324.

Turshen, M. (2001). The political economy of rape: An analysis of systematic rape and sexual abuse of women during armed conflict in Africa. In C. Moser and F. Clarke (Eds.), *Victors, Perpetrators or Actors: Gender, armed conflict and political violence* (pp. 55-68). London: Zed Books.

Algerian women in the liberation struggle and the civil war: From active participants to passive victims? *Social Research*, 69(3), 889–911.

Udovički, J. (1997). The bonds and the fault lines. In J. Udovički and J. Ridgeway (Eds.), *Burn this House: The making and unmaking of Yugoslavia* (pp. 11–42). Durham, NC; London: Duke University Press.

Udovički, J. and J. Ridgeway. (1997). *Burn this House: The making and unmaking of Yugoslavia*. Durham, NC; London: Duke University Press.

Udovički, J. and E. Štitkovac. (1997). Bosnia and Herzegovina: The second war. In J. Udovički and J. Ridgeway (Eds.), *Burn this House: The making and unmaking of Yugoslavia* (pp. 174–214). Durham, NC; London: Duke University Press.

Umutesi, M. B. (2004). *Surviving the Slaughter: The ordeal of a Rwandan refugee in Zaire*. Madison: University of Wisconsin Press.

UNHCR. (1998). *Information Notes on Bosnia-Herzegovina and other Republics*. Sarajevo, BiH: United Nations.

UNICEF. (2009). *Situation Analysis Report on the Status of Gender Equality in Bosnia and Herzegovina*. Sarajevo, BiH: United Nations.

United Nations, Special Rapporteur of the Commission on Human Rights, *Report on the situation of human rights in Rwanda submitted by Mr. René Degni-Ségui*, paragraph 20 of resolution S-3/1 (25 May 1994), available from http://hrlibrary.umn.edu/commission/country52/68-rwa.htm.

United Nations Development Program (UNDP) (2007). *Turning Vision 2020 into Reality: From recovery to sustainable human development*. National Human Development Report. Rwanda: UNDP.

United Nations High Commissioner for Refugees (UNHCR) (1998). *Refugees and Others of Concern to UNHCR - 1998 Statistical Overview*. New York: UNHCR.

Urdang, S. (1989). *And Still They Dance: Women, war, and the struggle for change in Mozambique*. New York: Monthly Review Press.

USAID. (2000). *Aftermath: Women and women's organizations in post-genocide Rwanda*. Washington, DC: USAID Center for Development Information and Evaluation.

(2001). *Civil Society in Rwanda: Assessment and options*. (No. 802). Washington, DC: USAID/Rwanda. http://pdf.usaid.gov/pdf_docs/Pnacm181 .pdf.

Utas, M. (2003). *Sweet Battlefields: Youth and the Liberian civil war*. Sweden: Uppsala University Dissertations in Cultural Anthropology.

Uvin, P. (1998). *Aiding Violence: The development enterprise in Rwanda*. West Hartford, CT: Kumarian Press.

(2004). *Human Rights and Development*. Ann Arbor: University of Michigan Press.

(2010). Structural causes, development co-operation and conflict prevention in Burundi and Rwanda. *Conflict, Security & Development, 10*(1), 161–179.

Uwineza, P. and E. Pearson. (2009). *Sustaining Women's Gains in Rwanda: The influence of indigenous culture and post-genocide politics*. Washington, DC: Hunt Alternatives Fund.

Van Leeuwen, M. (2001). Rwanda's *imidugudu* programme and earlier experiences with villagisation and resettlement in east Africa. *Journal of Modern African Studies, 39*(4), 623–644.

Verpoorten, M. (2005). The death toll of the Rwandan genocide: A detailed analysis for Gikongoro province. *Population, 60*(4), 331–367.

(2014). Rwanda: Why claim that 200,000 Tutsi died in the genocide is wrong. *African Arguments,* http://africanarguments.org/2014/10/27/rwanda-why-davenport-and-stams-calculation-that-200000-tutsi-died-in-the-genocide-is-wrong-by-marijke-verpoorten/. Accessed May 2017.

Verwimp, P. (2005). An economic profile of peasant perpetrators of genocide: Micro-level evidence from Rwanda. *Journal of Development Economics, 77*(2), 297–323.

(2013). *Peasants in Power: The political economy of development and genocide in Rwanda*. Dordrecht, Netherlands: Springer.

Vidal, C. (1969). Le Rwanda des anthropologues ou le fétichisme de la vache. *Cahiers d'études Africaines, 9*(3), 384–400.

(1974). Économie de la société féodale Rwandaise (the economics of Rwanda feudal society). *Cahiers d'études Africaines, XIV*(53), 52–74.

(2001). Les commémorations du génocide au Rwanda. Temps Modernes, (613), 1–46.

Viterna, J. (2013). *Women in War: The micro-processes of mobilization in El Salvador*. New York: Oxford University Press.

Vulliamy, E. (2012). *The War Is Dead, Long Live the War: Bosnia: The reckoning*. London: The Bodley Head.

Vyas, S. and C. Watts. (2009). How does economic empowerment affect women's risk of intimate partner violence in low and middle-income countries? A systematic review of published evidence. *Journal of International Development, 21*(5), 577–602.

Walby, S. (2005). Backlash in historical context. In M. Kennedy, C. Lubelska, and V. Walsh (Eds.), *Making Connections: Women's studies, women's movements, women's lives* (1993). Taylor & Francis, pp. 79–89.

Gender mainstreaming: Productive tensions in theory and practice. *Social Politics*, 12(3), 321–343.

Walsh, M. (1998). Mind the gap: Where feminist theory failed to meet development practice – A missed opportunity in Bosnia and Herzegovina. *European Journal of Women's Studies*, 5(3–4), 329–343.

(2000). *Aftermath: The impact of conflict on women in Bosnia and Herzegovina*. Washington, DC: Center for Development Information and Evaluation. USAID.

Walzer, M. (1977) 2015. *Just and Unjust Wars: A moral argument with historical illustrations*. New York: Basic Books

Wängnerud, L. (2009). Women in parliaments: Descriptive and substantive representation. *Annual Review of Political Science*, 12, 51–69.

Watkins, S. E. (2014). Iron mothers and warrior lovers: Intimacy, power, and the state in Rwanda, 1796–1912. PhD dissertation, University of California, Santa Barbara, Santa Barbara, CA.

Waugh, C. M. (2004). *Paul Kagame and Rwanda: Power, genocide and the Rwandan Patriotic Front*. Jefferson, NC: McFarland & Company, Inc., Publishers.

Waylen, G. (2009). What can historical institutionalism offer feminist institutionalists? *Political Science*, 1, 333–356.

Weber, M. ([1922] 1978). *Economy and Society: An outline of interpretive sociology*. Oakland: University of California Press.

Weitz, E. D. (2003). *A Century of Genocide: Utopias of race and nation*. Princeton, NJ: Princeton University Press. http://necrometrics.com/all20c.htm.

Wimmer, A. (2014). War. *Annual Review of Sociology*, 40, 173–197.

Wimmer, A., L. E. Cederman, and B. Min (2009). Ethnic politics and armed conflict: A configurational analysis of a new global data set. *American Sociological Review*, 74(2), 316–337.

Wings of Hope (2013). *Three Year Report 2010–2012*. Fondacija Krila Nade, Bosne i Herzegovina.

Women's Commission for Refugee Women and Children. (1997). *Rwanda's Women and Children: The long road to reconciliation*. New York: Women's Commission for Refugee Women and Children.

Women for Women International. (2004). *Women Taking a Lead: Progress toward empowerment and gender equity in Rwanda*. Washington, DC: Women for Women International.

Woodward, S. L. (1985). The rights of women: Ideology, policy, and social change in Yugoslavia. In S. L. Wolchik and A. G. Meyer (Eds.), *Women, State, and Party in Eastern Europe* (pp. 234–256). Durham, NC: Duke University Press.

(1995). *Socialist Unemployment: The political economy of Yugoslavia, 1945–1990*. Princeton, NJ: Princeton University Press.

World Bank. (1996). *The Priority Reconstruction and Recovery Program in Bosnia: The challenges ahead*. World Bank. http://documents.worldbank.org/curated/en/1996/04/696634/bosnia-herzegovina-priority-reconstruction-recovery-program-challenges-ahead-discussion-paper-no-2.

(1997). *Bosnia and Herzegovina: From recovery to sustainable growth*. Washington, DC: World Bank. http://documents.worldbank.org/curated/en/1997/05/694839/bosnia-herzegovina-recovery-sustainable-growth.

(1999). *Implementation Completion Report: Emergency landmines clearance project (Bosnia and Herzegovina)*. Europe and Central Asia Region: World Bank. http://documents.worldbank.org/curated/en/1999/06/728373/bosnia-herzegovina-emergency-landmines-clearance-project.

(1990–2012). *World Development Indicators: Rwanda*. The World Bank. http://data.worldbank.org/country/rwandap.

World Development Indicators: Bosnia. The World Bank. (1990–2012). www.worldbank.org/en/country/bosniaandherzegovina.

Yuval-Davis, N. (1997). *Gender & Nation*. London; Thousand Oaks, CA: Sage Publications.

Zajović, S. (2013). Feminist anti-militarism of women in black. In S. Zajović, S. Stojanović, & M. Urošević (Eds.), *Women for Peace* (pp. 71–108). Belgrade: Women in Black.

Žarkov, Dubrovka. (2001). The body of the other man: Sexual violence and the construction of masculinity, sexuality and ethnicity in Croatian media. In C. Moser and F. Clark (Eds.), *Victims, Perpetrators or Actors? Gender, armed conflict and political violence*. (pp. 69–72). London; New York: Zed Books.

(2008). *Gender, Violent Conflict, and Development*. New Delhi: Zubaan.

(2014). Ontologies of international humanitarian and criminal law: "Locals" and "internationals" in discourses and practices of justice. In D. Žarkov and M. Glasius (Eds.), *Narratives of Justice In and Out of the Courtroom: Former Yugoslavia and beyond* (pp. 3–22). London: Springer.

Zimmermann, W. (1995). The last ambassador: A memoir of the collapse of Yugoslavia. *Foreign Affairs*, 74(2), 2–20.

Zraly, M. (2008). Bearing: Resilience among genocide-rape survivors in Rwanda. PhD Dissertation, Case Western Reserve University.

Zraly, M. and L. Nyirazinyoye. (2010). Don't let the suffering make you fade away: An ethnographic study of resilience among survivors of genocide-rape in southern Rwanda. *Social Science & Medicine*, 70(10), 1656–1664.

Zraly, M., J. Rubin-Smith, and T. Betancourt. (2011). Primary mental health care for survivors of collective sexual violence in Rwanda. *Global Public Health*, 6(3), 257–270.

Index